Italian Women and International
Cold War Politics, 1944–1968

Italian Women and International Cold War Politics, 1944–1968

WENDY POJMANN

FORDHAM UNIVERSITY PRESS
New York   2013

Fordham University Press has no responsibility for the persistence
or accuracy of URLs for external or third-party Internet websites
referred to in this publication and does not guarantee that any
content on such websites is, or will remain, accurate or appropriate.

Fordham University Press also publishes its books in a variety of
electronic formats. Some content that appears in print may not be
available in electronic books.

Library of Congress Cataloging-in-Publication Data

Pojmann, Wendy A. (Wendy Ann)
    Italian women and international Cold War politics, 1944–1968 /
Wendy Pojmann. — First edition.
        pages cm
    Includes bibliographical references and index.
    ISBN 978-0-8232-4560-4 (cloth : alk. paper)
    1. Women's rights—Italy—History—20th century.   2. Feminism—
Italy—History—20th century.   3. Cold War.   I. Title.
    HQ1236.5.I8P65 2013
    305.42094509'04—dc23

                                                        2012039725

Printed in the United States of America

15 14 13   5 4 3 2 1

First edition

Contents

Acknowledgments

I very much enjoy research and writing, and I find the hours of both solitary work and engagement with the scholarly community to be fulfilling. Seeing my work published is always a thrill and brings to mind the many institutions, colleagues, friends, and family members who helped to make it happen. Of course, any errors or omissions remain entirely my own.

Getting to Italy many times to complete my research would not have been possible without financial support from the Committee on Teaching and Faculty Development at Siena College, which awarded me summer research fellowships in 2007, 2009, and 2010. I also greatly benefited from the 2008 Barbieri Grant (Trinity College Research Grant in Modern Italian History) and a 2010 Bernadotte E. Schmitt Grant from the American Historical Association.

While I was in Rome, Italy, my work was aided by the patience and competence of librarians and archivists at the Unione Donne Italiane, the Centro Italiano Femminile, the Lelio and Lisli Basso Foundation, the Gramsci Institute, the library of the International Women's House, and the Paolo VI Institute as well as by the receptive staff and spaces of the American Academy of Rome and the Library of Modern and Contemporary History. The excellent library staff at Siena College secured many obscure titles for me, which allowed me to move forward on my research while in New York.

My Siena College colleagues inspired me to achieve and maintain the high standards they exhibit in their own work. In particular, Laurie Naranch's and Vera Eccarius-Kelly's fiery feminist intellects kept me thinking about women and politics. Paola Bonissone worked with me to provide the best possible translations from the Italian. Bruce Eelman helped me to overcome my final bout of writer's block and finish the manuscript. Colleagues outside Siena, especially Francisca De Haan, Leila Rupp, and Robert Shaffer, were generous with their time and shared valuable research materials with me. Paul Breines has continued to mentor me ever since I was an inexperienced graduate student at Boston College. Helen Laville and Karen Garner made vital suggestions on the manuscript for Fordham University Press and were kind enough to share their identities with me so I could ask for clarifications. Fredric Nachbaur, Will Cerbone, and the Fordham University Press editorial board and staff offered welcome advice and assistance to see the book to publication.

My family extended every possible form of moral and logistical support. I was reminded about the importance of life outside the women's associations by my parents, Dave and Nita Pojmann; sister, Karen Pojmann; and my niece and nephew, Asa and Eze. My kitty, Tiger, kept my lap warm while I wrote. My mother-in-law, Maria Livia Talucci, offered her hospitality and unconditional sweetness. My husband, Andrea Parigi, has patiently listened to me talk about the Unione Donne Italiane and the Centro Italiano Femminile since 1996 and is always my main source of encouragement.

I dedicate this book to Giorgio Lombardi, whose gentleness and generosity helped it take shape in ways he may not have realized and whom I miss greatly.

Italian Women and International
Cold War Politics, 1944–1968

Introduction

The women of the left-leaning Unione Donne Italiane (UDI) and the lay
Catholic Centro Italiano Femminile (CIF) have long filled my thoughts
and many pages of my writing over the past decade.[1] It was not until I
was putting the finishing touches on an article, however, that I was
struck by an absence in my own research about these two women's associations, which were active throughout the post–World War II era.
Though I had explored the role of the associations in an Italian national
framework and had recently criticized their failure to incorporate the
experiences of migrant women, I had not really taken the UDI and the
CIF out of Italy and placed them in a global framework.[2] An examination of the national context in relation to the Cold War international
activities of the Italian women's associations, it occurred to me, would
warrant a book-length study. I wanted to better understand the ways in
which Italian women weighed in on the national political situation but
also how their work in Italy was informed by and influenced international developments.

The "missing" international piece of the histories of the UDI and the
CIF is the very one that makes them so relevant to the dynamics of the
Cold War and to the course of worldwide women's movements. While
much recent work in women's history has emphasized the multifaceted
experiences of women during World War II or the dynamism of the feminist movements of the 1970s, few studies have examined women as political actors during the in-between decades.[3] I want to suggest a more
continuous approach that considers the postwar era in relation to earlier
and later periods. The two Italian women's associations considered here
transformed women's experiences from the early days of an Italian
state through the contradictions of fascism and into the turmoil of the
Resistance. When they emerged from the war, stronger and more determined than before, the world was no longer the same. What had been

differences in vision about prioritizing women's political, economic, and social needs now took a new sense of urgency as the major world powers realigned themselves behind one of two new leaders, the United States and the Soviet Union. The choices women made about their political participation did not exist outside the influence of Cold War discourses and realties. The phenomenon of Italian bipolarism, or the nearly equal division of the Italian people into two camps—one procommunist and the other pro-Western—would shape Italian politics through most of the rest of the twentieth century.[4] It is no accident that the two largest autonomous Italian women's associations reflected but also contributed to the tensions of their times. The UDI represented the interests of women on the progressive communist and socialist left and had more than 3 million members. The CIF had 6 million members, most of whom identified as Catholic and traditional. The early leaders of both associations developed their political identities and commitment to women's emancipation especially during the antifascist struggles of the Resistance. The associations remained ideologically opposed, however, and they attracted women of very different backgrounds, particularly in their earliest years, when the typical UDI militant was a factory or agricultural worker, and the typical CIF member was a housewife from a bourgeois or formerly aristocratic family. Over time, the associations' memberships expanded to include broader cross-sections of the population and included the generations born during and after World War II.

A bipolar world also had important consequences for international women's movements. The women of the turn-of-the-century "international sisterhood" described by historian Leila Rupp may have had differences in vision because of their preferences for a socialist-inspired or bourgeois version of feminism, but in a world in which few women could vote, could own their own businesses, or could even divorce a husband, many women nonetheless found ways to help their "sisters."[5] After World War II, transnational cooperative efforts among women suffered because of Cold War hostilities, even though more women enjoyed new rights, including suffrage in most of western Europe. Historian Helen Laville has detailed American women's participation in international organizing in the Cold War era, noting a shift from alliances to competition among women of different nations. She argues that American women in organizations such as the International Alliance of Women and the League of Women Voters put their interests above those of women in other parts of the world and generally saw themselves as superior to women elsewhere.[6] Such a change in spirit marks a new age of contentiousness in which Italian women would play a part. Of course, in Italy, there was no national anticommunist unity. The Italian Communist Party remained a powerful opposition party for the duration of the period under consideration here and was arguably the most important communist party in western Europe. The UDI's and the CIF's explicit national and international cooperative efforts were thus minimal, occurring most often in regard to motherhood. Despite, or as I argue in later chapters, perhaps because of, their opposed political perspectives, the two associations sped up the advancement of women's rights in Italy by tackling a series of problems related to women's inferior political, social, and economic positions and extended their work to the international stage.

The intent of this book is to connect and synthesize the national and international histories of the UDI and the CIF between 1944, when the associations became active, and 1968, when the emergence of new social movements put younger generations of women activists into focus. I aim to demonstrate that the national and international contexts in which women's activists operated reveal the importance of women's associations across the traditional boundaries of the nation-state and call into question limited notions about the scope of women's political participation during the first decades of the Cold War. In my estimation, the flurry of women's political activity at the end of World War II may have diminished as new patterns of life developed in the postwar era, but women did not retreat to the confines of domestic walls nor back away from the challenges of public life. An ideal of the middle-class housewife came to prevail, and an underlying current of maternalism certainly carried through many legislative initiatives.[7] However, Italian women remained connected to their places of work, even if their workplace was the home, and they set the agenda for modernizing policies that would allow women access to a full range of careers and social services necessary to enable them to pursue their economic and social objectives. A small core of women entered the government, but many more filled important roles in the political parties, trade unions, church and community groups, and new nongovernmental organizations.

I cannot argue that women's international organizations always had a direct influence on policy, but I do want to suggest that they gave women a more powerful voice and introduced women's interests to a broader political arena. Did the women's organizations persuade the world's political leaders to end the war in Korea or halt the progression of the nuclear arms race? No, they did not. They did, however, point out contradictions between the discourse of peace and preparations for war and generally advanced a gendered notion that the world would be a less troubled place if headed by women. Perhaps more important, the international women's organizations demonstrated a continued interest in working with women around the world and seeking common objectives. What changed after World War II was that Cold War ideologies permeated the national women's associations' approaches to international issues of gender. For example, in the first years after the war, the UDI tended to view communist states, especially the Soviet Union, as open to women's emancipation, and they pointed to careers and opportunities in Russia that women in Italy did not have access to. The UDI, through its work with the largest postwar women's organization, the 36-million-member Women's International Democratic Federation, argued that instituting an international pro-Soviet propaganda campaign would show women that socialism and communism afforded them a better future. The CIF, in contrast, in some ways looked at the suburban American housewife as a model and favored especially international programs and projects that benefited mothers and children. Its focus on motherhood led the CIF to become active in the World Movement of Mothers, which attracted similar organizations from thirty countries worldwide.

The Italian women's associations made international alliances based on Cold War constructs, but they remained particularly committed to the women in their national associations. This, too, is important in understanding the dynamics of the Cold War in women's organizations and how they played out and were reproduced across national and international arenas. The UDI was one of the founding members of the Women's International Democratic Federation in 1945 and remained an influential member of its steering committee until 1963, when differences over the federation's pro-Soviet political positions led the UDI to loosen its ties to the international organization. The UDI implored the federation to move away from the trappings of international Cold War politics, especially because adherence to Soviet policies no longer appeared to the Italian women to be the best solution for peace. The UDI wanted the federation instead to focus on uniting national women's associations worldwide as it was attempting to do in Italy, where alliances between socialist and communist women had become strained by new political pressures. Similarly, the CIF's preference for the idealized American housewife had its limits. If embracing capitalism meant being able to provide a stable and happy home for their families, the women were happy to promote social and economic policies that favored it. If, however, capitalism spiraled into selfishness and disregard for Christian, especially Catholic, values, then it was worth reconsidering. According to the CIF, women's entry into the workplace and the benefits of the economic boom had to be carefully balanced with respect for the family and Catholic community. In most cases, the UDI and the CIF prioritized women's interests as defined by their associations and made gender the center of their organizing principles. Although the Italian associations developed important relationships with several international organizations—for instance, the CIF worked closely with the Rome-based Food and Agricultural Organization of the United Nations, and the UDI was very involved in the Paris-based international communist organization the Partisans of Peace—they dedicated a majority of their international work to women and held influential roles in the Women's International Democratic Federation and the World Movement of Mothers. As I demonstrate in the following pages, Italian women activists ultimately put their constituents above the direct interests of the political parties, above Cold War disputes, and above broader social trends despite the many pressures calling on them to do otherwise.

Keeping in mind the diverse political, social, and economic factors that the women's associations had to contend with, a key objective of this book is to connect the global Cold War timeline to events in Italy and to milestones in the Italian and international women's movements. In the following chapters, I show how Italian women negotiated the national political situation, which was driven by both national and international developments. Italy provides a fascinating case for a country study within a global context, particularly because of the "national/international nexus that characterized the political life of Washington and Moscow's lesser European allies during the Cold War."[8] However, most scholarship on the UDI and the CIF to date has been limited to examinations of their activities in relation to the Italian political parties, the Catholic Church, and the feminist movement.[9] Patrizia Gabrielli's extensive publications on the UDI and the CIF demonstrate an acute awareness of the complexities of Italian gender roles that allowed women access to new political rights through often traditional grassroots activities as caretakers.[10] Gabrielli has detailed and analyzed the ways in which the UDI's and the CIF's national and regional leaders sought to negotiate very delicate relationships with the Italian Communist and Socialist Parties and the Christian Democrats. Her work, however, has focused primarily on the local, regional, and national situations as informed by Italian society and politics and so has left the international dimension of women's activism relatively unexplored. Fiorenza Taricone, in her institutional history of the CIF, has situated the positions of the Italian women's association in relation to middle-class women in Western Europe and the United States, but she has not fully examined the CIF's international alliances during the early decades of the Cold War.[11] Essays in her coedited volume consider Italian women's movements in relation to international developments, but most of these focus primarily on European integration in more recent decades.[12] What is clear in the work of these scholars and further advanced by my study is that Italian women and their organizations interrogated the Italian system and developed tactics to achieve specific legislative and political aims. An examination of the impact of internal Italian politics on the UDI and the CIF thus remains central to my story.

Nevertheless, the growing scholarship on Cold War Italy has not generally considered women to be active political participants.[13] An important exception is Molly Tambor's characterization of the *sante rosse*, or "red saints," whose political activism from the Resistance until the elections of 1953 reflected their commitment to equal citizenship and democracy.[14] Tambor's enthusiasm for the women who joined forces to secure social services for Italy's devastated families at war's end and to guarantee women's formal political representation perhaps underemphasizes the political divisions among women's associations that were already well established before the elections of 1953. As I will argue below, even early instances of women's cooperation more often than not reflected deep ideological divides and mutual suspicions and did little to subvert the Cold War rivalries which, as Christopher Duggan has noted, immediately pulled the Italians into a three-way tug-of-war with the United States and the Soviet Union pulling on opposite ends and the Vatican yanking in its own direction.[15]

In fact, women remain largely outside consideration in most Cold War histories, other than as voters, despite the fact that women were also visible political actors pushing and pulling in their own ways and responding to competing political and religious tendencies. For instance, the formation of NATO in April 1949 generated international tensions and angered Stalin. The UDI and the CIF participated in the intense debate that preceded the Italian government's decision to join NATO. The UDI took an anti-NATO petition to the United Nations. And when in 1957 the Italian government agreed to allow the installation of NATO missile bases in northern Italy, the UDI led a massive protest on International Women's Day, March 8, to highlight the links between the women's and the peace movements. In many instances, the grassroots efforts of women's associations had direct relevance to national and international politics. There are many cases, however, in which events that appeared minimally connected nevertheless influenced each other. The pope's excommunication of socialists and communists in 1949 made it very difficult for the women of the UDI to convince devout Catholic women in Italy to join their association, but it united Catholic women worldwide against the threat of communism. The war in Korea (1950–53) led women's organizations to step up their efforts for peace and to initiate a campaign to send milk to Korean babies. The Soviet repression in Hungary in the watershed year of 1956 divided the Italian left and prompted the women's associations to rethink their political positions and alliances. On the timeline of women's rights in Italy, the UDI and the CIF led efforts for women's suffrage, the protection of workers and mothers, the enforcement of equal pay for equal work, and pensions for housewives. At the same time, they supported similar efforts internationally. In 1947, the CIF signed the World Movement of Mothers' *Mother's Charter*, which promoted women's legal equality in the household, and in 1953 the UDI signed the Women's International Democratic Federation's *Charter of Women's Rights* to promote women's economic independence. Each of these cases, and many others detailed in my study, demonstrate the interconnectedness of women and men in national and international politics and challenge notions that women's history during the Cold War was somehow outside the realm of world affairs.

Like historian Karen Garner, I am especially interested in women's nongovernmental organizations as key sites for women's political activism as opposed to examining women's more limited roles in appointed government positions or traditional modes of electoral politics. Garner's work on liberal women's organizations, in particular the World Young Women's Christian Association, has shown that women who engaged with the global governance systems of the League of Nations and United Nations faced structural discriminations that often impeded their assumption of formal political power inside these bodies.[16] Nonetheless, during the early postwar era, women's organizations gained consultative status in the UN, successfully advocated for gender-inclusive language in official UN policies, and introduced a specific global women's agenda to confront gender inequalities and promote human rights. Garner argues that informal power structures allowed women activists to seek "equitable power for women on feminine-gendered and liberal feminist terms that emphasized peaceful conflict resolution and nurturance, and employed moral considerations and humanitarian values as the foundation for national and international policy making in order to transform big-power politics."[17] While it may be easy to discount women's early postwar political influence because of the small numbers of women inside national and international governing bodies, the importance of women's organizations cannot be dismissed. The leaders of women's organizations developed complex relationships with a variety of male-led bodies across multiple contexts and in so doing revealed the complexities of gender relations and the need for autonomous women's organizations. For the Italian women's associations, the access provided to the United Nations through the special consultative status held by the Women's International Democratic Federation and the World Movement of Mothers was especially important during the early Cold War years since Italy itself did not become a member of the UN until 1955.

Long-standing and new differences in ideology and vision certainly led to debates among the national and international women's organizations, but it is not my intention to simply reconstruct old narratives of feminist conflicts. Of course, the women's organizations inherited key feminist questions of the early twentieth century that were often influenced by class and geographical divides and by conflicting ideas as to whether women and men were intrinsically different and so should operate in separate spheres. Some of the tensions that arose among the Italian and international women's organizations are informed by these disparate points of view, even because some of the same women transferred them into the new organizations. Seen this way, the UDI could be labeled a women's rights association, the CIF a social feminist association, the Women's International Democratic Federation a socialist organization, and the World Movement of Mothers a liberal feminist group. In my estimation, however, all the women's organizations at the center of my study operated as feminist organizations. While I may be challenged for applying the "feminist" label to these groups, especially because of their existence outside the boundaries of liberal (noncommunist) and secular (non-ecumenical) feminisms, each promoted women's rights and attempted to end multiple forms of gender discrimination. Francisca De Haan's work has done much to transform understandings of the Women's International Democratic Federation as a Soviet tool and its members as antifeminist minions. I agree with De Haan's correction of Karen Offen's overemphasis on the Women's International Democratic Federation's preference for "women's rights" over "feminism," since Offen's interpretation obscures the pro-woman program established by the federation during its 1945 Paris convention and carried through the signing of its *Charter of Women's Rights* in 1953 in Copenhagen.[18] Publications by Patrizia Gabrielli and others have sought to overturn similar characterizations of the UDI as a procommunist association that rejected feminism.[19]

On the other side of the Cold War divide, scholars have often viewed lay Christian and Catholic women's organizations as nonfeminist since these types of groups generally assume that women's first place is in the home, but even organizations such as the International Council of Women shared that particular conservative vision of gender roles while still advocating for equal rights. As Susan B. Whitney's work on youth organizations in interwar France has shown, even when they upheld marriage and motherhood as ideals for women, Catholic women's organizations, such as the Jeunesse Ouvrière Chrétienne Féminine, advocated for women's spiritual equality and offered young women opportunities to gain experience outside the home.[20] The CIF's commitment to the political and social advancement of women is well documented by both Gabrielli and Taricone. The history of the World Movement of Mothers remains largely unexplored by scholars, but recent work by Anna Scarantino on Maria Bajocco Remiddi and the Italian and international Catholic peace movement shows greater sensitivity to women's dynamic and complex roles in organizations that emphasized motherhood.[21] Instead of looking exclusively to reproduce recognizable points of contrast, then, I also discuss the many areas in which the women's groups overlapped. These include their use of propaganda and other political tools, confrontations with male political and religious leaders, and challenges in maintaining a clear focus on a unified set of objectives while responding to internal debates and pressures. At the same time, I explain how the women's work was embedded in a Cold War context that introduced new dynamics and historical circumstances into older ideological debates.

Finally, I hope to offer one small part of the story of the link between the "gendered internationalism" of the early twentieth century and the "transnational feminism" of the late twentieth century. The current state of women's international cooperative efforts has been defined in the wake of the fall of Soviet communism and the new challenges presented by globalization.[22] It is my contention, however, that a thread of commitment to women's rights runs through all the decades of the twentieth century and binds them in important ways. Leila Rupp noted a tendency of early women's organizations "to align with other women's groups," and that same trend can be identified during the era of the Cold War.[23] Women's studies scholar Mary Hawkesworth, for example, has emphasized how women's networks and alliances have continuously transformed feminist activism beyond the confines of national and regional interests over the past two hundred years.[24] However, the absence in her work of any mention of the role of the Women's International Democratic Federation or the World Movement of Mothers in women's transnational organizing reflects a long-standing tendency to favor certain kinds of women's organizations in analyses of transnational feminisms. In contrast, Francisca De Haan's continuing research is challenging notions in the historiography of international women's movements that the Eastern and Western blocs completely separated women's agendas and that the International Council of Women and the International Alliance of Women were neutral organizations, as opposed to the politically biased Women's International Democratic Federation. My study broadens and deepens De Haan's work by considering how the two blocs operated in the context of a western European country.[25] Nevertheless, it is evident from the women's studies scholarship that national interests and the division of the world from the poles of East and West to those of North and South have divided and continue to divide women.[26] The Italian women in this study attempted to reach out to their sisters around the world, but they remained part of a privileged western European culture and rooted in a set of traditions that reinforced ideas of European superiority. It is therefore worth considering which ideas reached an international audience and how they reflected and reproduced broader power structures.

Outline of the Book

The book is divided into six chapters and organized chronologically. I have attempted to create a periodization based on common tendencies in each range of years. Many themes are overlapping or continuous, but developments related to one or more major events in each period often shaped the activities of the women's associations. Organizing the chapters by theme alone would have resulted in needless redundancies and deemphasized the multiple levels of comparison that are necessary to construct a comprehensive picture of bipolarism in the women's movements. In each chapter, I highlight matters of current historiographical debate by drawing on the work of historians and other scholars writing in English and Italian. As relevant, I place my work in relation to influential texts in studies of contemporary Italian history, the Cold War, and women's movements.

The majority of my source material comes from the archival collections of the UDI and the CIF, the Gramsci Institute, the Paul VI Institute of Catholic Action, and the Lelio and Lisli Basso Issoco Foundation, all of which are located in Rome, Italy. I have also consulted recent collections of oral histories and images, which have mostly been compiled in the past several years by members of the associations. In addition, I benefited from materials about the Women's International Democratic Federation housed at the Sophia Smith Collection at Smith College and utilized the Archivia at the Casa Internazionale delle Donne in Rome. Although the materials are abundant, I cannot claim that they are exhaustive, and I do recognize some limitations in my study that result from them. For example, neither the UDI nor the CIF kept detailed data on official memberships, which makes it difficult to reach certain conclusions about changes in the size of the associations over time. Each chapter was assigned the task of issuing membership cards, but they did not always keep accurate records or report numbers to the national headquarters. There was also a certain degree of informal participation in the associations; many women attended some events or participated in a few initiatives but did not seek permanent membership. I should also point out that my approach to the source material is primarily from the points of view of the Italian, rather than the international, women's organizations. My study does not purport to be a comprehensive history of international women's movements since World War II but rather attempts to offer the Italian case as a means for understanding how work carried out in the nation-state, the primary site of women's activism, was translated to the international level during the divisive years of the Cold War. Finally, I recognize that the voices of the associations' leaders are the ones that can be heard most clearly. Since they are the women who most often participated in and reported on the international work of the associations, I have relied primarily on their accounts. This select group of women often had more money for international travel, spoke languages in addition to Italian, and benefited from higher levels of education than the rank-and-file members of the associations. Nevertheless, the leaders of the UDI and the CIF recognized the need to train their members, especially those interested in taking on more responsibilities in the associations, to effectively engage in national and international activities. They sent a few of them to specialized courses to help them learn more about the world of governmental and nongovernmental politics and the day's pressing issues.[27] When possible, I have attempted to include materials that shed light on the lives of other women who chose to become members of the UDI and the CIF since changes in their needs and desires are central to understanding how the women's associations established their agendas in line with broader tendencies in contemporary Italy. As historian Paul Ginsborg has shown, the remarkable processes of modernization, urbanization, secularization, and economic growth that occurred in Italy after 1943 is a story in itself.[28] The lives of the members of the associations are interwoven and informed by this story.

Chapter 1, "Daughters of the Resistance," examines the period between 1943 and 1946 from the armistice to the first free elections. I show that during this time, Italian women reinvented the women's movements of the late nineteenth and early twentieth centuries and transformed their associational lives to meet the demands of the new postwar era in the national and international contexts. In their new autonomous women's associations, the UDI and the CIF made important choices about their ideological frameworks, alliances with the Italian political parties, and the international organizations they worked with to construct a postwar world that would best represent their visions of an emancipated womanhood. The creation of two women's associations signified the divisive character of an emerging bipolar Italy and globe, but I want to demonstrate that a spirit of openness and cooperation also characterized these transitional years. The UDI and the CIF worked together on campaigns to assist Italy's families as they recovered from the war and to secure the vote and entry into government positions for women. Representatives from both associations attended the first international congress of the newly formed Women's International Democratic Federation in Paris in 1945 looking for ways to reach out to women worldwide. As I will explain, however, by the time of the Italian elections in 1946, any chance of overcoming political differences in favor of a united women's agenda had thoroughly ended with the Vatican's pronouncement that good Catholics could not also be good communists. The UDI retained its ties to the Italian left and took a leading role in the unapologetically pro-Soviet international federation, which led the women of the CIF to seek unions with women whose primary identity was as Catholics. The foundations and early years of the women's associations at the grassroots, national, and international levels form the focus of the first chapter.

Chapter 2, "Cold War Housewives?" analyzes developments between 1947 and 1949 when the Cold War became firmly entrenched in Italy as evidenced by the exclusion of the communists and socialists from Christian Democratic Prime Minister Alcide De Gasperi's cabinet, Italy's contentious membership in NATO, and the pope's excommunication of communists and socialists. I want to argue that despite a call for the return of women behind domestic walls, the Italian women's associations actually stepped up their mobilization efforts and worked tirelessly to design and implement social service programs for housewives and employed women and to participate in the great European and international debates that would affect Italy's political and economic future. I discuss the challenges that the women of the UDI faced as they attempted to construct a relationship with an Italian left dealing with opposition from the Vatican and U.S. President Harry Truman but not showing its full support for women's issues. At the same time, I consider what the favor of the Church and the Christian Democrats meant for the women of the

CIF. To place the Italian women's associations in their international context, I examine the CIF's contribution to the founding of an international Catholic organization, the World Movement of Mothers, in 1947 and the development of the UDI's role within the Women's International Democratic Federation. I analyze some of the first disagreements that took place among the Italian and international women's organizations, especially in regard to the housewife's role. Throughout the chapter, I explore how the women's organizations defined peace, democracy, and antifascism in relation to competing Cold War discourses.

In chapter 3, "Mothers for Peace," I consider developments between 1950 and 1955, when the women's associations launched a series of initiatives dedicated to peace and motherhood and experienced moments of cooperation across the Catholic/Popular Front divide. Both the UDI and the CIF sent delegates to the 1952 Vienna conference on the Defense of Children and to the 1955 World Congress of Mothers in Lausanne and worked together on an Italian consulting body on childhood issues. Although their activism and work together may appear limited to a construct of woman as defined by her "inevitable" role as mother, the UDI and the CIF actually demonstrated their political astuteness by bundling motherhood with other political messages and using them to reach younger women. The associations also called on their own cultural arsenals to counteract what they perceived as dangerous forms of entertainment arriving from the United States. Nonetheless, the associations' ideological differences were reinforced during this five-year period in large part because of national and international political developments. The war in Korea and events in Berlin elicited sharp responses from the Italian women's associations and influenced their positions in the international women's organizations. The UDI and the Women's International Democratic Federation, in fact, delivered a scathing report to the United Nations about American actions in Korea, whereas the CIF and the World Movement of Mothers developed a close relationship with Clare Boothe Luce, a fervently anticommunist American ambassador. The women's associations took the tense national elections of 1953 to the international stage by speaking on behalf of the political parties they supported at Women's International Democratic Federation and World Movement of Mothers events, an act that raised questions about their hard-earned political autonomy. By 1955, the UDI and the CIF had shown that a mini-détente was possible in a limited context but that the Cold War continued to overshadow effective widespread unity.

Chapter 4, "The Push for Autonomy and Women's Rights," focuses on the advancement of women's rights movements in the years between 1956 and 1959, when the UDI and the CIF accelerated their efforts in the national context to fight for labor legislation for women who worked inside and outside the home. Although neither association renounced its overarching positions on the primary roles and responsibilities of women, both opened up their platforms to account for a fuller range of women's experiences and needs. They reaffirmed their autonomy by directly confronting the political parties, trade unions, Catholic organizations, and the Vatican on outmoded ideas about gender. Campaigns in Italy for access to careers, pensions for housewives, equal salaries, and other reforms occupied the majority of the women's time, but they remained tied to international developments nonetheless. The disruption on the left caused by the Soviet invasion of Hungary in 1956 threatened to destabilize the membership of the UDI and the Women's International Democratic Federation and marked a watershed year in Italian politics. Italy's signing of the Treaty of Rome in 1957 opened the door to economic growth already evident by 1958 and signaled to the CIF and the World Movement of Mothers that the Europeans could overcome national divides and cooperate again as members of "Christian nations." The benefits of decolonization and the negative legacy of empire evoked responses from the Italian and international women's organizations as well. In chapter 4, I show that the UDI and the CIF advanced their objectives for Italian women while cautiously rethinking their national and international political alliances to best represent the interests of their members.

The years between 1960 and 1963 are the focus of chapter 5, "Opening to the Center." I will demonstrate that as global events of major interest, such as the 1960 election of John F. Kennedy in the United States and the first meeting of the Second Vatican Council in 1962, altered the course of the Cold War, the UDI and the CIF reaffirmed their commitment to women's rights in Italy and beyond. On the international level, the UDI became increasingly critical of the Women's International Democratic Federation's inconsistent Cold War politics and walked out of its 1963 congress in Moscow in protest. I show that this marked a significant shift away from decisive loyalty to procommunist international organizations and a return to a commitment to women's advancement. It also meant a renewed pledge to operate above the constraints of the Italian political parties of the left. Pope John XXIII's encyclicals supporting women's rights and the needs of citizens in poorer nations, meanwhile, invigorated the CIF, but grave financial problems threatened to put an end to the World Movement of Mothers. I explain that the CIF modified its positions in relation to broader changes—in this case the secularization of society and women's growing interest in roles beyond those of wife and mother. As this chapter demonstrates, the year 1963 was the last year that belonged to the historic postwar women's organizations, which were already beginning to note the great economic and social shifts occurring before them.

Chapter 6, "Confronting the Youth Generation," focuses on the important transitional years between 1964 and 1968. I suggest that as another generation of women activists began to take Italian women's movements in new directions, a reheating of the Cold War through the conflict in Vietnam and the Soviet repression of dissidents in Czechoslovakia reopened discussions about women's international role as agents of change for women's rights and peace. The UDI voted to become an associate member of the Women's International Democratic Federation and forged new relationships with women around the world, especially in Vietnam, and the UDI's oldest members pointed to similarities between Italian women's experiences during the Resistance and the struggles of women in the Viet Cong. The CIF, meanwhile, expanded its role in the World Movement of Mothers by assuming greater financial and administrative responsibilities. The association also stepped up efforts to reaffirm the organization's commitment to women's spiritual lives as a means of countering the effects of the new sources of generational disagreements. When Italian students occupied universities in 1966 to protest what they viewed as abuses of power by the status quo, the women's associations reacted at times with sympathy and at times with scorn. They also sought to transfer their own values to younger women in a time of crisis that was marked by opportunities for change. In this chapter, I will show that by the end of the 1960s, the Italian and international women's associations that had for so long defined themselves in relation to the hostilities of the Cold War would now have to confront a multitude of women's issues no longer so neatly tied to the ideologies of the earlier postwar decades.

1   Daughters of the Resistance, 1943–1946

In September 1944, tired from the destructiveness of years of fascism and war but energized by their commitment to Italy's liberation and optimistic about the future, a group of women gathered in Rome to form the Unione Donne Italiane (UDI). Their statement said in part: "Workers, farmers, housewives, women from anti-fascist parties, office employees, intellectuals, women without a party, and Catholics are animated by one wish—to liberate Italy from the fascists and the Germans. They have developed a unanimous, intense and enthusiastic project during the months of the Nazi occupation."[1] Little did the women know that their unity would quickly turn to division shaped by a postwar order known as the Cold War.[2] From their neighborhoods to the international stage and through their work in women's associations, Italian women would become active participants in the Cold War.

This chapter connects the multifaceted aspects of Italian women's political participation as it developed from September 8, 1943, when the Resistance began, to June 2, 1946, when the Italians held their first free elections with women voters. Italian women emerged from World War II with a new consciousness of their abilities as women, ready to participate in the reconstruction of their devastated country and to engage with women around the world seeking new roles. As members of nascent women's associations, women who had risked their lives to liberate their country now embarked on a different kind of struggle: one defined by the knowledge that an emphasis on women's emancipation would require a special commitment to autonomous organizing but also necessitate extensive cooperation with political parties and other types of organizations at all levels. The women's associations could not exist outside the influence of other forces, and as a result, they had to design their programs and ideologies in relation to them. Nonetheless, it would be incorrect to characterize the women's associations as subordinate to other, especially male-led, forces. Instead, women were driven by their own specific objectives even when they were in concert with the larger national and international political changes that surrounded them. Historians Anna Rossi-Doria, Anna Bravo, and Anna Maria Bruzzone have argued that the transition out of World War II and into the immediate postwar era was fraught with both joy and despair for Italian women who would be at the center of a surge of national political activity between 1943 and 1946.[3] As I will demonstrate, women's activism was not confined to the Italian context, however. The international stage, too, became a site for dynamic political engagements by women as the "international sisterhood"[4] of the late nineteenth and early twentieth centuries was transformed into a bipolar sisterhood led by women with new political rights.

Italian Women before World War II

Prior to the rise of fascism in the 1920s, Italian women had been part of the development of transnational cooperative efforts among women, which Leila Rupp has characterized as mainly an endeavor of European and European-origin women.[5] Like their counterparts in the late nineteenth century in the United States and Great Britain, Italian women questioned their subordinate social and cultural roles, made especially restrictive by the Napoleonic Code, and their exclusion from political and economic participation. They demanded a thorough examination of the *questione femminile*, woman question, through their participation in liberal, socialist, and Catholic women's associations and made connections with women worldwide in such organizations as the International Council of Women (1903), the International Alliance of Women (1906) and the Women's International League for Peace and Freedom (1915).[6]

Anna Maria Mozzoni (1837–1920) organized one of the first Italian women's associations, the Lega promotrice degli interessi femminili [League for the Promotion of the Interests of Women] in 1881 in Milan. It was founded on socialist principles of women's social and economic equality that had been influenced by French thinkers such as Charles Fourier. Mozzoni argued that the unification of Italy could be accomplished only by throwing out foreign aggressors, and she connected Italian liberation to women's liberation.[7] Despite the support of the newly formed Italian Socialist Party for social equality between men and women, the Lega preferred to operate outside the structure of the party and maintain its own distinct program of action. Mozzoni's role as a founder of the party but her own refusal to join it underscored the problem of political participation for women, who did not have the right to vote and were therefore excluded from formal politics. In many ways, Mozzoni's efforts represent the beginning of autonomous women's movements in Italy. Mozzoni, unlike her socialist contemporary Anna Kuliscioff (1857–1925), did not believe it was necessary for women to subordinate their feminist positions to the broader socialist cause. Under Mozzoni's leadership, the Lega's main activities focused on the protection of women, workers, and children. Those included career training and economic protection for women in feminized jobs, such as telephone and telegraph operators and schoolteachers; the establishment of an insurance plan for pregnant women; and charitable programs for orphans and disadvantaged children.

Italian socialist women under the leadership of such figures as Mozzoni and Kuliscioff became active in international women's organizations. In 1878, Mozzoni represented the Democratic Assembly of Milan at the First International Women's Rights Congress held in Paris, at which she delivered two speeches. In her inaugural day address, Mozzoni underscored the importance of the mission of the congress's working groups on education, morality, and economics and contested women's inferior position in European laws based on the Napoleonic Code. In her concluding remarks, Mozzoni implored women to work together to radically overturn inequality: "We will carefully walk together, we will conscientiously watch out for ourselves, because the individual satisfaction and glory we seek is not guaranteed: we want to knock down the walls of Jericho."[8] American women's suffrage activist Elizabeth Cady Stanton and French feminist Emily Venturi were among the many women dignitaries who attended events over the two-week conference held during the International Exposition and agreed to establish a permanent international committee on women's rights at the concluding grand banquet.[9] International recognition for Mozzoni and her ideas assured Italian women a presence at future international women's conferences.

Liberal Italian women also became activists in the late nineteenth century. In 1903, three groups of women from Rome, Piedmont, and Lombardy joined forces to create the Consiglio Nazionale delle Donne Italiane [National Council of Italian Women]. European women had begun to participate in international events organized by the largely North American–based International Council of Women founded in 1888, and they formed their own national groups linked to the council. German women took the lead in opening a chapter in 1894, after the international council's congress in Chicago, and Italian women in the National Council of Italian Women followed the British, Danish, and Dutch women in joining the organization. The Italian council's international participation was fairly limited, however, and the only area in which the Italian women took a leading role in the international council was in the Standing Committee on Emigration and Immigration.[10] Although the precise nature of the Italian council's national agenda varied during the early decades of the twentieth century, many of its activities were connected to philanthropic works and to a broadly defined progressive emancipationist movement for women based on the traditions of unification leader Giuseppe Mazzini. Led by Gabriella Spalletti Rasponi, a descendant of the Murat and Bonaparte families, the council appealed especially to moderate liberal women, often of aristocratic and upper-bourgeois backgrounds for whom a lay vision proved important in directing their cooperation with socialist women on matters such as equal pay and the opening of more professions to women.[11] Many communist women, however, rejected the group's bourgeois underpinnings, which maintained a split between public and private spaces and emphasized suffrage over the needs of women in the labor force.

Prior to World War II, Catholic doctrine had informed the development of lay Catholic women's organizations by emphasizing the separate roles and duties of women and men, which, in 1891, were reinforced by Pope Leo XIII in his *Rerum Novarum*: "Women, again, are not suited for certain occupations; a woman is by nature fitted for home-work, and it is that which is best adapted at once to preserve her modesty and to promote the good bringing up of children and the well-being of the family."[12] Although Catholic women had participated in activities sponsored by National Council of Italian Women, in April 1908 differences between conservative Catholics and liberals emerged at the first national congress of Italian women during debates over the education of girls, women's suffrage, the legal status of wives, rape, and women's work.[13] In 1909, a new Catholic association supported by the Vatican, the Unione fra le donne cattoliche d'Italia [Union of Italian Catholic Women], resulted from these divisions in vision and became the associational home for traditional Catholic women. During the 1920s, this organization was transformed into the Unione Donne di Azione Cattolica, the women's section of Catholic Action.

Italian women of diverse political perspectives and experiences overlapped in their struggles to promote the rights of women at the national and international levels as the twentieth century opened, but it was already evident by the conclusion of the First National Congress of the Italian Woman in 1908 that basic differences among bourgeois, socialist, and Catholic women would overshadow their common goals.[14] The rise of fascism in Italy during the late 1910s and 1920s further complicated women's self-organizing. Mussolini's regime successfully turned back many of women's political gains and promoted a maternalist ideology, even though some women who had not been involved in women's associations previously now had the opportunity to rise through the ranks of fascist organizations, such as the Fasci Femminili, or to enter public life through charitable work.[15] In fact, the fascist regime counted on the mass mobilization of women's forces to support and legitimize it while it undermined the activities of women's organizations rooted in the pre-fascist era. The liberal National Council of Italian Women was disbanded during Mussolini's dictatorship, and Unione Donne di Azione Cattolica, the lay Catholic women's union, was restricted to working on issues connected to motherhood and children and to cooperation with the Fasci Femminili. There was little hope for women to achieve their emancipationist or feminist goals, such as suffrage, equal pay for equal work, or increased access to higher education and professional careers. Fascist policies particularly harmed socialist and communist women. As historian Giovanni De Luna has pointed out, internal debates on the woman question among socialist and communist men and women, such as the need for separate women's sections inside the political parties, had not yet been resolved when political activists on the left were forced underground or into exile.[16] Despite some successful strikes carried out by women rice workers between 1927 and 1931, "after 1926, with the passage to clandestinity, the possibility for women to participate in conspirative life became even more drastically reduced because of the totalizing level of militancy required by clandestine structures."[17] Nonetheless, the experience of fascism led women's leaders such as Ada Gobetti (1902–68), Nilde Jotti (1920–99), and Marisa

Rodano (b. 1921), often under the influence of male family members, to question the direction of women in the Italian state.[18] New opportunities for women activists arrived not long after Mussolini made his disastrous alliance with Hitler and led the Italians into World War II in 1940.

Women during World War II and the Resistance

English- and Italian-language historiography has revealed the multiple complexities of the late war period, during which the Italians experienced three governments, two occupations, and a civil war that raged in central and northern Italy.[19] On September 8, 1943, Marshall Pietro Badoglio, who succeeded Mussolini after his dismissal by King Vittorio Emanuele on July 25, announced in a radio address to the Italian people that Italy had signed an armistice with the Allied government. Within a few days, the Germans occupied the northern half of the country and took control of Rome and other key cities. Badoglio was forced to reestablish his government in the southern city of Bari on the Adriatic coast. By September 23, Mussolini, then living in Salò, a small town on Lake Garda in the northern region of Lombardy, declared a new government, but he had lost most of his power and was under the tight watch of the Germans. Badoglio declared war on Germany on October 13. Now considered a cobelligerent nation by the Allies and rogue nation by the Germans, Italy was effectively divided into three governments: Mussolini and the Germans in the north, Badoglio and the king in Bari, and the newly formed Committee of National Liberation representing the antifascist political parties in Rome.

The Allies took an active interest in the future of the Italian government, which was already facing the necessity of moving forward under the leadership of the Committee of National Liberation parties—the Italian Communist Party, the Italian Socialist Party, the Action Party, the Democratic Labor Party, the Christian Democratic Party, and the Italian Liberal Party—or the monarchy and Badoglio. The Americans favored the antifascist parties, despite the vast range of political perspectives among them, since they considered the monarchy and Badoglio compromised because of their collaboration with Mussolini. The British, in contrast, were uncertain of the antifascist committee's ability to lead Italy, in part because of the ideological differences among the member parties, ranging from the communists on the extreme left to liberals in favor of parliamentary democracy and capitalism of the liberals.[20] Complicating the situation was the involvement of the Soviets, who, on March 13, 1944, recognized the Badoglio government and resumed full diplomatic relations with Italy. Historians have interpreted this move as an attempt by the Soviets to help the Italian Communist Party by contributing to political gridlock.[21] In fact, communist leader Palmiro Togliatti, exiled in the Soviet Union during the war, returned to Italy to lead the Italian Communist Party and expressed a willingness to go along with the decisions of the Badoglio government in the interests of ending the war and Nazi fascism. Before the war's conclusion, it was evident that a new set of political tensions would surface in Italy and that Anglo-American and Soviet influences would work their way into Italian politics.

Before the Italians could make any decisive choices about the future of the government, however, they still had to free the country from the Nazi fascists. The Allied High Command focused on liberating Rome, which it did by June 5, 1944, and on moving northward, where soldiers remained blocked in the Apennines by winter. Meanwhile, in the north, an organized resistance led by the Committee of National Liberation for Northern Italy sprang into action against the Germans. As a movement of citizens of all social classes, political viewpoints, and both sexes (estimates suggest that about 125,000 people were regular armed resistance fighters and that, of those, 55,000 were women), the Resistance marks a fundamental shift in the way the Italians envisioned themselves as political actors. The Resistance, despite its well-documented ugly moments of retaliation and brutal violence, proved the ability of civilians to rise in arms to defeat the enemy, and it showcased the many talents of Italian women.[22] As recent research has shown, women partisans in the Gruppi di difesa della donna [Women's Defense Groups] were anything but the mere assistants of men and were undertaking activities traditionally hailed as the most heroic—delivering messages, goods, and weapons and conducting reconnaissance missions. As Bravo and Bruzzone have convincingly argued, "ordinary" women engaged in the struggle to end the war through such actions as strikes and sabotage and by arguing publicly about the evils of fascism.[23]

Historians disagree about the relationship between women's participation in the Resistance and women's emancipation.[24] The conventional approach has been to glorify women partisans but to view their contributions in relation to traditional gender roles, especially maternal ones. From this perspective, women partisans were few and exceptional, and their activism ended with the war. Other historians, however, now recognize a historiographical gap connected to the mythology of the Resistance that has reinforced ideals of masculinity and femininity. According to these scholars, it is not that women disengaged from political life after the war but that very little attention has been devoted to the transitional years between the Resistance and the establishment of the first postwar government. Moreover, a maternal discourse proved to be empowering to women during the Resistance and would continue to inform the gendered approach of the women's associations. The idea of "choice" for women had not yet fully entered public consciousness, and the Italian people were suffering after years of hardship. Hunger, lack of adequate housing, and other shortages defined daily life as women struggled to care for their families and friends. Assistance came out of need during the war and in the immediate years after its conclusion. Nonetheless, in the Women's Defense Groups, women demonstrated a consciousness of gender inequality and injustice that went beyond their antifascist actions and called for a greater awareness of women's rights, especially for those of women workers, on a broader level. As women in the chapter of the group in Milan noted, "Next to the general claims of the working classes, it seems that only in a few factories have groups made demands relating especially to women. The problem of leveling wages among women, or in relation to those of men assigned the same tasks as women, exists nearly everywhere, but from what we know it has only been brought up at the Face in Milan."[25]

Resistance folklore was crucial to the founding of the Unione Donne Italiane, and the Resistance itself continued to serve as a defining historical moment even many decades after the war, especially when the UDI found it necessary to reunify the association during difficult times. Although the political left would prove defter in claiming a commitment to antifascism because of its Resistance legacy, the Catholics, too, including future leaders of the Christian Democrats, also pointed to their struggles in liberating Italy. Italian and Anglo-American historians, however, have noted that the Catholic Resistance was less marked by ideology and more defined by the practical necessity of assisting military forces in their fight against the Nazi fascists. When the Centro Italiano Femminile (CIF) later celebrated Resistance heroines, the connection sometimes rang more hollow despite the reality of the women's sacrifices and despite a relationship between the CIF and the Committee of National Liberation for Northern Italy that continued into the months after the war in Italy.[26]

The women who founded the UDI and the CIF drew upon their experiences in the Women's Defense Groups and other Resistance groups and benefited from their close connections to the leaders of the political parties that made up the antifascist Committee of National Liberation. The UDI formalized its structure in September 1944, just before the CIF, and attempted to attract women from all the antifascist parties despite the fact that just two of the fifteen members of the first executive committee were from the parties of the center right. The spirit of unity against Nazism that characterized the Committee of National Liberation was reflected in the UDI's expression of organizing all Italian women who had supported the antifascist struggle and recognized the particular sacrifices and needs of women as the war drew to a close. In May 1945, the readers of the UDI's newsletter *Noi Donne* learned that at a meeting in Milan, the Women's Defense Groups, which by then had seventy thousand members, chose to merge their remaining circles with the UDI to create a single national organization with the idea that it would be "stronger if dictated by all women in just one bloc."[27] As historian Jomarie Alano points out, "The formation of *Udi* provided a bridge between the *Gddd* and the postwar world, giving participants a women's organization in which they could continue their work after the liberation."[28]

Women partisans made up a key component of the UDI's membership, but the association's relevance to the postwar era had also been earned through its ability to point to the economic and social hardships shared by women who worked in the factories and the fields and who faced daily challenges in their homes as well. For example, Iside Bertaccini, born in 1928 in Ravenna, was a farmworker from a left-wing family who had participated in the Resistance. Wartime issues of the UDI's newsletter *Noi Donne* started to appear in Bertaccini's home, and slowly she and other young women began forming small groups and distributing the newsletter along with UDI membership cards. Her political activity and consciousness of her position as a woman attracted her to social organizing; she became the second woman member of the local agricultural cooperative. As a member, she explains, "I almost always brought forward women's battles and then they would say that I was a feminist and I would say,

'Look. I don't have anything against men. It's just that there are certain things you need to understand.'[29] In the UDI, Bertaccini found women who understood gender discrimination and recognized a need for an autonomous women's organization. Cooperatives and the political parties were not enough to fulfill women's dreams. Eda Bussolari, a field hand from Modena, said that she was "one of the communist women who was convinced that the communist party had made a large contribution to Italy's rebirth at the end of war," but she also saw that a women's association was needed "because it was a place where women without close personal ties could talk, argue, bring women together and ask them to read *Noi Donne*, and it was also a good way to learn how to reason in a feminine way without being sectarian."[30]

Soon after being founded, the UDI insisted that the provisional government accord full recognition of women's capabilities. In addition to asking for managerial roles on special commissions for motherhood and infancy, veterans' concerns, emergency assistance, and food distribution, the women of the UDI invited the government to hasten its efforts to purge the country of remaining fascists. They also warned about possible effects of returning veterans on the lives of women, stating, "We are asking the new government to give work to veterans but not to take bread away from women as a result."[31] While the transition out of the war remained a major concern for the women of the UDI, a number of objectives with a distinctly gendered component quickly became a primary basis of the association's early goals. Specifically, the UDI wanted to promote the "political and social elevation of woman" by fighting against prostitution and illiteracy while reforming the Civil Code, assuring women's full participation in all administrative and political bodies and seeking equal pay for equal work.[32] The UDI's purpose was thus not to flank or round out other organizations just by showing that women participated in them but to construct a separate agenda in which all women might partake.

However, as was the case in the Committee of National Liberation, disputes over political ideology and uncertainty about the future influence of the Soviet Union on the Italian Communist Party affected the direction of women's organizing. The liberal National Council of Italian Women was reconstituted in 1944 but failed to effectively connect with large numbers of activists of the leftist and Catholic women's movements and held onto only tangential international contacts in the postwar era, which meant it was not able to carry its prewar feminism across the multiple levels of activism targeted by the new women's organizations.[33] Of the antifascist parties, it was the Christian Democrats and the Communists who would compete for followers in the postwar era, whereas the Liberal Party became less electorally significant. In any case, already in 1945, male Liberal Party leaders asked women to leave the UDI, because they claimed such groups were no longer beneficial. "Unitary organizations were necessary and accomplished important tasks during the period of clandestine activity," they wrote, "but they are turning into an obstacle to the free and autonomous development of various directions of thought and indispensible methods for the attainment of an authentic democracy."[34] A spirit of unity was not forthcoming from women of the center right either. In October 1944, when Catholic women gathered in Rome to discuss the future administration of their organizations were invited to unite with the UDI, they rejected the proposal, preferring to form a federation of Catholic women's organizations, the CIF, stating: "The Centro Italiano Femminile is constituted by the union of all the women's forces (people, associations, bodies) that feel the duty to collaborate in unity and harmony, because society, coming out of the abyss of misery into which it plunged, is resuming its path of orderliness and Christian peace."[35] By early 1945, the Christian Democrats and Catholic Action pressured Catholic women to leave the remaining chapters of the Women's Defense Groups and work instead with confessional groups. Anna Minguzzi, a seamstress from Ravenna, recalls, "Once during a meeting of Catholic Action it was said that we were all passing into membership in the CIF."[36] Thus even before the Committee of National Liberation for Northern Italy took control of Italy on April 25, 1945, and the political parties began vying for control of the new government, important differences in vision surfaced among women's leaders and made the creation of a single large women's association improbable. Nonetheless, the women who formed the CIF, like those who created the UDI, recognized a need for an association whose main focus was women's issues. Grazia Gallone of Brindisi in Puglia points out that she and other early members defined the CIF's initial configuration as "'the woman question' because it was necessary to help and give moral support to her as the linchpin of the family and victim of a war that discharged on her all its tragic consequences and the problems of the daily life of her children and parents."[37] With a largely bourgeois Catholic base, the CIF began to develop its own demands for women, but, like the UDI, it emphasized the need to elevate women's moral and cultural status and ensure their representation throughout all political and social sectors.

Transitions at War's End

When partisans captured and killed Benito Mussolini and his mistress, Clara Petacci, on April 28, 1945, and hung their limp bodies in a gas station in Milan, they demonstrated the rage many Italians shared because of their years under the dictator. Anger soon joined uncertainty and loss as the government began to recompose itself. Historians and political scientists have remarked on the vast challenges Italy's political leaders faced at the end of war—the loss of more than 300,000 lives, economic ruin, physical destruction—that were exacerbated by Italy's inexperience as a unified liberal democracy.[38] Once able to work together, the antifascist parties of the Committee of National Liberation now found themselves at odds over what a new Italy should look like even though they "were agreed in acknowledging how the dictatorship and its structures had permeated the state, its bureaucracy, and the very marrow of its institutions."[39] While the communists and socialists blamed the capitalist bourgeoisie for its complicity in the rise of fascism and called for a complete overhaul of the government and the constitution, the liberals interpreted fascism as a temporary misstep and envisioned a return to the prefascist era. The Christian Democrats, however, wanted the new Italy to uphold the Catholic values of its history and work on a gradual change to the elements of prefascist Italy, such as an unequal distribution of wealth and the moral degeneracy that had contributed to Mussolini's rise.

Italian women shared in the problems of Italy's political future, not the least because the provisional government had granted them the vote.[40] Maria Eletta Martini of the CIF in Lucca recalls how women's suffrage and continued activism were closely connected. "The first of February 1945, while northern Italy was still fighting, the Bonomi government extended the right to vote to women. De Gasperi [leader of the Christian Democrats] and Togliatti [leader of the Italian Communist Party] were the most decisive in sustaining this new right. But, the problem was how women would react. Then the women's associations emerged outside the parties."[41] Although by no means supported by all Italian women and men, the leaders of the larger political parties and Pope Pius XII had, in fact, been convinced of the need for women's suffrage. Some of the smaller parties of the Committee of National Liberation, such as the Liberal Party, were concerned that women's suffrage would lead to more votes for the Christian Democrats, socialists, and communists, and therefore were reluctant to support it. Male political party leaders also engaged in some debate about women's political maturity, but ultimately there were no significant challenges to the extension of the vote. In a speech on October 21 organized by Maria Federici, the first president of the CIF, the pope reversed the Vatican's earlier positions on women's suffrage and argued instead that women would be likely to use their political power to uphold Catholic and family values.[42] As the pope saw it, the Vatican's attempt to renew the Italian nation as the center of the Catholic world would benefit from women's participation. The CIF agreed with the pope's vision and put forward the idea of women as a moral force that would vote with a Christian conscience and prevent another retreat from democracy. On the political front, the Christian Democrats were certain that Italian women would express a preference for their moderate evangelical message of gradual change over the communists' call for a radical break with tradition. The Christian Democrats may have at first expressed less support for women voters, but the party's leaders rightly hypothesized that women's suffrage would ultimately result in more votes for their party. The Socialist and Communist Parties had initially been more enthusiastic about women's political participation in principle but more cautious about the consequences of women's suffrage. Examples in other Western countries had shown that women tended to favor conservative candidates and that Italy's Catholic values would likely turn women voters in the same direction. Nevertheless, the women of the Women's Defense Groups and the UDI took the lead in reaching out to men on the left and pointing to women's contributions in the Resistance and the workforce, which they argued had earned them new political rights.

Historian Anna Rossi-Doria has remarked that the extension of the vote to women at the national level at the end of war passed without extensive debate but also without much celebration. It was as though the new government and the new women's associations took it for granted that this right would be extended to women. Rather than focusing their efforts primarily on the struggle for suffrage, which had begun in the late nineteenth century, women instead immediately turned their attention to confronting the political situation at hand. The women's associations took their new responsibilities as voters seriously and used their new political power to educate women about the political parties and the key issues at hand and to recruit new members to their associations. For example, the CIF made preparing women for the elections a top priority but always in relation to their other activities, such as stamping out immorality in the press, creating new schools for illiterate children, and setting up a national commission on childhood.[43] As a result, women could easily make connections between suffrage and public participation. Sample ballots and detailed instructions explaining the practicalities of how to vote appeared in the UDI's and the CIF's publications.

Given the dire circumstances of the Italian people at the end of the war, in 1945 and 1946, the UDI and the CIF put the immediate material needs of the Italian people at the top of their agendas and engaged in a number of cooperative efforts with each other and with other organizations and the government. For example, during the Christmas seasons of 1945 and 1946, they led efforts to collect food, clothing, toys, and other items for distribution to needy families.[44] The CIF's leaders had serious misgivings about the UDI and so chose not work with them on controversial social issues "for obvious reasons," but "in the realm of social services it was difficult to give a net refusal to collaborate."[45] In fact, the two associations frequently found at least some common ground on social services in coming years. Maria Federici encouraged women to use their new political voice to put pressure on the government to carefully plan the reconstruction of homes in safe and healthy areas and to offer special financial assistance to working homeowners.[46] Moreover, many women joined the CIF precisely because they hoped to help families left in terrible conditions in the immediate postwar period. Clorinda Morante of Avellino in the Campania region recalls that one day soon after the war's end she encountered local Catholic Action leader Italia Giordano, who had just become the CIF's regional president. Giordano said the moment had come for Catholics to turn their attention away from curing souls to curing bodies. She appointed Morante to the CIF presidency in Grottolella and asked her to run the cafeteria for hungry schoolchildren, a task "I accepted instinctually and with enthusiasm thinking about the service I could give to many families who in that moment were in great economic difficulty and I didn't worry at all about how or where to carry it out."[47] The UDI, too, implored the government to hear the voices of women throughout Italy, such as those of Sicilian women who "desperately ask for water because, just to get one drop, women in some villages must walk ten kilometers on foot."[48] The UDI also made plans to work for the protection of mothers and children worldwide and later contributed money from the Italians Abroad chapter of the Fur and Leather Workers Union in the United States and Canada to support Christmas activities for disabled children.[49] The women's associations were aware of the many demands on the first democratic governments but refused to allow the needs of families to be relegated to an inferior status.

Encouraged by the associations' successful collaborative efforts, UDI women attempted to dispel what they saw as misinformation about their association and its support for the left through repeated appeals to Catholic women. For example, at the UDI's First National Convention in October 1945, Adda Corti stated that "membership in the CIF or any other Catholic-confessional association does not prejudice minimally the full participation and adhesion in the organization and programs of the UDI."[50] Meanwhile, the editors of the UDI's *Noi Donne* published a dialogue in which a member of the UDI tries to convince her friend that joining the association does not require rejecting the Catholic Church or supporting the Soviet Union. "These falsehoods are meant to divide Italian women," the article said, "because, taken together, Italian women are an imposing force that scares the fascists and reactionaries."[51] The UDI's efforts would prove only minimally effective, however, since by the end of 1945, a *grande paura* [great fear] of communist-led armed insurrection had spread throughout Italy. The Italian Communist Party controlled large weapons depositories that had been used by the partisans, and violent acts of retaliation were committed against industrialists and landowners suspected of fascist leanings.[52] Class and religious differences informed women's associational choices, which were reinforced as the political parties launched a major propaganda campaign positing their major differences in advance of the first free national elections held in June 1946.

Women and the Elections of 1946

In June 1945, Italy's political class had chosen Action Party leader Ferruccio Parri to carry the spirit of cooperation of the Resistance into the postwar government, but Parri proved ineffective at taking control of a chaotic situation and easing the fears and tensions of the Italian people. Sharp divisions between urban and rural areas and north and south, and among the classes, prevented the promises of unity of the Action Party from materializing. By November, Parri was forced to resign, and Alcide De Gasperi of the Christian Democrats formed a government that stood closer to the political center. The Christian Democrats had not taken a large role in the Resistance or the CLN, but they enjoyed the backing of the Vatican and the capable leadership of De Gasperi, who "more than any other political figure of the time, sought to adapt his party to the multiform character of country."[53] With De Gasperi at the helm of the Italian government, the Allied Military Government expressed its confidence and handed over full control of the northern provinces by the close of 1945. De Gasperi also secured United Nations Relief and Rehabilitation Administration aid from the Americans. With De Gasperi enjoying the support of the major six parties, Italy entered into its first electoral period.

Recent scholarship suggests that Italy's history from the days of the Risorgimento through the post–World War II era is fraught with disunity.[54] The Italians carried both the "values of the Resistance" and the legacy of fascism into the period of recovery while at the same time being forced to embrace either the American model of liberal capitalism or the Soviet model of communism.[55] Rivalries among the political parties quickly produced a system in which "it was as though Italians occupied rival universes. The worker must be on the left. The practicing Catholic must be a Christian Democrat."[56] In March 1944, Palmiro Togliatti had returned to Italy from exile in the Soviet Union ready to lead the Communist Party he had helped to create, but he quickly found himself pulled in conflicting directions. On one hand, Togliatti supported Soviet leader Josef Stalin, had been active in the Third International, and firmly believed in the promises of socialism. One the other hand, Togliatti maintained that Italy would not enter a socialist era through violent revolution but rather through a gradual process that took into account its history as a Catholic nation. Pope Pius XII envisioned Italy as a model Catholic state but saw the communists and socialists as a threat to his vision. He launched a major propaganda campaign to persuade Italians to reject the Communist and Socialist Parties and to support the Christian Democrats. At the same time, President Truman made clear to De Gasperi that American aid was tied to a repudiation of the Soviets. A communist-led government would not sit well with the Americans, in part for ideological reasons but in part because of the need to reconnect its economy to Europe. De Gasperi worked through the Christian Democrats' "forced cohabitation" with the Communist Party and made it his objective to show the Italian people as well as the Americans that the Christian Democrats could be the party of capital.[57] Meanwhile, as historian Mario Del Pero has argued, leaders of the party, including De Gasperi, held onto an Italian nationalist vision and a distaste for the idea of the world being divided into blocs, even expressing the hope that "Italy could act as a bridge of conciliation between the United States and the Soviet Union."[58]

Within this complicated framework, the Italian people had two major decisions to make in the June 2, 1946 elections. The first was whether to form a Republic or continue the monarchy. The second was whom to elect to the Constituent Assembly. Although not necessarily apparent on the surface, linked to these choices was the future of the communist left in Italian politics. Supporters of the monarchy made the argument that continued monarchical rule would act as an effective deterrent to a communist takeover, but the Christian Democrats, knowing that its members were split on the question of the monarchy, downplayed the referendum in favor of stepping up efforts to ensure sizable representation in the Constituent Assembly. Enjoying the backing of the Catholic Church and Catholic Action, the party also turned to the CIF to reach out to women voters. The CIF focused its efforts on middle-class women voters and used the Church's rhetoric to turn women away from the left and the UDI. "In fact, the UDI, inspired by historical materialism is, like every other movement of agnostic or laicist inspiration, unacceptable to anyone who takes her principles and way of life from the directives of the Church," wrote an anonymous author in *Sempre più alto*," encouraging women to vote for the Christian Democrats.[59] The CIF's President Maria Federici followed suit in an article in the association's *Bollettino*, claiming that "voting for Christian Democracy is the only way to guarantee a victory for Christian forces over anti-Christian forces of disorder and violence that hide behind the democratic popular front."[60] The socialists and communists made every effort to show that they were also good Catholics, and the UDI attempted to correct the falsehood that they were an organization of nonbelievers by pointing out that they were "almost all practicing Catholics and that many take communion every morning and go to mass every Sunday."[61] The pope's insistence on the incompatibility of communism and Catholicism, supplemented by American aid, persuaded many religious voters to choose the DC.[62]

The left and the UDI therefore had much more success in persuading working-class voters concerned about their economic futures and antifascist voters worried about the rise of neofascist parties, such the Uomo Qualunque Party, that the Italians needed a dramatic break with the past to guarantee democracy and equality. The UDI campaigned for the Republic with flyers saying "for the rebirth of our country; for the defense of the family; for the protection of women workers; for the social and political advancement of women; and for the salvation of peace; vote for the Republic!"[63] On the question of which parties to select, the UDI sent a postcard to women voters with the message: "Vote for the parties that have accepted the UDI's program and which have always defended and will continue to defend your rights."[64] Although the names of the parties were not explicitly stated, the UDI's message was that only the parties of the left would genuinely advance an emancipationist agenda for women's full political, social, and cultural rights.

Women were not merely voters in 1946, however.[65] Two-hundred and twenty-six women ran as candidates for the Constituent Assembly: sixty-eight for the Communist Party; sixteen for the Socialist Party; twenty-nine for the Christian Democrats; fourteen for the Action Party; and the rest for the smaller parties. Among those elected to the first legislature were the UDI's Nilde Jotti, Lina Merlin, and Maria Maddelena Rossi and the CIF's Maria Federici and Maria De Unterrichter Jervolino. Each woman had a special history during the years of fascism that influenced her political approach. Nilde Jotti, running as a Communist Party candidate, was among the first generations of women to earn the *laurea* degree in literature. She had been a teacher when the war broke out and joined the Gruppi di difesa della donna to fight fascism. Lina Merlin of the Italian Socialist Party was also a teacher; she served two years in prison for refusing to take an oath of allegiance to Mussolini.[66] Maria Maddelena

Rossi, a communist, worked as a chemist in Milan until she was exiled in 1942 for clandestine antifascist activities. She reentered Italy after September 8, 1943, the formal birthdate of the Resistance, and continued her fight against fascism.[67] Maria Federici, a Christian Democrat, grew up in a well-to-do family and traveled with them to Sofia, Egypt, and Paris during the years of the rise of fascism. In 1939, her family returned to Italy, and Federici, inspired by Christian social thought, joined the Resistance in Rome, where she helped to establish a center to assist antifascists. Maria De Unterrichter Jervolino, also a Christian Democrat, was president of the women's section of the Federazione Universitaria Cattolica Italiana [Italian Catholic University Federation] in the 1930s, an organization that attempted to promote an intellectual Catholicism to counter fascist cultural hegemony. These women now looked to turn their public presence into a political one and put forward messages that would appeal to women voters.

The results of the elections proved the contentiousness of the postwar political situation but also the excitement of Italian citizens, 89 percent of whom came out to cast their ballots. The people favored the Republic by approximately 2 million votes and the left, the Communist and Socialist Parties, by nearly 400,000. The Christian Democratic Party won a little more than 8 million votes and dominance in the Constituent Assembly; female voters, especially in the southern and rural areas, voted in higher numbers for the party. Twenty-one women won seats as deputies; twelve of these were leaders in the UDI and the CIF.[68] The UDI congratulated the new women deputies and asked them to work for women's rights and interests despite ideological differences or adherence to different parties.[69] Togliatti, however, expressed concern over the fact that women voters had expressed a clear preference for Christian Democrats, stating: "Women already pay the consequences when they go to do the shopping and the unemployed when they are not able to find work because public work plans are not being carried out, and the consequences will be further paid in other areas of national activity."[70] Maria Federici of the CIF disagreed that women had voted against their own interests, but at the same time, she lamented the antiquated attitudes of some men who had discouraged women from voting, and she argued that there was still a lot of work to be done to educate women and men about politics and women's ability to understand the political system.[71]

Women's International Organizations at the Close of World War II

The observance of International Women's Day on March 8, 1945 brought warm wishes to the Italians from women abroad with a renewed spirit of optimism that had disappeared during the war years. The transformation of transnational cooperation among women was evident in the role International Women's Day had played over the more than thirty years of its celebration and pointed both to women's new political rights and to the challenges they would face as they emerged from the legacy of Nazism. International Women's Day can be traced to a 1909 socialist commemoration of National Women's Day in New York City that took place on the last Sunday of February. A year later in Copenhagen, during the socialist women's meeting that preceded the congress of the Second International, German socialist Clara Zetkin proposed an annual celebration of International Women's Day in March. The first European festivities took place on March 18, 1911, the anniversary of the Paris Commune, and focused especially on demands for women's suffrage.[72] During World War I, European women used International Women's Day to highlight their peace activism. In 1917, Italian women implored war-torn nations to come together in unity as wartime shortages caused widespread suffering, and in 1918, Austrian women organized a peace march that drew three thousand on March 8, the date that would become International Women's Day's official celebration. In the interwar period, European women further cemented the ties among labor rights, peace activism, and women's suffrage and cooperated in ceremonies in Spain, China, the Soviet Union, and numerous other countries. However, celebrations became more fragmented with the rise of fascism and the outbreak of World War II and led to a series of clandestine recognitions.

Beginning in 1944, women Resistance fighters in France and Italy used March 8 to recognize women's efforts during the war and to contemplate their roles in a democratic future. Italian women added symbolic significance to International Women's Day by distributing the yellow mimosa flower tied with a red, green, and white tricolor ribbon. As historian Jomarie Alano has noted, "the feast emphasized solidarity with women throughout the world and empowered the women of Italy with the strength that such awareness provided."[73] Ties with other women were, in fact, reinforced in 1945, when a message from Albanian women affirmed that "the ongoing collaboration between the groups of Italian partisans and Albanians against Nazi Germany has brought our people together."[74] *Noi Donne* reported on a March 8 celebration in London with women attendees from twenty nations proclaiming a right to "be able to participate in national and international political life."[75] In Italy, this possibility had become a reality since the granting of women's suffrage by the Constituent Assembly. The UDI's Laura Rossi expressed her enthusiasm for this new right with a recognition of the work that still lay ahead: "This March 8th, while we offer to give all our support to our comrades in the north still taking on Nazi fierceness, we celebrate our first win, the right obtained in the nascent Italian democracy to march side by side with men on the path to reconstruction."[76]

Cooperation between French and Italian antifascist women had begun even before the outbreak of World War II. In 1937, Italian women exiled in Paris began publishing the women's magazine *Noi Donne* clandestinely under the direction of Marina Sereni; it would later become the UDI's regular monthly. During the Resistance, partisans distributed *Noi Donne* in the German-occupied northern regions of Italy. The first public edition came out in June 1944. While in Paris, some of the women who would later lead the UDI began working with the Frenchwomen's association, the Union des Femmes de France. In October 1944, the UDI's executive committee wrote to the association to announce its formal formation and to point out the associations' common principles and experiences, including those of women partisans who served "on the mountains of High Savoy and in the Province of Cuneo and by the united actions of our women to assist the combatants for liberty."[77] Like the UDI, the Union des Femmes attracted many left-leaning, antifascist women who envisioned a postwar world that would grant them greater political, social, and cultural rights. To make their vision a reality, the women of the French organization looked beyond their own national context and commenced plans to establish an international women's organization that would encompass the national women's movements of countries around the globe. In June 1945, women representatives from Great Britain, Belgium, China, Spain, Yugoslavia, Italy, and the Soviet Union joined with the Frenchwomen to form the Women's International Democratic Federation with temporary offices on the Champs-Élysées in Paris. They immediately announced "the preparation and organization of an international congress of women with the object of working towards a coordination of the activities of women throughout the world on the following essential program: To destroy fascism and ensure democracy in all countries. To work for a happy life for future generations. To give women the rights that are set out in the International Women's Charter."[78] The international federation quickly established itself as a major postwar international women's organization; its leaders recognized that the world had been forever changed by the years of fascism and total war. Accomplished French physicist and educator Eugénie Cotton, the organization's president from 1945 to 1967, led the organization on a path of commitment to antifascism, peace, and women's rights.[79]

European women, especially Italian women, sought to contribute to Cotton's vision while the Women's International Democratic Federation established its reach and immediate goals. A delegation of twenty-nine Italian women—including Ada Gobetti, Camilla Ravera, and Rosetta Longo from the UDI and Maria Jervolino and Anna Giambruno attending as observers for the CIF and Christian Democrats—joined approximately 850 women from forty countries at the federation's first congress in Paris in November 1945. Given the divisive national political climate, the women of the CIF and the Christian Democrats had hesitated to join the UDI women in Paris until they were assured that participation at the congress did not mean they had to join the organization.[80] Italy was one of the countries on the international federation's executive committee, and UDI women filled roles in several subcommittees—Gobetti on the commission on the consolidation of democracy, Ravera on the commission to draw up the federation's statute, and Corti on the commission to study women's legal and economic positions. During the congress, Ravera delivered a speech about Italian women's roles in the antifascist struggle, and Maria Romita discussed the problems facing Italy's children at the end of the war.[81] As would be the case at future congresses, a great deal of ceremony and celebration accompanied the work at hand. One UDI delegate reported that "the great hall of the Palais de la Mutualité offered a spectacle that one cannot forget" because of the diversity of faces and fashions, including clothing that ranged from the "simple American elegance" of the African American women to the polished boots and fur hats of the Soviet delegation. The Italian women expressed their enthusiasm for this exchange of races, cultures, and points of view.[82]

The Italian delegation was one of the largest groups at the congress in Paris. The UDI, encouraged by the number of Italian women participants, attempted to represent the conference as politically neutral and open. *Noi Donne* reported, "Italy knew how to present itself as a nation in agreement in which various associations of women workers—without regard for class, political ideas or religious faiths—work together with one common scope: to raise the lot of our country and hasten its reconstruction."[83] In fact, very little marked the conference as overtly procommunist. Rather, a strong antifascist discourse dominated the event. A Greek delegate, for instance, spoke about the resurgence of fascism in her country, where the jails were full of "patriots," and the participants from all nations made a general call to end Franco's regime in Spain. Even in the oath taken by the delegates that concluded the congress, there was a noted absence of pro-left or pro-Soviet discourse. As historian Francisca De Haan has pointed out, "The just and peaceful world [that the Women's International Democratic Federation] believed in was based on the continuation of the wartime antifascist alliance between the Soviet Union and the Western powers."[84] Instead of focusing on their differences, the women's groups of various nations vowed to "create the conditions indispensable for the harmonious and happy development of our children and future generations; annihilate fascism in all its forms to create a true democracy; to guarantee to the world a lasting peace, the only guarantee of happiness for our homes and our children."[85] The resolutions adopted by the federation established its objective also to participate in the United Nations, formed just one month before the international women's congress. The federation hoped to offer a counterweight to the Liaison Committee of Women's International Organizations, which had been influential in the League of Nations but was now unable to organize a major international conference of its own.[86] The Women's International Democratic Federation also planned to oversee the coordination of a women's agenda in its individual member countries. As the UDI's central committee explained in a *Noi Donne* article, the federation "must be a large, mass international organization capable of mobilizing the masses of women of all countries and capable of weighing heavily in the decisions of the various governments."[87]

Despite their politically neutral discourse during the international congress, many of the federation's leaders were known to be committed communists. As a result, several members of the Italian delegation, such as

Action Party member Maria Calogero, expressed misgivings about joining an organization that appeared to equate democracy with communism.[88] Calogero claimed, in fact, that viewpoints straying from the political positions of the far left had received little attention from the federation's core leadership. Maria Federici agreed, and in her report to the CIF's regional offices about the Paris conference she wrote, "In November we received an invitation from the UDI to participate in the International Congress in Paris to found an international league of women. After a great deal of reflection the Central Committee of the CIF decided not to participate but to send an observer, Dr. Maria Jervolino. The Congress turned out to be in a predominantly communist style, so much so that the Italian delegation, except for the UDI, abstained from giving its adhesion."[89] The CIF, in fact, did not join the Women's International Democratic Federation. It looked instead to develop international cooperative relationships with Catholic women's organizations, and it joined the World Movement of Mothers in 1947.[90] The left/right split that had separated the women's associations in Italy was being replicated at the international level since women were making choices about their political alliances that lined up with their ideological outlooks.

The Italian women's associations reached out to women worldwide and began to construct channels to connect their grassroots, national, and global agendas. Lina Merlin, like many other women leaders, held that international networks were needed to reinforce and deepen the work that already overlapped in local and national contexts. Merlin explained that "by connecting ourselves to other associations informed by the same spirit, the influence [of the association] will make itself heard in the world with the highly human objective of helping people find the way of peace toward progress."[91] Coordinating efforts across diverse environments required special organizational structures and a strong sense of purpose. Both the UDI and the CIF, which had established their headquarters in Rome, maintained close contact with their regional branches. The UDI operated much like the mass political parties. It established a central office led by the association's president and executive committee, which set an overall agenda for the association and oversaw the planning of its major initiatives and annual national conferences. However, regional UDI circles had a fair amount of freedom to respond to local needs and were welcome to introduce ideas to Rome they believed translated well to the national context. The association also encouraged, but did not require, double and even triple militancy: that is, simultaneous memberships in the UDI and in the political parties, trade unions, and agricultural cooperatives. There continues to be some question about the degree of the UDI's status as an autonomous association, especially since so many of its leaders were, in fact, double militants in the UDI and the in Popular Front parties and because the Italian Communist Party contributed to the UDI's budget from its founding until 1982, when the UDI completely rejected communist funds. However, my argument that the UDI was not a flanking organization of the Communist Party and was sustained by thousands of rank-and-file members without any other political ties has been upheld by historians such as Perry Willson, who affirms that both the UDI and the CIF were much more autonomous than the women's sections inside the political parties and "mobilized plenty of much needed support for the efforts of women parliamentary deputies to push through important legal reforms."[92] In other words, autonomy did not mean complete independence, and it did require the establishment of a network of alliances with a variety of other bodies, including the political parties and trade unions and social service and labor organizations. The UDI also recognized the need for work on the global level, and in November 1945 it created an international subcommittee, which included eminent figures such as Marisa Rodano and Rita Montagnana, to better coordinate its multilevel activities and to focus on specific national and international aims. As reports on the situation of women across the country arrived in Rome, the UDI communicated them to the regional UDI circles and to the subcommittee. National organizing was based on goals including peace, an end to the Allied occupation, the continued fight against fascism, and economic recovery. On the international level, the committee outlined precise gender-based plans to work for legal equality for women in the family and workplace, economic equality in the form of the right to work and to a fair salary, and political equality through women's suffrage.

The CIF, in contrast, was structured as a federation of twenty-six different women's groups that kept in touch through special reports to the Rome office and in stories that appeared in its nationally distributed journal *Il Bollettino di attività del Centro Italiano Femminile*. Entire Catholic women's groups with special interests or a special focus, such as the Gioventù Cattolica Italiana [Italian Catholic Youth—1898], could join the

CIF. The CIF preferred, however, to act as an umbrella organization that kept track of the specific needs of women related to their local situations, such as the availability of housing, and tied them to national circumstances, such as the availability of resources. In each case, the CIF prioritized Christian, especially Catholic, affiliations, a trend that would continue on the international level. The CIF cultivated relationships with women's organizations such as the conservative French Catholic Unione Féminine Civique et Sociale, which prior to World War II had campaigned for a wage for working-class mothers who returned to the home and had also supported preferential hiring practices to favor male heads of household.[93] In 1946, the CIF sent delegations to two international congresses in Paris: the French Catholic women's union's "The Mother, Builder of Human Progress" and the National Union of Family Association's "World Congress of the Family and Population." At the former, the CIF expressed its willingness to take on "an immediate effort to adapt legislative norms to a better understanding of the mission of the mother." At the latter, Maria Federici delivered a speech on the economic situation of Italian families and underscored the problem of salaries barely sufficient to sustain one or two people, let alone an entire family.[94] At both congresses, the CIF committed the association to an international component of its work. Both the UDI and the CIF showed consistency in forming their objectives, messages, and political strategies and easily adapted them to the specific contexts in which they operated. Maintaining strong local visibility in Italy's cities and towns and a central headquarters in the capital city while developing an international presence allowed the associations to reach women with overlapping interests and needs.

Conclusion

The international activism of Italian women has its roots in the nineteenth century, when liberals, socialists, and Catholics joined in struggles for suffrage, fair employment, and social equality with noted international organizations such as the International Council of Women and the Women's International League for Peace and Freedom. Although women's leaders held different perspectives on the causes of women's oppression and often sought different solutions to it, women's historians such as Leila Rupp have generally characterized the period before World War I as one of cooperation based on a shared notion of a sisterhood. In democratic Western nations, such as England and the United States, women secured the vote at the conclusion of the Great War, and in European countries such as France and Italy, married women won recognition as holding legal majority. The rise of fascism in Italy, Spain, and Germany interrupted women's progress on feminist objectives, whereas the spread of communism promised to offer supranational equality for women and the working classes. The outbreak of World War II deepened political divisions and created new ones that women would find more challenging to overcome. As the United States and the Soviet Union became weary of the balance of power being created in a postwar world, tensions between the emerging superpowers extended to other countries and influenced their national affairs. The Italians, especially, were affected by a developing bipolar world as conditions apparent at the global level replicated themselves in Italy. The Italians had to determine not only how to cope with the legacy of fascism but also whether the American or the Soviet economic model would best help them recover from the fascist and wartime eras.

Italian women participated in political debates that concluded World War II, and they looked for opportunities to share their ideas with women beyond their borders. Women's rights suffered under the leadership of Benito Mussolini, but women did not back away from challenges during the fascist period, and they rapidly advanced their causes because so many women participated in the Resistance. As the provisional government struggled to regain a place for democracy, it granted women the right to vote and to share the governing of the new Republic. Nascent women's associations, the Unione Donne Italiane and the Centro Italiano Femminile, established themselves as autonomous, politically active and socially engaged organizations ready to promote the interests of women from the tiniest local context to the international stage. Nevertheless, the establishment of these two associations points to the fears, misunderstandings, and losses that accompanied women and men out of the war. The Italian women who founded the UDI and the CIF were largely Catholics and mostly workers and mothers. They wanted to reach out to suffering families and eradicate fascism while helping women to secure their equality with men. Despite the similarities among these women, however, the ideological Catholic and communist divide that had existed before the advent of fascism was deepened and transformed by the realities of the developing national and international political system. Calls for unity were therefore undermined and transferred across local, national, and international contexts. An acute awareness of existing gender roles and the special needs and interests of women contributed to the formation of the women's associations. However, affinity on many issues did not necessarily extend to common points of view on the role of religion or to the experience of class, issues that defined the founders' visions of their groups and determined their national and international alliances. Women's leaders approached each other and were open to dialogue, but the materialization of the Cold War resulted in cautious interactions and ultimately separate paths for politically energized women.

2   Cold War Housewives? 1947–1949

In July 1949, the women's section of the Italian Communist Party sent a report to the party's central committee concerning the key problems it faced in expanding the communists' appeal among Italian women. In its report, the women's section listed "incomprehension and weakness of group work and, in particular, that of the UDI—insufficient initiatives—weakness in our actions towards Catholic organizations—confusion on the religious problem" among the women's main challenges.[1] The report went on to speculate that the UDI was weak because not enough women understood its purpose. Most UDI members at the time were housewives rather than part of the paid labor force, and the writers lamented that the provincial UDI branches were not attracting enough laborers to the UDI or to the Italian Communist Party. Meanwhile, as its membership continued to rapidly expand, the lay Catholic CIF was finalizing the results of its survey on women and housework and childrearing and finding that Italian women had an overwhelming preference for being housewives.[2] Outside and inside onlookers of both the Italian women's associations suggested that in the immediate aftermath of World War II, Italian women were choosing a life of domesticity. But was this in fact the case? After years of work to ensure the political, social, and cultural participation of Italian women, had the UDI and the CIF become, in fact, associations mainly for housewives? If so, could national and international political pressures be blamed for pushing women into traditional roles?

This chapter seeks to respond to these purposely provocative questions with a resounding "no." Although women's momentum may have slowed following the elections of 1946 and after two years of especially intense political activity, women did not disappear from national and international political life, and their associations did not become clubs for women who just wanted to exchange recipes or cleaning tips. On the contrary, between 1947 and 1949, the UDI and the CIF began to better delineate the objectives of their associations and to construct their national and international alliances accordingly. Social assistance work and economic recovery defined the local work of the women's associations, particularly because, as historian Luisa Tasca has shown, the development of state-run family policies and social services in the immediate postwar years was uneven at best.[3] At the same time, the development of a bipolar national and global system influenced women's political activism. Renata Talassi, a home laborer and militant from Ferrara, was quite aware of the complexity of the situation facing Italian women in the late 1940s. She recalls, "The battles at the time went in two directions. There were the social questions, assistance, especially for needy people or families and for babies. Then there was the political horizon, the great theme of peace. Already in 1948, the division of the world into blocs, the terror of the atomic bomb, the Cold War . . . this was the other side. I remember all the banners signed by hand, the petitions, the demonstrations."[4] As Talassi's words make clear, far from withdrawing from the political debates that came to characterize what were arguably some of the most intense years of the Cold War, women mobilized without hesitation. From such matters as the framing of the new Italian Constitution in 1947 to the decision as to whether to enter the North Atlantic Treaty Organization (NATO) in 1949, the women of the UDI and the CIF expressed their members' concerns and put pressure on the political parties and international bodies to represent them.

Italian women also continued to play a role in international women's movements; the UDI expanded its leadership in the Women's International Democratic Federation, and the CIF became a founding member of the World Movement of Mothers. The Italian women's associations found it increasingly difficult to cooperate with each other, however. Even when their core interests overlapped, such as on matters pertaining to social assistance for mothers and children, the permanence of a divided Italian state took hold with the momentous elections of 1948 and left the UDI and the CIF at odds with each other, competing for members and for a vision of postwar womanhood. The women's associations constructed particular discourses of democracy and peace in relation to gender that were informed by the key national and international political developments of the late 1940s. For the UDI, as for other left-wing peace movements of the time, peace and democracy was framed to support the people's democracies, especially the Soviet Union.[5] However, the women's discourse was characterized as much by fear of a return of fascism and the losses to freedom that such a political system had meant for Italy's women as by their enthusiasm for Stalin and Soviet policies. The UDI wanted Italian women to have the opportunity to find security and fulfillment in an economically and socially just society and was convinced that the only way to achieve it was through campaigning for disarmament. The women of the CIF looked to the past as well, but because they wanted to see Catholic principles and traditions carried into the postwar era; they also agreed with the position adopted by the Christian Democrats that Catholics must be at the vanguard of defending the values of Western civilization and upholding individual liberties. The CIF's discourse and actions therefore tended to favor a conception of woman as a mother who protected Christian civilization above all else. By throwing their support to the side of the Christian Democrats and the Americans, the women of the CIF assisted in constructing a democratic capitalist nation that favored the modern nuclear family and its separation of gender roles.

Postwar Recovery

Following the elections of 1946, the Italians struggled to rebuild their country's political and economic systems and repair infrastructure damage. Nearly 10 percent of housing, 60 percent of state highways, 40 percent of railroads, and 90 percent of the merchant marine had been destroyed during the war.[6] Agricultural losses amounted to at least 550 billion lire, and industrial damage accounted for 450 billion lire.[7] The Italians' living standards had suffered as well. Meat consumption was 24 percent lower than its prewar level; 11.8 percent of the population lived below the poverty level; and 11.6 percent were considered poor.[8] Historians now recognize that because of the massive buildup of Italy's industrial infrastructure before and during the fascist era, such figures appeared more devastating to contemporaries than they actually were.[9] Nonetheless, a lack of raw materials and inadequate transportation networks left the Italians seeking solutions that would continue to depend on foreign aid.

In January 1947, Alcide De Gasperi, the prime minister and a Christian Democratic leader, traveled to the United States to meet with President Harry Truman. The Italians were already receiving hundreds of millions of dollars of aid from the UN in the form of raw materials, machinery, fuels, and food supplies, but they needed more. De Gasperi counted on building a relationship with the Americans to secure Italy's economic future. The Americans were ready to open the coffers to the Italians but wanted political reassurances from them. When De Gasperi arrived in Washington, D.C., without Pietro Nenni, the foreign minister and a socialist, the Americans took it as a positive sign. The talks went fairly well, and De Gasperi returned to Italy with promises of more money from the Americans. The precise nature of the arrangements between De Gasperi and Truman, and especially whether De Gasperi's exclusion of socialists and communists from his cabinet in May of that year was a precondition for an infusion of American money, remains a source of disagreement among historians.[10] What is clear, however, is that the Americans feared a communist takeover in the Mediterranean as British influence diminished there. The Americans were also seeking new outlets for trading their industrial and consumer products to shore up their own economic development and prevent an economic collapse in Western Europe.

By March, Truman had outlined his doctrine for Soviet containment and knew he could not risk losing Greece and Turkey to the communists. Italy's strategic position and its potential to be a strong trading partner and ideological friend to the United States was not lost on government officials in both countries. Truman needed De Gasperi's support to counter the influence of PCI leader Palmiro Togliatti and the socialist Nenni, whose parties had united in January in a newly constituted Popular Front alliance. Truman would not tolerate a communist government in Italy, and De Gasperi could not risk losing valuable aid to rebuild Italy; the January meeting between the two leaders thus proved crucial in the months and years to come. When in August 1947, the U.S. secretary of state, George Marshall, released the first estimates for the European Recovery Program, the so-called Marshall Plan, Italy stood to receive hundred of millions of the $29 billion to be distributed to European countries over four years beginning in 1948, but this meant that the Italians had to come up with a comprehensive long-term economic plan to present to the Americans. The Italian plan, as economist Vera Zamagni has argued, did have some positive effects on the economy, but its inability to effectively resolve the country's unemployment problem "constituted the central issue in the disagreements between the Italian and American governments over the use of Marshall Plan funds."[11] The Americans believed that the popularity of the Italian Communist Party was mainly related to the country's economic and social problems. Between 1947 and 1950, by overseeing a series of economic reforms and new industrial projects, the Americans hoped to effect a policy of "positive containment," that is, to make Italy part of the Western bloc through a process of conversion.[12]

As De Gasperi was deepening his relationship with Truman and the Americans, Togliatti was attempting to consolidate the communist base among the working classes while holding on to his alliance with the Christian Democrats. Historian Paul Ginsborg has argued that while the communists were successful at growing the ranks of the party, they failed to become essential to the government by "making the political arena, and in particular their alliance with the DC [Christian Democrats], the exclusive terrain on which reform would be achieved."[13] Togliatti miscalculated the Christian Democrats' potential to become a progressive force and found himself and the Popular Front cut off in the parliamentary system following the Popular Front's exclusion from the government. The left's hostility to the Marshall Plan, perceived by a majority of voters to be a positive part of Italy's reconstruction, backfired and made the Italian Communist Party look out of touch with the gravity of Italy's economic situation. The U.S. cinematic propaganda campaign to sell the ERP, with its images of American autoworkers driving their own cars to work and shopping shelves full of consumer goods, had been difficult for the masses to resist.[14] As a result of such communist miscalculations, "the period from 1947 to 1949 was one of almost unrelieved bad news for the left. The PCI [Italian Communist Party] fell into an isolation never desired by Togliatti."[15] The Italian Communist Party, which had stood at the threshold of power in 1945 and 1946, now found itself politically marginalized as the Christian Democrats and the Americans led the Italian people further away from the possibility of revolutionary change.

The response of the UDI and the Women's International Democratic Federation to such national and international political and economic developments was less than favorable but also revealed their conflicted positions. On one hand, the founders of the UDI insisted on maintaining the autonomy of the association and did not want it to become a mouthpiece for any political party.[16] On the other hand, many of the UDI's leaders held communist and socialist economic and political positions and so were weary of the Americans having too large a role in European recovery, which the Christian Democrats appeared to be accepting. Moreover, many of the UDI's most politically active members, such as Togliatti's wife, Rita Montagnana, and his long-term companion, Nilde Jotti, were also dedicated communists who supported the Communist Party and the Soviet Union and Stalin. As a result, it proved difficult at times for the UDI's leaders to find a balance between their staunch defense of communist positions held by many UDI members and their desire to forge ahead on an agenda for women's emancipation. According to historian Patrizia Gabrielli, this sort of conflict sometimes resulted in even greater criticisms of the opposition than those emerging from the political parties themselves.[17]

The UDI's leaders entered into a strong anti-American discourse that carried into their work with the Women's International Democratic Federation and built on elements of the Popular Front's propaganda. Rather than viewing the Marshall Plan as an aid package to help rebuild Europe, the women of the federation called it a "tool of expansionist and capitalist economics" used by the "American imperialists" to distract the world from deeper endemic problems and to position U.S. military forces in Europe.[18] As Rosa Fazio Longo, a member of the federation's executive committee, saw it, "Today, the imperialists would like to see the economic and political subjugation of Italy; in the future, they would like to make our territory a depot for the atomic bomb, a launch point for their bombers, and to transform our ports into naval bases and use our men for their war games."[19] The women of the federation were doubtful about America's potential to lead the world through an economic recovery and predicted that a deep crisis was imminent in the United States because of massive spending in preparation for war. The federation presented inaccurate statistics claiming that the U.S. budget for 1949 called for spending 79 percent on the military and just 21 percent for civil needs. A *Noi Donne* article, which more accurately reported 35 percent of the U.S. budget allocated for military spending, nonetheless praised the Soviets for guaranteeing a 39 percent share of their budget for economic reconstruction.[20] According to federation and UDI reports, Soviet leader Josef Stalin was reducing military spending and investing in the rebuilding of schools, homes, hospitals, and cultural institutes to improve the lives of Soviet citizens while developing the state-controlled economy. Based on such examples of spending for the good of the people, the UDI preferred to follow the lead of the Soviets rather than the Americans to guarantee Italy's economic future and freedom from a foreign military presence.

The CIF, in contrast, was pleased to see that De Gasperi was building a strong relationship with the Americans and that he was veering Italy away from cooperation with the extreme left. De Gasperi had been courting the CIF since the association formed in 1945 and was frequently a featured speaker at CIF events. In a 1946 speech to the women of Christian Democracy, which several CIF members attended, De Gasperi noted the reluctance of many women to become involved in any form of politics because they viewed participation in the political parties as leading to "a reduction in individual liberty."[21] Instead, De Gasperi argued, politics needed women more than ever because of their "spirit of sacrifice . . . of charity and of reconciliation" that would move Italy forward as the world transitioned out of the period of fascism and war. As historian Cecilia Dau Novelli has pointed out, De Gasperi's words resonated with the women of the CIF, who "came from an experience in which they had been considered more like soldiers under the orders of an army than as free-thinking subjects."[22] De Gasperi represented a Christian-infused democracy to the women of the CIF, and he engaged them in interesting exchanges about possibilities for Italy's future, particularly in regard to social assistance work and politics. Early CIF member Anna Maria Pazzaglia from Bologna recalls that she and other women easily related to De Gasperi's words: "The CIF not only took care of projects for little kids but succeeded in building on the Christian foundation of our association. . . . It was culturally ready to take on the big themes of political life at the time."[23] De Gasperi and the Christian Democrats had the CIF's full support for the country's reconstruction and development—hence, for accepting Marshall Plan funds and resisting the spread of communism.

This is not to say that no debate about the United States took place in the Catholic CIF, however. Pope Pius XII, although ultimately in favor of American aid, had raised important questions about American priorities that many CIF women shared. International relations expert David Ellwood has pointed out that the Italians' acceptance of Marshall Plan funds raised a conflict in values for social Catholics. "At the same time as the Marshall Plan propaganda was purveying a vision of life which was economic, private, consumerist, limitless and available for emulation," he wrote, "the Vatican and Christian Democrat politicians were encouraging the emergence of a strong state which was socially-oriented, collective and welfarist."[24] The CIF, much like the Christian Democrats, moved toward the Americans in many areas, especially because of the help they offered, but not all CIF women venerated the American way of life. Clementina Bertini Passalacqua of Cosenza recalls that one her first responsibilities was to distribute used clothing that the Americans sent to Italy, while Cesarina Mittini credits the Americans with helping CIF in Novara to reopen its daycare centers.[25] But, in the early days of recovery, their focus was on Italy's families, not on emulating the Americans. In other words, recognition of and appreciation for American actions did not automatically translate into the adoption of American models.

Even the most fervent supporters of capitalist enterprise knew that for economic recovery to move forward in Italy, the government had to help Italian workers get back to work and curb rising inflation. Success was mixed, however. By the summer of 1946, factory workers, manual laborers, farmers, and sharecroppers had become frustrated by unemployment figures that had risen to 2 million after the demobilization of wartime production and by unfair work contracts that favored landowners and private monopolies. In the urban areas of the center and north, ex-partisans and workers staged protests and strikes, while in the south and rural areas sharecroppers made demands for new agreements on land usage, production, and debt settlements.[26] In most cases, the agricultural and working classes did not benefit from their mobilization. However, as Ginsborg has remarked in regard to the legacy of the struggle of the sharecroppers, "A tradition of collective action and cooperation had been established; family and collectivity had been drawn sharply together; the young had contested the dictatorial power of the old, the countryside that of the city."[27] The communists and the agricultural division of the CGIL trade union, the Federterra, benefited also from their role in assisting rural workers and saw substantial gains among voters in these areas in future elections.

The women of the UDI took part in the struggles of agricultural workers and gained experience mobilizing for peacetime political collective action. Women participated in great numbers at the many agricultural congresses that took place throughout Italy in 1947, which underscored the UDI's assertion that "there are vindications that women will bring to these meetings of the people."[28] In addition to asking for the removal of "gift" giving and other obligations that sharecroppers were expected to present to landowners, the women of the UDI made it clear to male peasants, farmers, sharecroppers, and day laborers that women were doing the same hard work as men and so should be represented on their farm commissions. They also appealed to the language of family and collectivity by pointing to the high infant mortality rate among agricultural workers and by asking for protections for pregnant women and new mothers. Work and women's difference, as characterized by women's role as mothers, informed the UDI's approach to important social questions as the association transformed its activities from wartime into reconstruction and sought to build its base alongside the main political and labor organizations of the left. In its membership campaigns in 1949, the UDI even decided to allow women whose primary affiliation was with another organization, such as the agricultural collectives, to simply purchase an UDI stamp, a *bollino*, they could attach to another membership card, thereby building the association's base—the UDI was attempting to reach 2 million members—and recognizing multiple levels of social and political mobilization.[29] Calling for women to come together, the UDI exclaimed: "Let's unite women farm hands and share croppers, small property owners and tenant farmers, of the north and the south, from the mountains to the plains, along with everyone who works the earth, in a grand association to win the redemption of the countryside, a life of work and of freedom, and a future of peace."[30] Its leaders wanted the UDI to become a mass association for women that would cross geographical and class divisions and unite women behind a platform of women's interests. In fact, in many areas, UDI chapters were headed by women without any specific political affiliations. Ansalda Siroli, an agricultural worker from Emilia-Romagna recalls, "back then they tried to put the UDI in the hands of independent women so the association would not be seen as an association of the party."[31]

The CIF was also represented in the Federterra, but as historian Maria Casalini has argued, the association maintained a presence in certain organizations less because of a desire to cooperate with the UDI or other organizations of the left than because of a "basement competition to corner vaster segments of consensus."[32] The CIF's mass mobilization indeed took a different direction, focusing mainly on the continuation of assistance programs the association had initiated during its first three years of activity. In 1948, the CIF announced its *giornata del sole* [day of sunshine] campaign to spread public awareness of childhood tuberculosis. The success of the event throughout Italy led the CIF to open the Case del Sole [Sun Houses] after acquiring land and buildings, most at what were considered "healthy" elevations of three hundred to four hundred meters above sea level, to house children sick with tuberculosis.[33] By 1949, the association had opened twelve children's tuberculosis centers in various parts of the country. Since the CIF conceived such programs as the Case del Sole in a spirit of Catholic service and charity, they did not view them as overtly political. Nonetheless, the women of the CIF proved they could mobilize women and men and raise large amounts of money for their programs from other Catholic organizations, private companies, and individuals.[34] For many Italian women, joining the CIF meant aligning themselves with an association that cared for Italy's vulnerable families in a Christian framework. This, too, was a useful propaganda tool. By the end of the 1940s, it was clear that the UDI was a force for women who worked outside the home and the CIF for mothers and children, but both associations focused on the needs of all women and ventured into each other's "territory" nonetheless.

Housewives and Workers

Agricultural and industrial workers joined the UDI in large numbers, but the association did not want to discount those women who did not neatly fit into categories that tended to vote for the Popular Front parties and so extended its efforts to reach women who self-identified principally as housewives. The Italians had not suffered the great population losses of the Germans—Italy reported about a 1 percent loss of its prewar population compared to a loss of approximately 10 percent in Germany—and, unlike Germany, Italy did not experience a large discrepancy in the male to female ratio after the war, with figures remaining consistently at a slightly higher number of females in the pre- and postwar eras.[35] Nevertheless, women deprived of male support in the household usually fared worse than their male counterparts. To show their support for housewives who had lost their husbands during the war and to highlight the stories of women who had been left in precarious familial situations, the UDI featured the founding text of the new Association of Women Heads of

Household in its newsletter.[36] Military and civil widows, the UDI argued, had a right not only to their husband's pensions but also to special job training and preferential hiring to help them to support their families and, additionally, to state support for their children's schooling and health care. The UDI also recognized the insecure situation of housewives who took on forms of paid labor in the household while managing their other tasks. Whether entrepreneurs, artisans, or piece workers, women who worked outside the home often found themselves without representation or the ability to organize for better pay, job training, or assistance programs. The UDI suggested improving women's access to cooperatives, eliminating middlemen, and creating women's sections inside artisan's organizations such as the Confederazione Nazionale dell'Artigianato [National Confederation of Artisans].[37]

For women whose main activity was caring for their homes and families, the UDI took the lead in working with housewives to establish special associations for them. In the summer of 1947, the UDI reported on the founding of the Association of Women Housewives in Pisa, which was just one of many similar associations forming throughout Italy to guarantee the housewife that "her daily ongoing work be recognized, that she be guaranteed assistance when pregnant or ill and that she be assured a pension in cases of disability or in old age so as not to be a burden to her children or to have to ask for charity after a lifetime of work."[38] The UDI argued that the state should establish special insurance and pension funds to support Italy's 10 million housewives because in the current capitalist system, the Italian economy could not function without women's household labor.

Even in later years, the association never wavered from the position that all labor, paid or not, deserved recognition and compensation from the government. The women of the CIF disagreed, however, and that disagreement led the two women's associations into a decades-long conflict that revealed their opposed viewpoints and pointed to the different segments of the female population their associations attracted. Like the UDI, the CIF was also helping to create housewives' associations, but instead of turning to the state for financial support, the members were themselves putting monthly sums—typically between 50 and 100 lire—into special accounts. About this sort of arrangement, the UDI asked: "But how many women will be able to pay this quota? And what advantages are there for them to be united in associations, when an insurance plan such as this one, in addition to offering few guarantees, can also be obtained individually from any kind of insurance agency?"[39] The CIF's response came in the form of a series of conferences, surveys, and publications about housewives, most of which led the association to the conclusion that they were not like other types of workers since, in addition to cleaning, cooking, and performing other household tasks, they contributed an affective component to their households as *angeli del focolare* [angels of the hearth] and took on an educative role as teachers of their children.[40] According to the more conservative members of the CIF, being a housewife was an honorable calling that had been threatened by industrialization and the war; women should now return to the home and reassume their duties.

The CIF's president Maria Federici took a more open position on the question of women's responsibilities and called on Italian women to communicate their preferences about housework and childrearing to the association so that new programs could be established to help them overcome the most challenging and isolating parts of their work.[41] In fact, after receiving extensive feedback from its members—more than 100,000 women responded to a questionnaire that appeared in the March 1949 issue of the *Bollettino*—the CIF expanded the roles of its housewives' associations to teach women home economics information relating to cleaning, teaching and entertaining their children, first aid and health, cooking, and balancing the family budget.[42] Housewives associations offered women support networks and a place to share experiences; they were much more than insurance brokerages. By providing women with certain tools, the CIF enhanced women's work inside the home. Whenever presented with the option of whether to work inside or outside the home, the CIF hoped women would fulfill "God's mission" and choose the former.

Discussions and debates concerning women's work and the role of housewives were not limited to the national context. The CIF's housework survey took center stage at the International Days on the Family congress in Rome in September 1949, when participants from twenty-seven countries engaged on the theme of the family economy in the uncertainties of the modern world.[43] By March 1947, the CIF had received an invitation to attend the Third International Congress of the Union Féminine Civiques et Sociale held at UNESCO in Paris and titled "Mothers Work for Human Progress."[44] The CIF's individual invitation to the congress signaled its independence from the Women's Union of Catholic Action, which had been the major organization for Catholic women activists before and during the war. The CIF joined Catholic Action and the Union Féminine in arguing that women's primary mission should be within the family. Founded in 1925, the union was a social Catholic organization whose primary goals were twofold: "on the one hand, to revalorize motherhood through public education and, on the other, to construct economic and social policies that would enable women to stay in their homes."[45] The union continued its mission in the post–World War II era as the World Movement of Mothers, the name it was given at the conclusion of the Paris convention with Frenchwoman Geneviève d'Arcy as its first president.

The drafting of the Movement of Mothers' *Mother's Charter* codified the new international organization's interpretation of the role of mothers in linking all facets of human society. As described in the charter, "A mother is the most powerful influence on the cultural, economic and social life of the family and society. A mother, therefore, determines the moral and spiritual values of an entire nation and impacts on the ethos of the international community. . . . It is vital that public opinion and policymakers in all countries recognize and value the priceless contribution of mothers throughout the world."[46] According to the charter, men and women had equal but complementary roles within the family; the family—defined by the presence of a husband, wife, and children—was a natural social formation that should be aided by organizations and governments. The charter stated that "the union of a couple in marriage and the fertility of their conjugal life are subject to their conscience alone and may not be imposed nor impeded by legislation, political institutions or economic planning."[47] The implication was that any attempts to interfere with the traditional family in which gender roles had been clearly defined should be stopped. According to the Movement of Mothers, the economic and social planning suggested by some socialists and communists, even for example in the kibbutz that formed in Palestine in the 1930s and 1940s, which would redefine gender roles and remove primary care giving responsibilities from the biological parents, ran contrary to human nature, religious tradition, and the modern state.

Such positions received sharp criticism from the Women's International Democratic Federation, which viewed the Union Féminine Civiques et Sociale, in addition to the Entente Mondial des Femmes pour la Paix and Le Conseil Internationale des Femmes, as organizations promoting the return of women to the kitchen and eliminating their social and political lives "just like the fascists did." According to the federation and the UDI, "the activities of these organizations represent a very serious threat to peace and to the international women's democratic movement. Behind these organizations there are propagators of war."[48] Their disdain for these women's groups was also evident in their refusal to participate in an international UNESCO congress organized by the Entente in October 1947 and by the UDI's failure to even mention the meeting in *Noi Donne*. Political scientist Anna Scarantino has argued that the Women's International Democratic Federation's "snubbing" of the Entente even reduced the peace organization's effectiveness in the international arena in later years. Given the UDI and the Women's International Democratic Federation's failure to interact with the Entente and the Union Féminine Civiques et Sociale, Scarantino has questioned the sincerity of their stated desire to become unitary organizations for women with antifascist histories who were genuinely determined to prevent another war.[49] While I do not share Scarantino doubts, it is clear that a particular discourse suggesting that women had a "natural" calling and were complementary to men, or one that held that women were not suited to public life, alarmed the women of the UDI and the Women's International Democratic Federation. Both organizations were still coming to terms with the losses that women's movements had suffered during the interwar years and World War II. The years of fascism in Italy under Mussolini had come to an end, but fascism had not been completely discredited.[50] Fascism in Spain, in the meantime, was still a stark reality and indicated that the Europeans needed to remain vigilant to prevent its spread.

To begin to effectively put behind them the constraints on their freedom that fascism had reinforced, the leaders of the UDI and the Women's International Democratic Federation argued, women needed a political and economic system that would empower them and allow them to construct new gender roles based on mutual respect. They idealized a sort of Stalinist maternalism, which had been promoted in feminist circles in the mid-1920s by German socialist Clara Zetkin. In this model, the socialist worker-mother labored outside the home but benefited from an array of social services that gave her ample space to devote to the emotional well-being of the family; she was a "hard and fast synthesis of productivity and morality."[51] The same ideal persisted into the period of reconstruction when UDI leaders such as Maria Maddelena Rossi claimed that Soviet women were so far advanced in the areas of work and social services that she and other Italian women felt "embarrassed in comparison next to them."[52]

Work outside the home in capitalist countries such as Italy offered women opportunities for greater economic independence, but many found it difficult to keep their jobs once they became pregnant. The women's associations recognized this conundrum and examined ways to help. In June 1948, the CIF published a special insert in the *Bollettino* on the legislative proposal for the Protection of Working Mothers. The women of the CIF upheld their traditional position that it was better for women to be housewives than paid laborers, but they stood behind Pope Pius XII's words: "Woman is indeed kept outside the home not only because of her proclaimed emancipation but often also because of the necessities of life, by the continual worry of obtaining daily bread. It is therefore in vain that one preaches for her return to the hearth as long as the common conditions persist that constrain her to stay away."[53] The CIF's leaders understood that the difficult economic times of the immediate postwar era had led many women into the workplace, at least temporarily. Maria Federici therefore worked with Teresa Noce and the other women parliamentarians to draw up protective legislation for women in the labor force who had children. The key details of their proposal were enlarging the categories of women who would receive protection; making longer periods for maternity leave with better economic compensation; establishing feeding rooms and day care facilities for young children; and, providing women who were entitled to sick leave benefits with health care benefits when pregnant.[54]

The UDI and the CIF were able to work together on the legislation because of the proposal's emphasis on maternity, but the associations and the women who represented them in the government faced sharp criticisms from the political parties and businesses trying to increase productivity and cut spending. Nevertheless, the associations mobilized their activists in Italy going beyond their traditional methods of collecting signatures and money in favor of the proposed law. They vowed, "We will launch bigger demonstrations, festivals, awards, and gift give-aways, tying the laws to the particular requests of women in each specific place . . . day care, a preschool, a clinic, a school."[55] Teresa Noce reported on the Italian women's efforts at the 1948 Women's International Democratic Federation's convention in Budapest where she pointed out that protective legislation was needed to bring Italy's labor practices into line with its new constitution, which guaranteed not only the equality of men and women in general terms but also entitled them to the right to work and the right to an equal salary for equal work. "When you read the text of our constitution and when you compare it to constitutions of other countries, you think that our constitution offers great possibilities for social and civil progress."[56] In other words, the basis for equality existed; it was now time to see it practiced. Women's consciousness of their special roles as workers and as mothers in this particular case crossed political lines and led to success when the law titled the "Physical and Economic Protection of Working Mothers" took effect in 1950. The women's associations proved their ability to reach the masses of Italian women and to put aside other disagreements when necessary. Few such occasions arrived, however, since it was difficult to ignore new developments in the Cold War.

The Constitution and the Elections of 1948

According to the women who had taken part in the antifascist movements at the end of the war, only peace and democracy could offer all women new opportunities for advancement. What those terms meant precisely became contested terrain, however, as the divisions of the Cold War took hold in Italy and worldwide. Generally speaking, the Western bloc, led by the United States, upheld individual liberty as the cornerstone of democracy and peace. From this perspective, as long as the Soviet Union denied civil liberties to its citizens in favor of maintaining its hegemony in a one-party system, it could not be considered a democracy. On the other side of the divide, the defenders of the Soviets argued that they were taking the lead to prevent the resurgence of fascism and a new war and so were supporting peace. Adding another dimension to the discourse of peace and democracy was the Vatican, which saw the family unit as the basis

for social justice. Proponents of Catholic social doctrine promoted egali-
tarianism as a fundamental element of recovery and progress.[57] The
women of the CIF believed peace and democracy would be guaranteed in
the new Italian Republic by way of its new democratic constitution, which
was approved in 1947 and went into effect in January 1948.[58] Peace to
them meant not only the end of the war but also the reinforcement of
Christian values and the continuity of Italy's Catholic history reflected in
the government. Maria Federici represented her CIF and Christian Democracy constituents' interests as a member of the Constitutional Commission and reported on the ongoing discussions about the drawing up of
the new constitution. In an article in the CIF's *Bollettino*, readers learned
that the new constitution would espouse a general principle of the separation of church and state by granting each its own missions but would also
allow established Christian traditions to continue.[59] The Christian Democratic Party, which had garnered most of the CIF's members' votes in
1946, fought to have Catholicism confirmed as the official state religion
and succeeded, after an intense battle with the socialists and communists, in having the Lateran Pacts of 1929 incorporated into the new constitution as article 7. Catholic values for the promotion of peace therefore
included such civic principles as compulsory religious education in public
schools but also social legislation, such as the sanctity of the family. Although the women of the CIF viewed marriage and the family as "natural" conditions strengthened by religious sacraments rather than as matters
to be legislated, they nevertheless supported laws to prevent breaking up
families.[60]

Communist and socialist UDI members on the Constitutional
Commission—Teresa Noce, Nilde Jotti, and Lina Merlin—disagreed vehemently with these constitutional measures, arguing that they undermined democracy and assigned too much power to the Catholic Church.
To sustain a working relationship with the Christian Democrats, Palmiro
Togliatti had persuaded the communists to vote in favor of declaring
Catholicism to be the state religion. To the dismay of the socialists, all
communists in Parliament, with the exception of the UDI's Teresa Noce,
followed Togliatti's lead.[61] Noce argued that the declaration of a state
religion in article 7 violated article 3, which stated: "All citizens have
equal social status and are equal before the law, without regard to their
sex, race, language, religion, political opinions, and personal or social

conditions." With a special place awarded to Catholicism, Noce asked how non-Catholics would fare. On the question of the sanctity of the family, the UDI supported Giovanni Grilli's proposal to allow for the dissolution of marriage. Togliatti had not been inclined to pursue any issues that could be used by the Christian Democrats as evidence that the left wanted to destroy the traditional family, and he wanted the UDI and the women's section of the Communist Party to back away from potentially incendiary legal measures. Grilli's proposal did not win enough support anyway, but the UDI continued to pressure the communists to rethink their positions on separation and divorce for decades to come. For the time being, the UDI questioned whether its vision of democracy—that women must be granted full economic and social rights as individuals—was being represented in the new government. The UDI's leaders also grappled with the contradictions inherent in stressing the need for women's emancipation, on one hand, and making sure Italian women understood that supporting socialism did not mean that they had to stop being good wives and mothers, on the other.[62]

Questions regarding the meanings of democracy and peace would be further contested as Italy entered its next election season with voting scheduled for April 18, 1948. Despite the attempts of Togliatti and other communists and socialists to govern with the Christian Democrats, De Gasperi booted them from his cabinet, citing his need for solidarity to effectively govern the state. Given the compromises the Communist Party had made in an effort to appease the Christian Democrats and the havoc that had wreaked on the relationships among the parties, the Popular Front was in no mood to concede the elections to the Christian Democrats. All the political parties understood the global significance of the 1948 elections, which meant that "never again, in the whole history of the Republic, was a campaign to be fought so bitterly by both sides, or to be influenced so heavily by international events."[63] Perhaps most telling was the overt interference of the American government and the American people in the elections. Since President Truman could not risk a communist victory, he relied heavily on the use of propaganda surrounding American aid to be sure the Italians understood that help was contingent on a democratic outcome. The threat of American military action loomed just beneath the surface. Outside the government, ordinary Italian Americans and Hollywood stars wrote letters to friends, relatives, and even unknown Italians imploring them to vote for the Christian Democrats, at times stuffing a few dollars into the envelopes.[64]

Inside Italy, the Catholic Church, led by Pope Pius XII, joined forces with the Christian Democrats and mobilized lay organizations, such as Catholic Action, the Centro Italiano Femminile, and local parishes, to reach Italian voters. The CIF's Maria Federici endorsed the Christian Democrats in the association's *Bollettino* and promised to deliver the party 6 million votes from women who realized that "voting for the DC was the only way to combat the anti-Christian forces of disorder and violence."[65] Just to be sure women cast their votes correctly, the *Bollettino* article included an image of the party's logo, a shield with a cross inside with the word *Veritas* written across it, as it would appear on the ballot.[66] Because of the pope's admonition that voting for the Popular Front was tantamount to voting against Christ, many Catholic voters came to believe that "the choice was not between political parties or philosophies, but between heaven and hell."[67] The formation of a group of progressive Catholics who aligned themselves with the Popular Front, the Movimento Cristiano per la Pace [the Christian Movement for Peace], did not have a significant influence on voters despite the campaigning of women such as Ada Alessandrini, who left Christian Democracy because "it had betrayed the ideals from which it was born," and she became a militant UDI leader and activist in the Women's International Democratic Federation.[68]

In part because of the Americans and the Vatican standing firmly behind the Christian Democrats, and in part because of the Popular Front's inability to clearly define and communicate its plan of action, the results of the elections were decisive. The Christian Democrats won 48.4 percent of the vote, more than 12.7 million ballots—an increase of 5 million over the previous elections in 1946. The Popular Democratic Front garnered 31 percent of the votes, with 8.1 million ballots cast in its favor. The last opportunity for the left to reverse the momentum of De Gasperi and the Christian Democrats had been lost. The elections signaled to the victors that voters wanted political and economic stability as well as a secure alliance with the United States and its other Western European allies. For the left, in contrast, the victory of the Christian Democrats signified a definitive turn away from the possibility of revolutionary socialism and a need to unify the parties differently. Only for a brief moment in July 1948, following the attempted assassination of Togliatti, did the more radical communists and socialists take insurrectionary action. Without the support of the communist leadership, however, the militants were forced to retreat, and the left to accept the political outcome.

The members of women's associations campaigned for the political parties and for their own women candidates during the election season and analyzed the results in relation to their particular programs for women and interpretations of democracy and peace. In terms of women's political representation, women won forty-five seats (7.1 percent) in the House and four seats (1.2 percent) in the Senate. Christian Democrat Angela Maria Cingolani Guidi entered the cabinet as the first woman undersecretary of commerce and industry. Women more than doubled their presence from the twenty-one members of the 1946 Constituent Assembly but actually just maintained their ground in terms of overall percentage since the number of elected parliamentarians grew from a total of 556 to 945.[69] At the UDI's second national convention in June 1948, Rosetta Longo delivered a detailed opening address in which she noted the powerful electoral influence of the Vatican, the United States, and lay Catholic organizations such as Catholic Action and the Centro Italiano Femminile, but stated that she did not wish to dwell on the results of the elections. Instead, according to Longo, the women of the UDI needed to move forward to defend women's rights, especially to work and to a fair salary. Making significant advances would necessitate that the members of the UDI "ask our leaders something we have never asked of them before, that is to truly be political leaders, to embed themselves in all demonstrations, agitations, and movements that will take place in Italy."[70] Moreover, the UDI suggested working more closely with the Alleanza Femminile, the women's section of the Popular Front, even if the UDI would remain autonomous and "at the vanguard of all women who struggle for the triumph of democracy."[71] The UDI's leaders were upset by the results of the elections, but they decided they would not be held back by them and would instead move forward on their immediate goals, including the campaign for international peace in cooperation with the Women's International Democratic Federation. The losses of 1948, moreover, had the unintended consequence of bringing more women into the association. Gabriella Vergoni, for example, recalls that "after the 18th of April and the defeat suffered, which I call the bump on the head, I decided to participate in a more serious way. I joined the communist party and I started going to the UDI."[72]

The women of the CIF, in contrast, were thrilled with the results of the elections. They witnessed their own mass mobilization produce the desired outcome. "The electoral campaign—begun in a hot, if not explosive climate, because of outcomes that could have caused our country to divert from its path—was organized and conducted by the women of the CIF with a full understanding of the moment, with solid tenacity in their work of waggle and persuasion, fully intent on victory. From the big cities to the small towns, Christian women did their best with assiduous propaganda. . . . Let's say that victory required six million votes from our women. Six million were reached."[73] The CIF remained independent of the Christian Democratic Party, which had its own women's section, and of the Vatican and Catholic Action, but like these other religious and political bodies, the CIF connected Italy's moral and material progress to global anticommunism and cooperation with the United States. As the CIF's national council recalled in a summary of its main activities between 1945 and 1949: "In 1948, re-entering the political struggle with much more harshness than that which had characterized the elections for the Constituent Assembly, the CIF retained its strict duty to intervene . . . since other results would have had a decisive importance for the destiny of the country and its Catholic Church."[74]

International Peace and Democracy

In the late 1940s, conflict dominated the international political scene. Chinese leader Chiang Kai-Shek lost ground to the communists as they mounted a full-scale offensive against the nationalists. Despite American support, Chiang Kai-Shek's government was forced off the mainland and created the state of Taiwan, while Chinese communists sought an alliance with the Soviets. In the Middle East, new Jewish settlers in Palestine proclaimed the state of Israel, leading to a continual state of open hostilities with surrounding countries. Josef Stalin expanded Soviet influence in Europe through the installation of satellite governments in Poland, Hungary, Romania, Bulgaria, Albania, and Czechoslovakia. The violence surrounding the communist coup in Prague in February and March of 1948, some argued, contributed to the defeat of the Popular Front in Italy since many revolutionary socialists and communists had labeled it a victory, but it also drew attention to the powerful tools Stalin had at his disposition. In the Mediterranean, a popular uprising of Greek communists had already led to civil war, which was followed by British and American intervention. In Spain, fascist leader Francisco Franco continued to hold on to his power. In Italy, neither De Gasperi nor Togliatti wished to pursue the authoritarian and heavily church-influenced model offered by Spain or face the social unrest caused by the civil war in Greece and thus remained committed to the new Italian constitution and to their parties' principles of antifascism.[75] National and international politics came into dramatic conflict, however, when the Americans asked the Italians to join NATO in 1949.

The UDI took several actions in the international realm to uphold its vision of peace and democracy. The CIF occasionally responded to some of the UDI's national initiatives but distanced itself from the UDI on the international level. The UDI sat on several national and international committees, for instance, to support the Palestinian and Greek people and decry Franco's regime in Spain, whereas the CIF did not. The UDI's leaders intended to "show our women that the struggle for peace we are conducting is a struggle, not only of the Italian people but also of many other people; we must let women here know about the lives of women in other countries and explain how they are organized in democratic movements and in which forms they carry out the struggle for peace."[76] Issues of Noi Donne in the mid- to late-1940s featured stories about, for example, Greek communist women and the hardships they and their families faced during the British- and American-backed conflict; Dolores Ibárruri, La Pasionaria of the Spanish Civil War, who became a vice president of the Women's International Democratic Federation in 1945 and continued to lead her country's fight against Franco's regime; Chinese communist women supporting Mao's efforts to secure a people's democracy.[77] A kind of political naiveté runs through each of these features; there is no question that the communists are the defenders of peace and democracy and that the Western bloc is the perpetrator of war.

This same line of reasoning can be found in the UDI's preparations for the International Day of Peace held on November 30, 1947—not coincidentally the second anniversary of the founding of the Women's International Democratic Federation. Organized to build momentum for the group's December 1948 congress in Budapest, the day of peace also opened the UDI to criticisms from the women of the CIF who had been invited to participate in its celebrations.[78] Since the invitation included the phrase that the Western powers "try to show that a war against the USSR and the people's democracies is natural and inevitable," it did not gain much favor with the CIF, which responded with the message that "the initiative, the messengers, and all the machinery is of Marxist inspiration and flavor and therefore of a mindset that today is being expressed in a totalitarian and warmongering form being put into effect and that has already submerged half of Europe."[79] The CIF made clear that, unlike in Paris in 1945, it would not send any delegates to the upcoming Budapest congress.

As historian Francisca De Haan has pointed out, the Women's International Democratic Federation's second congress reflected the direct influence of the Cold War, characterized by a more overt expression of pro-Soviet politics "at the expense of both a positive agenda and women's rights."[80] It was also a moment for showcasing the hospitality of the Hungarian communists. When the eighteen Italian delegates arrived at the convention in Budapest, they were treated to rooms in the nicest hotels and showered with gifts.[81] Maria Maddalena Rossi, Rosetta Longo, Giuliana Nenni, and Rita Montagnana officially represented the UDI, and UDI members Teresa Noce and Ada Alessandrini attended the convention as representatives of the trade union, the Confederazione Generale Italiana del Lavoro, and the Movimento Cristiano per la Pace [Christian Movement for Peace], respectively. Jone Cortini served as the Italian delegate of the Women's International Democratic Federation. Despite the pleasant reception and well-appointed surroundings, however, ongoing international conflicts and ominous threats hung over the heads of the women assembled from fifty-one nations in the Hungarian parliament building; their discourse revealed the nastier qualities of the Cold War. Taking a direct hit at the United States and Great Britain, the leaders of the Women's International Democratic Federation accused the Western powers of disobeying the principles of Yalta and Potsdam, trying to halt the advance of the people's democracies, and challenging the independence of colonized nations.[82] Magda Jóboru, chief secretary of the Union of Hungarian Women, opened the convention with the following politically charged words: "I warmly greet the delegates of our neighbor, the chief defender of peace and democracy, the Soviet Union, with special affection. I warmly welcome the heroic Chinese, Greek, French, and Spanish women, delegates of the peoples who are bravely fighting against the imperialists." She closed her speech with a rallying cry of "long live the peace-loving women of the world! Long live the great leader of the world's peace-front and the front of democracy: Marshal Stalin!"[83] There could be little doubt that the sort of peace and democracy the Women's International Democratic Federation had in mind meant support for Stalin's Soviet Russia and a denigration of the American-led Western bloc. The UDI's Rosetta Longo concurred, arguing: "To prepare for war, the American imperialists, with the complicity of the Christian Democrats, are looking to economically subjugate our country and to weaken our democratic liberties."[84] However, it was not only anti-Americanism that permeated the women's discourse but also admiration for the strength and determination of the Soviet people at the end of World War II. As historian Christopher Duggan has noted, the pro-Soviet orientation of many Italian communists and socialists was directly tied to "the victory at Stalingrad, as the supreme ideological and material headquarters of the fight against fascism."[85] In fact, when UDI member Giuliana Nenni, who was also a member of the Italian Socialist Party, expressed her admiration for the Soviet women who had heroically defended their cities and were now engaged in rebuilding them, it so touched the women of the Antifascist Soviet Women's Committee that they later quoted her. Resistance and antifascism were woven into the Italians' pro-Soviet discourse.

Although perhaps obscured by intense Cold War positions, a women's agenda did emerge during the congress, as did further affirmation of the Women's International Democratic Federation's purpose and the UDI's place within it. Ada Alessandrini, for example, expressed a particularly favorable impression of the new international democratic women's movement. "The Budapest congress, much more than an international meeting, can truly be considered a global women's conference," she said, because even if women spoke in their native tongues and brought their own religious, political and cultural customs with them to Budapest, "they harmonized their efforts in the organicness [sic] of a truly organic project." Alessandrini acknowledged that the Italian delegation was not very large but asserted that it represented all the women of Italy, especially the hundred thousand subscribers to *Noi Donne*; she urged readers to send questions to the magazine about the UDI's international presence.[86] Rosetta Longo highlighted the Women's International Democratic Federation's strides forward; she recalled that when women went to Paris in 1945, they were uncertain of their ability to make the federation "a strong and powerful organization, capable of carrying out its tasks and making itself heard in the political world." After Budapest, Longo was comfortable reporting that after just three years of activity she could say that the federation had become strong and powerful and was "the only international women's organization that [was] truly democratic."[87] Teresa Noce recapped the progress that Italian women had made since the days of the Resistance, pointing out that they now voted, sat in Parliament, and had gender equality written into the constitution. Now it was time, she argued, to be sure that the path toward women's emancipation remained unimpeded and that the rights to work and to a fair salary be guaranteed.[88] Working together, the Italian delegation believed, the UDI and the Women's International Democratic Federation could advance the overlapping struggle for peace and women's rights at home and around the world.

The socialist and communist women's Cold War mobilization across multiple levels is most evident in regard to their opposition to the Atlantic Treaty, which was also discussed at length in Budapest. During, and partly because of, debates over Italy's entry into NATO, the national and international political climate changed from one of lukewarm cautious cooperation to one of heated open opposition. NATO was an important part of the U.S. strategy to contain communism, but as Del Pero points out, there was not unanimous support in U.S. political circles for Italy's entry. President Truman and diplomat George Kennan opposed it, citing the strength of the Italian Communist Party and its close ties to Moscow as valid reasons to keep Italy out. Nevertheless, other voices, such as that of Secretary of State Dean Acheson, convinced the naysayers that Italy's exclusion from NATO would "weaken the De Gasperi government and pro-western governments."[89] For De Gasperi, inclusion among the NATO countries signified reentry into the international arena but also meant further acceptance of a bipolar world and possible peace treaty–breaking remilitarization.[90] Nevertheless, the advantages to Italy's political position and relations with the United States led De Gasperi to seek ratification of the pact. Togliatti and the communists fully opposed it and put the full scale of their resources into action to stop it.

Women of the UDI launched a massive campaign to collect 6 million signatures against Italy's membership in NATO, which would give the left further backing in its demands for neutrality. UDI leaders had already successfully led a similar initiative in 1948, when the association sent a petition with 3 million signatures to the United Nations in support of nuclear disarmament, and they were confident they could now extend the association's reach and mobilize even more women, especially given the urgency of the upcoming vote. UDI volunteers used the opportunity presented by their petition initiative to talk to women door-to-door and attempt to open their minds to the possibility that most propaganda circulating at the time favored the Christian Democrats, the United States, and NATO.[91] Editorials written by UDI members in *Noi Donne* against the Atlantic Pact, such as one by Dina Rinaldi, claimed that President Truman and French statesman Robert Schuman's "words of peace were just an electoral strategy, a way to use the aspirations of the people to lead them gradually into war."[92] Expressions of opposition to NATO ranging from rank-and-file UDI members to well-known actresses and members of Parliament appeared in numerous issues of *Noi Donne*. Socialist Party leader Pietro Nenni even offered his own insights in the magazine, arguing that the American and Soviet people all wanted peace but that moves on the part of the United States to exert its economic and military power in Europe were interfering with that possibility. He asked women to continue their mission for peace.[93] All of these personal appeals to the women of Italy, however, were muffled by those of the pope, who intervened in the matter by stating in a public radio address on Christmas Eve that nations should unify in defense against threats from other countries. The CIF used the pope's words in its own propaganda efforts. Opposition to NATO failed; Italy entered into the Atlantic Pact in April 1949. The UDI's efforts did not stop, however. After Italy's ratification of NATO, the association sent a letter directly to President Truman to let him know that millions of Italian women had opposed the actions of their government and that they did "not want counter-opposed blocs of states but one united organization of all nations" representing all the people of the world.[94]

Conclusion

By the end of the 1940s, Italy was very different from what it had been at the close of World War II. A new constitution reaffirmed the Vatican's role in postwar reconstruction, and the victory of the Christian Democrats in 1948 assured Italy's ties to the Western powers, led by the committed anticommunist United States. The power of the left in government diminished, as did the possibility of a violent communist takeover. Economic recovery moved slowly ahead, but some stability appeared close at hand. While citizens of other democratic countries with longer histories of liberalism dreamed of "a return to normalcy," the Italians faced a new reality in which not only the world, but the Italian nation-state, was divided into opposed blocs. In the Italian case, however, the choices were not capitalism or communism but communism or Catholicism. For the political parties of the center and right led by the Christian Democrats' capable De Gasperi, American influence through the Marshall Plan and NATO was hard to resist. The prime minister was credited with helping to boost the Italian economy and regain a place for Italy on the international stage. The Americans offered the Italians viable models for capitalism and their related social and cultural life. The left, however, moved ahead on less unified ground, with some leaders completely rejecting the West and embracing the Soviet model and others looking to infuse at least some aspects of socialist ideals into the emerging Italian system.

Messages concerning women's rights and roles arrived from both sides of the political spectrum, with most male political leaders asking women to assume subordinate roles in both public and private life despite the provision for women's full equality in the new constitution. Conservative forces called on women to assume their duties in the household and contribute to Italy's future as housewives who sustained their families and provided the community with good citizens. Even politicians who leaned more to the left asked women to support the traditional family, whether by giving up such radical objectives as permitting divorce or by accepting that working conditions and pay might favor male workers, since men were supposed to sustain the economic life of the family.

The Italian women's associations positioned themselves according to their own understandings of the actual political, social, and economic situation in Italy and beyond. The standpoint of the CIF that women's primary mission was in the home squared up more evenly with Church doctrine and public discourse. The CIF's leaders, however, recognized that many women worked outside the home because of necessity and understood that a strong and healthy economy was a precondition to the sole breadwinner model. The association therefore looked for ways to help and sustain mothers and families at the local and national levels while the economy transitioned out of the war. Since many of the CIF's leaders, especially its dynamic president, Maria Federici, were themselves recognizable political and public figures, the association did not call on women to give up a public role and take on a lone existence in the home. Instead, the CIF summoned women to volunteer to help others or to work in the service sector where their special feminine qualities would guide them. The CIF also continued to support Christian Democracy and trust in its alliance with the Americans and membership in NATO to help fulfill the promise of economic growth for all allied Christian nations. The CIF's same vision extended to its work with the new World Movement of Mothers, an international organization committed to women's equality through their complementarity with men.

The UDI, in contrast, took a much different stance on women's roles. According to the UDI, women had an important productive role to fulfill that was best met through their full and equal employment. In solidarity with the Women's International Democratic Federation, the UDI looked to the Soviet Union and the people's democracies for examples of states that provided social services to women with jobs outside the home. They also criticized organizations such as the CIF and the World Movement of Mothers for advocating an ideal of domesticity that recalled the suppressions of fascism. Moreover, fearful that the Western powers were preparing for a war against the Soviet Union that could result in nuclear destruction, they initiated a massive peace campaign and attempted to block the expansion of NATO. The Italian women experienced the influence of broader political disaccord more directly, however. Many UDI members supported the Popular Front parties, but not all did, and many women realized that the Popular Front's support on some issues, such as equal pay or divorce, was far from universal. As a result, the UDI had to learn how to move forward and advance its own agenda without being influenced by outside forces that required compromise. Whatever their ultimate visions, the UDI and the CIF proved they were much more than social organizations for housewives. They assured Italian women a public presence and strived to guarantee that the ideal of equality established by the constitution would be upheld. Equally important, the women's associations took on a challenging double role: providing social services and sustaining a political voice in a trying time of recovery.

3   Mothers for Peace, 1950–1955

In July 1955, the World Congress of Mothers gathered in Lausanne, Switzerland. Clotilde Cassigoli, a Florentine housewife and Catholic Action member, delivered an emotional speech imploring women around the world to put aside their differences and cooperate as mothers. Cassigoli recounted a traumatic experience during the Resistance of seeing the bodies of seventeen partisans who had just been executed pass before her eyes. Then, almost as if nothing had happened, "life went back to normal and then the sun shone again on my beautiful Florence, but for those seventeen mothers, like many others, their sons didn't come back."[1] Cassigoli had made it her mission as a mother to fight for disarmament and peace so that other mothers would not have to suffer the loss of their children to conflict and war. Cassigoli was conscious of not quite fitting in at the conference, which had been organized by the leftist Women's International Democratic Federation, but she said, "I haven't heard a single word here that has offended my profound sensibilities as a Catholic woman." In fact, Cassigoli had ignored detractors who "say that where people speak a lot about peace, disarmament and neutrality, and condemn the atomic bomb, it means that there are communists, socialists, and all those people who are sometimes labeled 'sons of darkness'."[2] In no way did Cassigoli see a conflict between her religious views and the political views of the conference organizers; they were all united under common objectives. Did Cassigoli's address at the World Congress of Mothers signal a change in direction in the realm of international organizing that would now allow women of the left and women of the center and right to put Cold War hostilities to the side? Were women in Italy and around the world constructing new bonds based on common understandings? Had international political developments led women to rethink their objectives?

While Cassigoli's comments at the congress highlight several key themes that characterized the overlapping interests of Italian and international women activists on opposed sides of the political spectrum in the early 1950s, they cannot be taken to represent a widespread spirit of sisterhood. The lines of the Cold War had by now been clearly demarcated and left little space for cooperation between women who came from the divergent associational worlds of Catholic and socialist/communist women's movements. As Cassigoli's case illustrates, however, a few moments in which women were able to work together and put aside their differences did surface between 1950 and 1955 but almost exclusively on the terrain of motherhood and childhood. This chapter explores the construction of the discourse of motherhood and peace in relation to the continuing efforts of the UDI and the CIF to provide Italian women with the necessary tools to lead productive and happy lives that would be replicated in the global context in their work with the Women's International Democratic Federation and the World Movement of Mothers.

In just this five-year period, the women's associations held numerous conferences and events under the rubric of motherhood and peace. In Italy in 1950, the UDI organized its celebration of International Women's Day, "For the Joy and Tranquility of your Family, Defend Peace," and the CIF followed in 1951 with its annual conference, titled "Problems Relative to the Life of Children." The international women's organizations stayed on topic with the World Movement of Mothers' congress in 1953 in Brussels, titled "The Educational Responsibilities of Mothers" and with the congress in Lausanne in 1955. The women's associations, in collaboration with numerous other national and international bodies, produced questionnaires, reports, special studies, and many other pages of documentation on the state of mothers and their children focusing on such international political events as the war in Korea (1950–53) and examining cultural production coming from the United States through films and comics. In Italy, the women's associations proved that bipolarism was still thriving as the Italians entered a particularly contentious election period in 1953, and the UDI and the CIF appealed to Italian women to support the political parties that most supported women, children, and peace. I intend to pull apart the many layers of the discourse and actions surrounding motherhood and peace to show that although the women's associations approached their activism from intensely diverse frameworks, they all placed mothers and children at the center of their efforts for mainly political reasons and used them to attract new and more active members to their associations. The communist and socialist UDI women and their affiliates in the Women's International Democratic Federation were attempting to counter the propaganda efforts of the Vatican, the Christian Democrats, and the American-led NATO bloc that labeled communists as destroyers of religion and family. The women of the CIF, in contrast, were trying to ensure that Catholic values did not lose their importance as many Italians and other people around the world embraced American capitalism and entertainment.

National and International Context

The Italian elections of 1948 ushered in a period known as the *quadripartito*, the four-party coalition, under the lead of the Christian Democrats and Alcide De Gasperi, which lasted until the next national elections in 1953. The Christian Democrats and its coalition allies—the Social Democrats, the Liberals, and the Republicans—believed the decisive defeat of the Popular Front would bring the sort of stability to the government that was needed to consolidate democratic institutional structures and develop the economy. Political cooperation among the coalition parties, however, was incomplete: the Social Democrats and progressive Catholics favored the nationalization of major industries and a planned economy, whereas the more conservative members of the Christian Democrats and the Liberals preferred a leaner state apparatus that guaranteed individual liberties and a capitalist economy.[3] Nevertheless, as historian Giuseppe Mammarella has noted, "although the members of the four-party coalition were divided by ideological and programmatic questions, their common alliance against the Communist menace generally proved stronger than the causes of division."[4] The Popular Front had been defeated, but it certainly had not disappeared. The Italian Communist Party attempted to better define its positions, which appeared to necessitate even greater loyalty to the Soviet Union, as the party expelled members who no longer conformed to Soviet cultural and scientific directives. Nevertheless, the party continued to draw support from industrial and agricultural workers and maintained an upper hand in its relationship with the Socialist Party, which remained largely subordinate to the communists until 1953.[5]

An escalation in the Cold War followed the Soviets' detonation of their first atomic weapon in August 1949 and led to a strategy of "negative containment" in Italy.[6] In April 1950, Paul Nitze, director of policy planning for the U.S. State Department, delivered a top-secret National Security Council paper (NSC-68) to President Harry Truman. The document, of which Nitze was the principal author, argued that "the Kremlin's policy toward areas not under its control is the elimination of resistance to its will and the extension of its influence and control."[7] Nitze provided evidence that the "Soviet Union is developing the military capacity to support its design for world domination."[8] Nitze's report led the Truman administration to take direct action in foreign policy and step up its militarization. Secretary of State Dean Acheson traveled to western Europe, considered especially vulnerable to Soviet attack, to strengthen NATO and assure the French and British of American military capability in an effort to prevent them from adopting a position of neutrality. In Italy, NSC-68 resulted in a shift in U.S. policy and a new determination to undermine and eventually outlaw the Italian Communist Party. Resistance from Prime Minister De Gasperi as well as the Americans' inability to reach their goals, however, limited the effect of new American strategies in Italy.[9] In East and Southeast Asia, in contrast, Acheson's team cultivated relationships with friendly governments by sending military and economic aid while supporting the French in Vietnam and defending Taiwan from the Chinese communists. It also looked to retain a U.S. military presence in Japan even after the occupation had ended.[10]

The Soviet Union, meanwhile, was also stepping up efforts to secure its international position after having lost the contest over Berlin and West Germany.[11] Stalin was torn between following the position promoted by moderates such as Georgii Malenkov, which proposed trying to reach an understanding with the Americans and their allies before moving toward direct confrontation, and that of Soviet hardliners such as Lavrenti Beria, who favored taking a more aggressive stance toward the West while supporting communists elsewhere. Stalin's inclination to bolster the Soviet Union's international influence became apparent in February 1950, when he and Mao Zedong signed the Sino-Soviet Treaty of Friendship and Alliance, which refocused Soviet attention on East Asia and away from Germany and Europe. The peace treaty with Japan at the end of World War II had stipulated that the Korean peninsula be divided at the 38th parallel, with the USSR temporarily occupying the North and the United States overseeing the South from its Asian headquarters in

Tokyo commanded by General Douglas MacArthur. Stalin began arming the North Korean People's Army with tanks and artillery and, in April 1950, agreed to provide Kim Il Sung, the ruler of the Democratic People's Republic of Korea, with the military support needed to unify Korea under communist rule. A communist Korea, Stalin reasoned, would "improve the Kremlin's strategic position vis-à-vis Japan, preserve Communist solidarity in Asia, and divert American power from Europe."[12] On June 25, 1950, Kim Il Sung's troops invaded the South, surprising the American government, which had done little to arm or train the small South Korean Army despite an increase in disputes along the border. The United States rushed to the UN Security Council and had the North Koreans labeled the aggressors in the conflict and then asked member states to send military assistance to the American troops already stationed in East Asia. The Korean War broke out as the first hot conflict of the Cold War.

The Korean War

Peace activists around the globe became increasingly alarmed by the direct hostility between the governments of the United States and the Soviet Union, the drive to build new and more powerful nuclear weapons, in particular the hydrogen bomb, and the outbreak of the first military conflict between communists and noncommunists in a strategic location. The Soviet Union and the Italian Communist Party successfully exploited the new political climate caused by NSC-68, the subsequent U.S. weapons buildup, and the start of the Korean War; they launched a massive peace campaign that crossed national borders and involved several Catholic organizations. The Communist Party's peace petition garnered 16 million signatures and gave the communists new credibility as the "true defender of peace and democracy." By drawing on people's fears of a nuclear war and pointing to U.S. military actions, European communists drew new supporters to their anti-American cause.[13] Given the Soviets' nuclear weapons testing and buildup, however, the Soviet-supported Partisans of Peace dropped its antinuclear activities shortly after its March 1950 Stockholm conference and left other international communist organizations in a conundrum.[14]

The war in Korea elicited an especially forceful response from the Women's International Democratic Federation and the UDI. In 1951, the federation sent twenty-one women "of different countries, of different nationalities, of different religious beliefs and different political views" to Korea "to tell conscientiously and truthfully to the women who delegated us to this commission and to all the common and peace-loving people of the world the facts as we have seen them."[15] The federation's president, Eugénie Cotton, sent the organization's disturbing and detailed report, "We Accuse," to the United Nations on June 11, 1951 on behalf of the federation's 91 million members. The report demanded that "those who are responsible for the crimes committed against the Korean people be charged as 'war criminals' as stipulated in the Allied Declaration of 1943."[16] Most of the individual reports the women compiled recounted the experiences of North Koreans during the period between October and December 1950 when United Nations troops led by General MacArthur made their farthest advance into North Korean territory.

"We Accuse" serves as a defining document for the international communist/socialist women's movement especially because of its emphasis on both the civilian women and children who became victims of the so-called limited war and on the savageness of American, British, and Syngman Rhee troops, who appeared frenzied by anticommunist rage. In chapter 5 of the report, Elisabetta Gallo, an Italian Communist Party member, and three other women from China, Belgium, and Czechoslovakia gave chilling accounts of the stories of two women:

Sin Yenk Ok, 46, a peasant woman living in Kyeng-San Ri Street in Wonsan said that her daughter-in-law, aged 25 and in the 9th month of pregnancy (who had been chairman of the women's organization in her district for the last two years) was arrested on November 18, 1950. She was beaten for being a "red"; five days later she was exposed publicly in the town square. Her child, about to be born, was killed when a rod was thrust into her womb. The mother died at once. This done [sic] by two Americans and one Syngman Rhee man.[17]

Li Kum Sun, a peasant woman aged 38, member of the Women's Organization, living in Sedon-Ri (in the city of Wonsan) told us that she was arrested with her month-old infant on October 25, 1950. She was taken to Kal Ma Ri suburb, in the town of Wonsan. Every night she was beaten on her back and stomach when she was brought in for interrogation. On November 10 she was freed. Five days later her child died.[18]

In both of these descriptions, the brutalized women were peasants, mothers, activists in local women's associations, and presumed communists. The succinct factual way in which the authors recounted the treatment of these women at the hands of American and Syngman Rhee troops actually constructs their experiences as particularly horrifying; their arbitrary arrests, followed by repeated beatings and the deaths of their unborn and newborn babies, expose the vulnerability of mothers guilty of nothing more than living in a "people's democracy." The Women's International Democratic Federation delegates offered no other commentary or context. They communicated the essentials to build a case for peace and against the "foreign invaders."

Attempts to produce a change in the United Nations' approach to the conflict proved futile. The UN had to handle the Korean War successfully to lend itself further credibility as it passed its first five years in existence, but the Soviets had already boycotted the body, making communication nearly impossible. The UN's recognition of the Taiwanese government headed by Chiang Kai-Shek and its refusal to acknowledge Mao's government in Beijing enraged Stalin, who saw the United Nations as another source of American power. The Soviet boycott, however, meant that Russia could not use its place on the UN Security Council to veto the use of force requested by the United States to push the North Koreans back to the 38th parallel. The Women's International Democratic Federation's closeness to the Soviet Union had further repercussions for the organization. In January 1951, the Union des Femmes Françaises and the federation were asked to leave Paris because of their campaigns against the French colonial war in Vietnam, in which they had asked French mothers to prevent their sons from fighting in the conflict. The federation moved to East Berlin, where it remained for the duration of the Cold War.[19] Though it may have had the backing of the women from twenty-one nations who traveled to Korea during the conflict, the Americans benefited from the participation of the troops of sixteen member states and the South Korean army. For all the reports the federation could produce of atrocities committed against the North Korean people, the South Koreans could generate their own and show that they had no desire for Kim Il Sung's version of democracy, which they had already rejected in UN–supervised elections in 1948. Although it had been compiled in the spirit of ending the war and granting "self-determination for the Korean people and the right to settle their own affairs," "We Accuse" had a procommunist, pro-Soviet framework that made it easy to label as propaganda. The most damaging result, however, was felt by the Women's International Democratic Federation itself. In 1954, at the urging of the United States and supported by Great Britain, the federation lost its consultative status at the United Nations.[20] The federation's ability to forge a women's agenda for peace and women's rights at the UN had been compromised, "thus effectively shutting down a discussion of women's role in peacemaking in the [Commission on the Status of Women] forum."[21]

In Italy, Elisabetta Gallo delivered presentations throughout the country about the federation committee's observations in Korea and the organization's attempts to change the course of the conflict.[22] The UDI reached out to the Union of Korean Women to ask what could be done to help mothers and children who were suffering as a result of the war. The campaign "a can of milk for a Korean child" emerged from their correspondence, conceived not only as a way to provide relief for Korean children but also as a means to advance the UDI's peace agenda. The discourse of the campaign remained emotionally charged and focused on the lives of mothers and children, as demonstrated by such descriptions as "she looks for the breast of her dead mother" and "Korean babies die near the cadavers of their mothers."[23] A poster designed for the campaign features a plump Italian peasant mother with a baby in one arm and a can of milk in the other reaching out to a skinny Korean mother holding her own baby. The ruins of a bombed building appear in the background.[24] In this case, too, there is no overt political message, but the supporters of "a can of milk" listed on the right on the image include the UDI, the women's commission of the CGIL trade union, the Federbraccianti, and the National Committee of the Partisans of Peace—all organizations of the left. The link among peace, motherhood, and the left is subtle but clear.

The CIF did not become directly involved in the discourse surrounding the conflict in Korea, mainly expressing sadness for the loss of life it caused. Instead, the CIF preferred to support mothers and children in Italy.[25] The Christian Democrats eventually backed the U.S. position on Korea, even though De Gasperi had initially commented on the political naiveté of the Americans and on Italy's desire for peace. The Italians did not send any troops to Korea because Italy was not yet a member of the

United Nations.[26] In response to the inroads the communists had made in appealing to the Catholics' sense of peace, the Christian Democrats created the National Solidarity Campaign for Peace and Security and reminded the Italian people that the war had been sparked by the disruption of peace by the North Korean communists.[27] The Italian Red Cross sent medical personnel to attend to casualties. The Vatican took an ambiguous stance on the Korean War, which proved that it "was having difficulty choosing between different moral claims."[28] In July 1950, a few months after the war broke out, Pope Pius XII issued "On Public Prayers for Peace." Article 12 proclaimed:

> As a matter of fact, there have never been lacking, either in ancient or in more recent times, those who tried to subjugate the peoples by the use of arms; on the other hand, We have never ceased to promote a true peace. The Church desires to win over peoples and to educate them to virtue and right social living, not by means of arms but with the truth. For "the weapons of our warfare are not carnal, but mighty to God" (II Cor. 10, 4).[29]

By not making an explicit statement about the politics of the Korean conflict, the Vatican was attempting to put forward the possibility for a third way. As Renato Moro has argued, in 1950 and 1951, there was an "emergence of a 'dialogue' about 'peace' between Catholics and communists," which transitioned into a Catholic "peace offensive" between 1952 and 1955.[30] Catholics were at first unsure about the issue of peace but reclaimed and reframed it in the spirit of Catholicism once the communists backed away from trying to attract Catholics to their cause.

Childhood and Culture

The politicized discourse of childhood became a central feature in the cultural analyses of the UDI and the CIF and their international allies and one that they tied to the discourse of peace. The Italians voraciously consumed American films, magazines, and comics, which rapidly poured into Italy after the nylon stockings and chewing gum that had accompanied American soldiers to southern Italy in 1943. By 1952, the European edition of *Reader's Digest* regularly circulated into the homes of half a million Italian families, and, by 1953, Italian cinemas had acquired more than five thousand American movies.[31] The Americans had clear economic and political motives for ensuring the distribution of American entertainment in Italy. Economist Emanuela Scarpellini has argued, in fact, that the Americans recognized the Italians' reluctance to simply apply American economic and political models and therefore used culture as a way to open new channels and convince the Italian people of the advantages of the "American way of life," which included mass consumption.[32] To make cultural inroads and shape young people's perceptions of the United States, the U.S. government offered grant money to Mondadori, publisher of *Topolino* (Mickey Mouse), to interest Italian children in other beloved American characters. The comic's new digest format derived from the same machines that were printing *Reader's Digest*. The Americans also funded the construction of American-Italian research institutes and libraries, such as the Center for American Studies in Rome, to attract educated Italians, who might otherwise have been drawn to the intellectual circles of the socialists and communists. Soviet cultural production had little chance to compete in a climate of such enthusiastic reception to American products, and as Stephen Gundle has argued, the leaders of the Italian Communist Party "never really grasped the appeal of either mass culture or the consumer society" and so had only limited success in countering American cultural models.[33] As a result, communist youths developed an interesting convergence of antipathy for American politics and enthusiasm for American culture, which they did not experience as a contradiction.

Although the Italians were especially receptive to the arrival of American entertainment, perhaps more so than other western Europeans, the flood of American cultural goods aimed at children troubled the leaders of both the UDI and the CIF. Historians have shown the broad reach of American consumption in western Europe during the early postwar period, but have sometimes had a tendency to overlook the importance of long-standing cultural traditions in the reconstruction process.[34] In Italy, the Vatican and Catholic Action had very direct influence on television programs, which resulted in censorship that sometimes took bizarre forms, as in the substitution of the term "interesting state" for pregnancy. At the same time, however, new Italian cultural expressions, such as the San Remo musical festival that began in 1951, celebrated the "eternal" figure of the Italian mother in songs such as "All Mothers," which declared that "all the mothers of the world are beautiful" and compared their wombs to the Virgin Mary's.[35] For the Italian women's organizations, the need for continuity and community informed their responses to American consumerism as it applied to mothers and children. The individualism and materialism inherent in American models conflicted with the CIF's emphasis on the Catholic family and the UDI's socialist model of cooperation. As a result, both associations began a careful examination of the cultural transformation of childhood taking place because of the influx of American products and entertainment. Their discussion fit within a larger trend found in the *cronaca nera* of the time that was constructing the figure of the "lost youth" of modernization.[36]

In May 1951, the UDI organized a discussion with Catholic organizations "on the problem of the harmful influence that comics have on the moral education of children. Six million copies are distributed each week and worm into our children the seeds of violence, sexual excitement and war as an indispensable means for solving conflicts among peoples."[37] The UDI was especially concerned that Italian children were being exposed to "warmongering" films and literature that promoted the glory of war and sent the message that peace was for weaklings. The CIF objected to the moral content in American entertainment that appeared to encourage children to value violence and the accumulation of wealth over the bonds of family and society. In response to an essay written by a thirteen- or fourteen-year-old American boy that recounts his fantasies of being part of a murderous gang of bank robbers, a speaker at the CIF's Fourth National Convention in 1951 pondered how a boy who "belongs to the good American middle-class; lives in a clean and honest environment where neither corruption not vice has ever reigned" could write such "terrible things." His conclusion was that "he saw all of this, learned it, got to know it, at the movies."[38] Both associations wondered if the myth of America had fueled the most salacious and selfish parts of the Italian psyche at a time when energy was needed to continue the country's recovery. As the women's associations saw it, the world portrayed by Hollywood was a distant fantasy for the 50 percent of Italians whose homes in 1952 still lacked running water and for the ninety-three thousand who were living in shacks, caves, or other forms of temporary housing.[39] Conditions were especially abysmal in the south. Children in Naples, one report showed, were crowded into rooms of ten people and suffered much higher rates of tuberculosis and cancer than did children in other parts of the country.[40] The women argued that with so many children living in poverty, their efforts should be directed at improving the health and well-being of Italy's children and other children around the world.

With that objective in mind, the associations sent an Italian delegation to the International Conference on the Defense of Children held in Vienna in April 1952. Of the 103 delegates who attended the conference, the majority (57) were members of the Popular Front parties, and 21 were members of the UDI. Five Christian Democrats and one member of the CIF, Caterina Maza Castelli, attended. Among the conference's Italian sponsors were Raffaele Caporali, president of the Senate Commission on Hygiene and Health, and Mario Venditti, former undersecretary of public education. In the months preceding the conference, numerous health care experts, government officials, and representatives of nongovernmental organizations, including the women's associations, met in various locations throughout Italy. They produced more than fifty reports describing children's living conditions, and they agreed to defend the rights of children in Italy and at the international level. The major objectives of the conference included, in addition to improving children's health and housing conditions, combating juvenile delinquency, protecting children "from the pernicious influence of immoral literature, radio broadcasts and films," and organizing "suitable recreation for them."[41]

Despite the pro-child framework of the conference and participation by men and women of a variety of political affiliations, the pro-Soviet perspective of the key speakers frequently surfaced, contributing to the Cold War political propaganda that entered into discussions of women and children at the international level and keeping the Italian women's associations heedful when reporting on what the opposition was doing. Italian psychologist Nicola Perrotti, for example, delivered a talk on children's health around the world in which he concluded that "general comparisons show that while in the United States and England, and even in Sweden, care for children has remained stationary and little or nothing is being done to fill the gaps or decrease the inequality of treatment, in the USSR, on the contrary, social assistance is dynamic because it is continuously progressing and tends to perfect services for all children."[42] On the subject of the influence of the media on childhood development, a German woman doctor, Dr. Groscurth, reported, "In the USSR there is a great variety of literature and books for children. Their educational value is remarkable, because they arouse confidence in the dignity of man, in his creative capacities in all fields of endeavor. . . . The thoughts of the Soviet child are directed to creative work, happiness and brotherhood."[43] In the language of these two speakers and many other delegates, the Soviet Union was a model state for the physical and moral development of children, whereas the United States and other Western democracies fell short. The fact that in May 1952, immediately after the conference, the UDI and the CIF designated members to sit on a national consulting body on children's issues called the Consiglio nazionale permanente per la difesa dell'infanzia [Permanent National Counsel for the Defense of Childhood] should be taken not as a sign of cooperation between the women's associations but as an indication of their continued vigilance. When women from both the UDI and the CIF participated in the drafting of legislation to regulate the distribution and viewing of movies by children and agreed to elect members from the associations to sit on an appeals committee regarding objections to censored films, they did so to ensure that the other association did not have an advantage.[44] Their common points of view were ultimately obscured by politics.

Nevertheless, the Italian women's associations shared a passion for looking after the welfare of children, and they embraced the opportunity that their children's programs gave them to continue making inroads into the homes of ordinary Italians, especially those with small children. As a report compiled by the CIF notes, "The participation of mothers in social and civic life has a slower pace than the participation offered by single women. The most active mothers . . . are the ones [whose children] are the most advanced in age. It's more difficult to involve mothers with small children in social-civic activities."[45] The key to expanding the associations' appeal to women with young children was to involve them and their children in activities sponsored by the associations. Political affinity became an important subtext of the associations' assistance and cultural programming once they had made the first contacts. The CIF's leaders were particularly skilled at bridging the gap between children's programs and the social-political involvement of mothers. The CIF's Case del Sole program continued to be a huge success and, by the early 1950s, the association was assisting more than 1.6 million Italian children in daycare centers, after-school programs, summer camps, and other outlets.[46] The CIF furthered

its work in the cultural arena by carrying out extensive research on the
effect of films on children and then developing the Cinema per Ragazzi
[Cinema for Young People] program, which CIF representatives reported
on to a favorable response at the International Congress for the Protection
for Public Morality held in Cologne in May 1955.[47] The association organized screenings of age- and theme-appropriate films for young people in
centers throughout Italy. The idea was to be sure that children were not
exposed to "immoral" entertainment while making the CIF's name
known to mothers who might then become interested in attending other
CIF events. At the screenings, the local CIF leaders distributed materials
about upcoming events, such as seminars about caring for the home and
family.

The UDI took a similar approach to compel women who attended
events for children to take a larger role in the association. One UDI chapter, for example, reported in 1954 on the children's performances of
dance, singing, and poetry readings it had organized and then listed a
series of events the women had planned for the upcoming year.[48] In most
instances, the chapter held one event for mothers and children and another event on a political matter or initiative for women's rights in the
same month. In January, for example, the local UDI organized a children's
party during which members distributed care packages of donated goods
and held a conference on the rearmament of Germany. In March, the association sponsored both a parade of young women getting married during the year and a debate on the new Italian family. In August, the center
threw a going-away party for children attending summer camps and then
sent women to the northern lakes region to distribute Noi Donne at various vacation spots.[49] In each case, mothers could easily make the correla-
tion between programs for their children and engagement in the women's
movement. Although UDI leaders may not have had the American cultural arsenal behind them or the benefit of the Vatican funding that went
to the CIF's programs, their use of festivals, arts, camps, and publications
nevertheless helped them to make women see the connection between
entertainment and the life of the association. Both the UDI and the CIF
reaped the benefits of appealing to the full range of individuals' lives and
interests, which was also a strategy used by the political parties to create
the illusion of the party as an extension of the family.[50] For mothers, such
ideas resonated especially forcefully and helped them to see associational

and political activities not as something self-interested that took them away from their families, but as a part of their daily lives.

Mother's Rights

As the women's associations developed programming for children and broadened their appeal among young Italian mothers, they also refined the nature of their national and international efforts. The leaders of the associations understood that they could relate the personal, local level to the broader international one. As historian Mariuccia Salvati has shown, after the collapse of the fascist state, political parties took on new roles as symbols of national identity and as democratic institutions; they "built up their respective influences by emphasizing the feeling of belonging to a large, integrated institution and to its protective network of relief organizations."[51] The same idea can be applied to the UDI and the CIF, which cooperated with the political parties but also established their own networks in the absence of well-developed state-run social services. Like the Germans in the early 1950s, the Italians, too, coped with poor housing conditions and shortages that especially affected children and their mothers.[52] Sociologist Maria Cacioppo has pointed out that the 1950s was characterized "by a notable scarcity of resources at the disposition of the great majority of people, and by a substantial stability of family forms and living standards."[53] The Italian women's associations tried to help fill these absences and bridged social service and politics at the same time. The CIF's leaders, for example, astutely pointed out the relationship between daycare programs and social-civic involvement. The organization reported, "It's about the activities offered to these mothers that are completely voluntary and that start from their own interests for the nursery schools and then pass them on to rouse the interests of other women (all of whom belong to the common classes whether urban or rural workers) in other communities outside the family or school: the neighborhood community, the City, the Province, the nation-state, the European community, etc."[54] Neither association, in fact, confined its efforts to just one class or only to the Italian situation. Members of the CIF, for example, along with several other Catholic organizations, were even invited to take a special five-day course on Catholic and international life organized by Catholic Action. The one hundred participants learned how major international governmental and nongovernmental organizations operated and expanded their knowledge of how actual global political and economic circumstances affected the operations of international Catholic organizations. As the CIF recognized, too often "a lack of qualifications in various areas (e.g., religious and moral training, professional cultural training, knowledge of foreign languages, technical competence) lead Catholics to have to forgo important tasks in international life."[55] The women's associations recognized that participation in the international arena required special competencies not necessarily developed in the national context alone or shared by women with different class and educational backgrounds.

The UDI and the CIF thus worked to deepen the reach and effects of their activities, but their discourse continued to be shaped by the polemics of Cold War politics and competing ideals of womanhood as defined by their distinct ideological perspectives. In an article about a text titled "The Zetkin Course for the Emancipation of Woman," being offered for sale by the Italian Communist Party, the CIF's Clara Valente critiqued long-standing socialist interpretations of gender roles, arguing that the far left had accepted a gendered division of labor in preindustrial times but rejected it when applied to the modern family, favoring instead a matriarchal structure that derived from women's free engagement in relationships outside monogamous marriage—a possibility Valente found extremely unsettling. She moreover rejected the notion that women were subjugated in the modern family. In her opinion, the Christian view of the family that "if the man is the head, the woman is the heart" should inform both theoretical and practical approaches to family policy in a Catholic country like Italy.[56] The CIF's leaders agreed but also sought ways to extend their vision beyond the Italian context. One such example emerged during preparations for the 1953 World Movement of Mothers international convention in Brussels, when the CIF demonstrated how it could develop its work from the grass roots to the international level and simultaneously build upon its philosophical and religious foundations. The World Movement of Mothers instructed its member associations to distribute questionnaires to members on the educational responsibilities of mothers. The surveys posed, among other questions, what services mothers believed their children needed to help them avoid confronting the same difficulties they had faced as girls, what they identified as the biggest challenges in educating their children, and which associations or institutions they believed were the most helpful to mothers. To reach a broad comparative sample, the CIF divided the questionnaires by unpaid women (especially rural mothers and the wives of white-collar workers), and women with jobs outside the home (especially artisans, professionals, and commercial employees), and distributed them throughout the country. Based on the hundreds of responses received from the CIF's regional offices, the CIF's new president, Amalia di Valmarana (1950–62), prepared a summary report titled "Family, Social, and Civic Education: Social Conditions Which 'Facilitate' or 'Hinder' Education of Youth," which she then presented at the conference in Brussels and used to develop the CIF's local and national programs.

Despite the diversity of the respondents and their answers, Valmarana used the questionnaires to reinforce her perspectives on women and the family rather than to reconsider them. In fact, Valmarana led the CIF away from the high degree of political engagement that had characterized Maria Federici's leadership toward a more contemplative reengagement on questions regarding women's work inside and outside the home.[57] The war had contributed to the re-formation of traditional family structures because of the loss of life, wartime affairs, and relocations it caused, but the CIF continued to think of the family as a unit consisting of a husband, a wife, and their children. According to the CIF's study, only a nuclear family could produce healthy citizens. As stated by Valmarana: "If a family is constituted in a regular way, and its life has a normal and peaceful rhythm, if harmony reigns between wife and husband, and also between parents and children with regard to love and authority, the child will accept moral and disciplinary rules willingly."[58] To achieve a balance in the family, Valmarana argued, society had to offer its citizens economic and moral health and social freedom. On the first point, Valmarana asserted that families needed "a complete system of social protection" against unexpected events, such as illness, disability, or death, which could threaten their normal budget and result in role reversals. "In an economically healthy society," she wrote, "the head of the family is at work and his income is entirely sufficient to satisfy the needs of the family budget. . . . The economic measures taken in some countries to facilitate the mother being permanently at home, indicate that an economic problem is at the base of women's work."[59] In other words, the CIF maintained that most of its members who worked outside the home did so because of economic necessity, a necessity that had arisen because of a lack of sufficient economic development. It was now time to work to achieve the sort of growth needed to allow women to remain in the home—much like that which was occurring in the United States. Historian Elisabetta Vezzosi has explained that for Italian women who had been employed in low-level positions in the agricultural sector or as home pieceworkers, "the life of the housewife was considered a symbol of freedom and independence rather than of oppression."[60] The World Movement of Mothers welcomed Valmarana's comments to reinforce its own position that women's ideal place was in the home and that a dynamic capitalist market was the most likely guarantor of that possibility. The two women's organizations had approved of the creation of the European Coal and Steel Community in 1950, and the CIF, in particular, acknowledged De Gasperi's further moves toward European integration. A stronger European marketplace, they argued, would stimulate growth and lead to a freer, more dynamic economy that could become as important globally as that of the United States and could diminish the communists' ability to compete.

The UDI and the Women's International Democratic Federation disagreed with the CIF and the World Movement of Mothers' perspective on economic development and women's roles. The international federation's executive committee drafted a resolution on women's rights that argued, "Women in capitalist countries still do not have equal rights with men. In the Constitution and other legislative acts in numerous capitalist countries women's rights are formally recognized but the conditions for their realization have not been created."[61] According to the federation, only women in the Soviet Union, China, and East Germany had benefited from their governments' granting the right to work and the right to an equal salary because the "correct" economic conditions had been implemented. Rina Piccolato, a member of both the federation's executive council and the UDI, reported at the federation's Bucharest meeting in July 1952 on the difficult situation of Italy's 5 million women in the workforce. Piccolato did not broach whether women should be working outside the home. Instead, she noted that a lack of respect for Italian women workers contributed to their lower status in the workplace and that "our government's politics for rearmament and war comes from the domination of the big industrial monopolists . . . expanding their excessive exploitation and layoffs."[62] Piccolato informed the federation's council that, in Italy, the UDI was organizing a seminar series on the rights of women workers in conjunction with the CGIL trade union, which would help women understand their own situations in relation to those of women in other parts of the world. In particular, the UDI wanted to "show Italian women through our delegates, meetings, and activities, hope and confidence in the situation of our happy sisters in the Soviet Union and people's democracies" and proposed that the federation hold an international convention on the rights of women.[63] The UDI and the CIF both looked to develop consistent messages that would be understood by a housewife in Milan or an agricultural worker in Bari and then be extended across regional and national borders.

The associations' publications helped activists to do just that. Since they had control over editorial content, the UDI and the CIF's leaders could frame their printed materials as they wished. Internal disagreements, however, surfaced about the content and purpose of the women's magazines in the early 1950s, which led to important changes in how their publications were laid out and distributed. The editors of Noi Donne, led by Maria Antionetta Macciocchi sought to ensure that their now well established publication remain "a paper of struggle, propaganda and the organization of the democratic women's movement" instead of a bourgeois women's magazine.[64] Nevertheless, Noi Donne reflected trends of the day and, between 1951 and 1955, moved from being composed primarily of political articles to featuring more content about entertainment, culture, and daily life. Noi Donne's writers made the connections between peace, motherhood, and children easily palatable to its readers, who were happy to see a publication that would, in Macciocchi's words, "defend the lives, health, and education of our children, of our adored sons and daughters."[65] In fact, the number of images of and stories about children increased dramatically during the early 1950s while the UDI continued to criticize U.S. foreign policy and discuss the lived conditions of women workers in Italy, again tying together the multiple facets of women's lives. Noi Donne featured pictures of the adorable babies of the magazine's readers in special column called "Little Angels of Peace" and ran an advice column called "Answering Mothers."[66] The women of the Soviet Union continued to serve as models of emancipated mothers when the UDI stepped up efforts to counter the propaganda of the center-right. The magazine was also an effective transmission device between mothers and daughters. Lorenza Bartolotti of Ravenna recalls that *Noi Donne* was always in her house when she was growing up in the 1950s: "My introduction to the UDI was certainly mediated by the fact that my mother belonged to the UDI and my own reading of *Noi Donne*. My mother subscribed to *Noi Donne* and it arrived each week. I always waited for it, especially for the part with letters from readers."[67] The UDI's leaders fell short, however, of achieving the perfect balance they wanted to see between support for the worldwide social-communist movement and women's rights and the female public's desire for the latest films, stories, and fashion. Patterns for sewing Soviet-styled clothing and recipes for favorite Russian dishes thus coexisted with serial installments of romances, such as "Senso" [Sense], which recounted the lives of the members of an aristocratic Florentine family and articles about Hollywood stars and other international celebrities.

The CIF struggled with similar issues. The *Bollettino* and *Cronache e Opinioni* had served the association mainly as information tools for CIF members. The *Bollettino* had been printed modestly in a quasi-missalette format, and *Cronache*, although more attractively formatted, remained focused on reporting CIF activities and offering short informative articles about Catholic doctrine, saints, and other matters of interest to religious women. Now, however, the association wanted to extend its print appeal as the UDI had done with *Noi Donne*; the result was *Stella*. Historian Fiorenza Taricone has described the magazine as the "umpteenth attempt at modernization that the CIF proposed in a complex society precisely because it appeared to be conformist."[68] *Stella*, Valmarana and others hoped, would offer Italian women a viable alternative to *Noi Donne*. As Valmarana explained to American ambassador Clare Boothe Luce, *Stella* "constitutes a weapon in the hands of women's forces to rebut an immoral press in the political, social and educational areas. The publication would like to orient the less knowledgeable masses in a democratic direction, with social consciousness and good taste and reaching advanced ideals that constitute the foundation of civil life."[69] The CIF's new publication received as much criticism as praise from its members and the leaders of other Catholic organizations, however. Carmela Rossi of the Women's Union of Catholic Action noted that *Stella* did not have a strong enough religious component, that it overemphasized fashion and underemphasized current events, and that the writing was not engaging. Valmarana responded to Rossi's criticisms and agreed the magazine needed modifi- cations.[70] The editors were not able to develop a more satisfying layout, however, and the magazine was pulled for lack of money. The CIF's mem- bers appeared to be more content with a magazine that reflected the pur- pose and direction of the association rather than with one that followed the trends of other women's magazines.

Further occasions in which the Italian women's associations could broaden their reach and differentiate their political views and alliances surfaced in relation to the celebration of International Women's Day dur- ing the early 1950s. Although the UDI and the CIF had both observed the day at the end of World War II, the CIF and women's section of Catholic Action now wanted to seek the assistance of the Vatican to establish a new Day of the Christian Woman. A letter addressed to the pope ex- plained: "One would like that Christian Woman's Day give importance to its being informed by a principle of Catholic women's unity and existing in contrast to the women who celebrate the day of March 8, which by now has assumed a Marxist-Leninist tone."[71] The themes of past March 8 fes- tivities between 1950 and 1954 in Italy had included peace, family, and childhood, but the socialist origins of International Women's Day and its appropriation by the UDI and the women's section of the Popular Front kept most CIF, Catholic Action, and Christian Democratic members away from activities connected to the day. The Vatican was happy to offer money and public relations campaigns to help the Catholic associations organize the Day of the Christian Woman in "an annual convocation of all Italian Catholic women in order to make them aware of today's urgent and grave needs, so that they better know how to act to benefit society" and praised the CIF for being an effective and important association for uniting Cath- olic women.[72] While the political parties were battling with each other, the Catholic women's associations claimed, Italian women "knew how to and wanted to create a peaceful atmosphere, in the home and outside it, on which democratic customs and democracy itself are constructed."[73] The Day of Christian Women became the politically and religiously cor- rect celebration for women of the Catholic center and right.

The UDI did not view the CIF's alternate celebration as particularly peaceful or unifying and accused Amalia di Valmarana of being too quick to renounce work with groups such as the UDI, which the CIF president had labeled as a home for atheist materialists. In an article about the CIF's further severing of ties with the UDI, Maria Antonietta Macciocchi asked if all the CIF's members were necessarily also Christian Democratic voters. She also questioned whether they recognized that nearly 50 percent of Italians voted for the left and that of those voters about half were women. Furthermore, Macciocchi pointed out that Catholicism and socialism were not mutually exclusive, stating that "unity is therefore being rejected with a real and large part of the female population that is, what's more, mostly Catholic."[74] If the CIF was not interested in working together on International Women's Day, the UDI interpreted it as a sign of the Catholics' non-cooperation and willingness to sacrifice women's emancipation to political and social conventions. Giuliana Dal Pozzo commented, "What woman asks for today for her dignity as a citizen and as a worker influences the progress of society; that's why we think it's absurd to say society's not ready, let's wait." She suggested that CIF women follow the example of the saints they venerated and named St. Catherine, to whom a recent CIF congress had been dedicated, as an example of a woman who moved forward to achieve peace and unity despite obstacles placed in her path.[75] The polemics between the UDI and the CIF continued; their special days of recognition for women further severed their ability to bridge the Catholic/Marxist divide.

Elections and New Directions

Clashes between the women's associations in the early 1950s derived in part from their involvement in a particularly contentious election season in which the political parties accentuated their different values on issues including family and peace and counted on their female bases to help them to victory. The Christian Democratic Party had lost some ground in the administrative elections of 1951 and 1952 and expected to have to campaign aggressively to retain its absolute majority; party leaders needed grassroots mobilization and the full participation of women. In October 1952, the Christian Democrats proposed a new electoral policy—a legislative trick of sorts that would grant 65 percent of seats in Parliament to the coalition of parties that secured 50.1 percent of the votes. The left quickly labeled the proposal the *legge truffa* [swindle law]. The Popular Front's opposition to the law did not stop its passage, but it did reenergize the left, which targeted the *legge truffa* as evidence of the Christian Democrats' undemocratic practices. Moreover, the Popular Front criticized Christian Democracy on its foreign policy, pointing out that De Gasperi and other party leaders often seemed to ignore international initiatives that indicated that some progress toward peace was being made in favor of following the lead of the United States. The consequences to Italy, the left argued, included massive spending on unnecessary rearmament that could have gone instead to protect workers and families and to build the economy. The timing of British Prime Minister Winston Churchill's speech in Locarno, Switzerland, in May, which seemed to suggest that international tensions were on the decline, could not have come at a better time for the Popular Front parties. They used the words of Churchill, a close U.S. ally, to support their arguments that the worldwide political mood had shifted. Moreover, a speech by newly appointed American ambassador Clare Boothe Luce imploring the Italians to vote for the DC but also hinting at negative consequences for Italian-American relations if they did not, received a cool response from the Italian public. Threatening language from a high-ranking U.S. diplomat further undermined the Christian Democratic Party's case that Americans' main interest was peace. The newer, less revolutionary tone of the Popular Front carried more weight with voters than did Luce's position. The coalition led by the Christian Democrats won the elections, but with 49.85 percent of the votes. The *legge truffa* was repealed the next year, and De Gasperi's political career ended.[76]

As they had done in 1948, the UDI and CIF reached out to women voters to encourage them to vote for the Popular Front's and the Christian Democrats' coalitions, respectively, and again drew from familiar messages about the role of women and mothers in Italian life. This time, however, the UDI was driven by a need to show the left that it could count on women voters since some male members of the Popular Front had blamed their losses in 1948 on the granting of women's suffrage.[77] As a result, the communist members of the UDI took special care in fostering their relationship with the Italian Communist Party and its women's section, even sacrificing their autonomy in international activities to do so. For example, in 1952, the UDI's Maria Maddalena Rossi sought advice from the party's secretariat about which English-speaking delegate to send to a celebration of International Women's Day in London and which two UDI women should go to Latin America to take part in a study by the

Women's International Democratic Federation on the defense of child-hood. Acknowledging the current national political tensions, Rossi added, "We understand how difficult it is for our movement to go without capa-ble management for such a long period, but the reasons that accompanied our request convinced us to present the problem to you."[78] In other words, how could the women who were most involved in national party politics still be fully engaged with their global agendas for peace and protecting working mothers and children? Attendance at the 1953 congress of the Women's International Democratic Federation in Copenhagen from June 5 to 10 presented further challenges along these lines because the elec-tions were to be held on June 7. The UDI women who went to Copenha-gen would not be able to campaign in the critical days leading up to the elections and would not even be able to vote. After a series of letters be-tween Carmen Zanti, a communist and UDI member who worked full time in the federation's headquarters in Berlin, and the UDI's leaders in the Rome office, the UDI finally decided to send an Italian delegation as soon as the women had been able to vote on election day.[79] At the federa-tion's congress, communist UDI women made sure to publicly discuss the Italian elections and to remember lo zio [uncle] Palmiro Togliatti in their conversations with the other delegations. The construction of the left as an extended family, complete with a smart and friendly uncle, effectively functioned at the international level as it did within the Italian context, especially given Togliatti's international stature.

The CIF campaigned for the Christian Democrats but, believing its preferred political party had a comfortable lead, did not dramatically change its activities in the period leading up to the elections, other than publishing Stella. Italian women, the CIF leaders argued, still held tradi-tional Catholic values and a Christian sense of justice and had, perhaps, been put off by what they saw as the UDI's "woman as worker only" dis-course, undermining the significance of the role of mothers. The CIF had attempted to show that it would support women workers within the com-plex framework of their personal lives and emphasize the challenges they faced in balancing work and motherhood. Amalia di Valmarana, more-over, expressed her disdain for the misdirected words of the left that la-beled "necessarily fascist every state that is not communist" and insisted that "the Italians must dread and prevent groups on the extreme right and the extreme left from becoming protagonists in the Italian Parliament."[80]

Extreme positions, she argued, destabilized peace. The women of the CIF miscalculated, however, and in the 1953 elections more than 50 percent of the 14.9 million voters chose the Popular Front parties. More than half of Italian women voters did not vote for the Christian Democrats. The UDI attributed the results to its position that the socialists and communists did a better job of recognizing women as both mothers and workers. The CIF, according to the leftist association, was not only unrealistic in suggesting that women should be able to leave the paid workplace but also insulting in assuming they would automatically choose the domestic sphere over the public one.

At the Women's International Democratic Federation's Copenhagen congress, the UDI signed the *Charter of Women's Rights* affirming mothers' right to work and to the services they needed to do so, such as maternity leave and daycare centers and free medical clinics.[81] The federation underscored its view of the militarization of the Cold War that directed money away from women and children and toward the arms race, stating that "it is necessary to improve the basic conditions of life for the people, develop the construction of healthy homes, and increase the means for social works. These measures become possible by reducing war budgets and committing these funds to the service of life and the happiness of families in a world where peace is guaranteed."[82] Meanwhile, the CIF reaffirmed its adherence to the World Movement of Mother's *Mother's Charter* at the June conference in Brussels and made clear that it did not view the Christian Democratic Party coalition's losses as a sign of Italian women's dissatisfaction but rather as a message that the left still had a strong grassroots movement that the Catholics would have to take more seriously in the future. Nevertheless, the CIF could not help but be disappointed at the showing of the Christian Democrats' female candidates, who lost seven seats in the legislature, and with the female Catholic electorate in general, which cast fewer votes in 1953 than in 1948 for female candidates.[83] The CIF's Paola Gaiotti commented that the elections showed a troubling trend of movement toward the extremes, which she attributed to a lack of understanding, mostly on the part of Italy's working and peasant classes, about the De Gasperi government's economic achievements and the effect they would have on Italian families. She told the *Cronache*'s readers that this meant Catholics and the Christian Democrats had to lead an even greater effort to defend Italy's democracy.[84]

However, the end of De Gasperi's career, and shortly thereafter his life (August 1954), meant the loss of a powerful CIF ally and ushered in new uncertainties for the association and its future relationship to the Christian Democrats' leaders.

Conclusion

The Eisenhower administration (1953–61) was disappointed by the Italian elections. Clare Boothe Luce threw her support toward the parties of the right, hoping to push Christian Democracy in a more conservative, more fervently anticommunist direction. She even expressed, as one historian put it, "the willingness on the part of the United States to support extreme measures such as the outlawing of the PCI [Italian Communist Party] and the arrest of its main leaders" to reach an end to the "communist menace" in Italy.[85] Tired of what appeared to be the Christian Democrats' strategy of using anticommunism as a means to secure American money without following through on its promises, Luce offered Prime Minister Mario Scelba a chance to take stronger measures against the communists. He did not deliver, however, and his government collapsed in 1955. In the meantime, international tensions had diminished following the death of Josef Stalin in March 1953 and led to a period of détente in 1954 and 1955 as Soviet leaders contended to take the helm of the government and publicly expressed a desire to work for the end of the Cold War. After a July 1955 meeting in Geneva that included U.S. and Soviet representatives, Soviet propaganda began to refer to the "spirit of Geneva" as a source of trust among the great powers.[86] The Eisenhower administration regarded the new Soviet language as potentially dangerous, however, suggesting it might lead the United States and its allies to let down their guard. In December 1955, the admission of Italy to the United Nations along with fifteen other countries, including some cobelli‑ gerent nations now in the Soviet orbit, signaled nonetheless "a favorable international situation that Italy was able to exploit to obtain direct and indirect support from various friends in the small circle of European countries of the day and within the broader framework of the Atlantic Alliance."[87] The year 1955 thus marked a shift in the Italian political climate, and the U.S. response to it and marked the potential for peace in the Cold War.

The UDI and the CIF experienced a small détente of their own in 1955 as they renewed their commitments to creating conditions for peace that would allow a stable environment for workers, mothers, and children to continue to grow. Both associations turned to Parliament to draft new legislation to uphold women's equal status in the constitution by opening all careers to women and guaranteeing equal pay for equal work. They took the same issues to international bodies where they pointed out that work outside the home and motherhood were not so easy to distinguish. According to the UDI's Giuliana Nenni, the Christian Democrats had been largely to blame for deep divisions in the Italian women's movement. Now, however, it appeared to her that the CIF was taking up objectives similar to those of the UDI and making changes in its approach to questions of motherhood, women and work. In an article in the Women's International Democratic Federation's *Women of the Whole World*, Nenni wrote, "For the first time, the Centro Italiano Femminile sent the International Work Bureau a letter in which it recognizes the right of women to choose whether to work outside or inside the home."[88] In fact, the CIF was responding to the changing needs of its members just as Italy entered a phase of rapid economic growth that would make the second half of the 1950s a period of especially intense focus on women workers. Its own Maria Federici had, after all, been the first to sign the 1950 law guaranteeing protection for women with paid jobs.

For the time being, moments in which Catholics and communists could share the same spaces, as Clotilde Cassigoli did in Lausanne, were rare and not transformative, but they did result in declarations of a shared commitment of women of the left, center, and right to motherhood and peace. In its "Message to the United Nations Organization," unanimously adopted at the World Congress of Mothers, the women of the Women's International Democratic Federation affirmed that children "have the right to grow up and develop in happy conditions. This is why the mothers appeal to the United Nations Organization, whose work they follow with great interest. They hope that the United Nations will fully realize the objective it set itself when it was founded—to safeguard new generations from war."[89] The fact, however, that Cold War politics had directly interfered with the federation's ability to continue to present its objectives to the UN revealed the uncertain influence held by all the women's organizations. The discourse of motherhood and peace served to unify and strengthen women's movements, but as a product of women's activism retained its gendered dimension. The national and international women's organizations used creative strategies that included special programs and language to bring more mothers into their folds. They also successfully advanced the notion that peace was a precondition for a tranquil family life and therefore was necessary for the good of all nations that viewed the family as the basic social unit of the community. The women's organizations were not, however, able to institute significant or long-standing cooperation across political lines or to sway world leaders to place motherhood above their other interests. Progress and regress thus continued to delimit the women's agendas for a new era.

The Push for Autonomy and Women's Rights, 1956–1959

In March 1956, Maria Maddalena Rossi, president of the UDI, sent a letter to Amalia di Valmarana, the president of the CIF, inviting her to the Fifth Congress of the Italian Woman, to be held in Rome in April. Rossi highlighted the UDI's distribution of a questionnaire, referred to as a referendum, designed to help the association get a better idea of public opinion on women's position in society. The referendum posed such questions as: Should women work outside the home? Did housewives have the right to a pension? Was it fair to require that female and male workers be paid the same salary for the same jobs? After noting that the CIF had been a proponent of polling women and asking them to reflect on their lives, Rossi continued her invitation to Valmarana by stating that the referendum "confronts the most current problems of Italian women today, placing them in relation to all aspects of society—it cannot interest just one segment of public opinion or one segment of Italian women. We have full trust in your interest and that of the whole association you direct."[1] In her response to Rossi's letter, Valmarana agreed that the themes of the questionnaire "cannot but interest anyone who takes women's problems to heart." Valmarana objected, however, to the framework in which the referendum had been constructed. She wrote, "Allow me to make the observation that the schematics of these questions are such that they exclude concepts, opinions, and principles for which the responses may not be so categorical as the same schematics logically require."[2] Moreover, Valmarana believed that some of the questions "do not take into account situations or contingent reasons that also have an undeniable weight or those, such as in the case of the family, of social assistance or other projects whose realization is already under way." No CIF delegates, Valmarana informed Rossi, would attend the Congress of the Italian Woman, given the UDI's limited understanding of who the "Italian woman" actually was. The UDI, however, continued to see itself as the truly representative association of all Italian women and reported in *Noi Donne* that the eight hundred women who attended the congress in April "represented millions of women of all of Italy, of every social class and every religious creed, who in this moment . . . fight with energy for their emancipation, for a more just society, and for the structural renewal of our country."[3]

The subtlety in this exchange of correspondence between the leaders of the Italian women's associations is significant for several reasons that will be explored in this chapter. First, it shows the continued importance of grassroots organizing, which would be expanded in the second half of the 1950s as women's leaders proposed several new pieces of legislation. Some of the central legislative initiatives of interest to the women's associations were equal salaries for equal work, pensions for housewives, the prevention of unjust firing practices, and the loosening of divorce laws. The UDI and the CIF debated each other and the political parties, the Church, and other institutions and organizations as the Italians grappled with their traditional notions of gender in a rapidly growing nation. Second, Rossi and Valmarana's exchange points to the importance of national consciousness between 1956 and 1959 as the Italian woman became the almost exclusive focus of the UDI and the CIF. The flurry of legislative activity kept the women's associations engaged mostly at the grassroots and national levels, although they applied their general concepts to the international situation and addressed the question of women's positions in countries undergoing the turmoil of decolonization. Third, Valmarana's decision not to accept Rossi's invitation underscores the ideological disparity—no longer centered mainly on the left-right split but now extended to a particular vision of gender—between the two associations that would become more precisely articulated by the end of the 1950s. The UDI began to use the language of emancipation, suggesting that it was an instrument for progress and not an end in itself; the CIF, meanwhile, reaffirmed its commitment to Christianity but looked to integrate civil rights with its Catholic mission.

In this chapter, I intend to show that the differences in the activism, ideologies, and perceptions of autonomy between the UDI and the CIF shifted from being defined mainly in relation to their Cold War political alliances and broad concepts of postwar Italian life to being shaped by the associations' own attempts to construct theories of gender and extend their independent public roles. Of course, international developments figured in the national context and contributed to the associations' delineations in theoretical and practical terms. The tone of the Cold War in Western Europe lessened in intensity between 1954 and 1955, but a new series of events in 1956, including the Suez crisis and the Hungarian uprising, threatened to lead to dangerous international interventions or to war. The signing of the Treaty of Rome in 1957 also affected European relations and economics. So although the Italian women's associations turned their main attention away from the international arena for a few years, it would not be correct to suggest that they no longer took an interest in international affairs or that events outside Italy did not affect them. Instead, as I will demonstrate, the associations' careful crafting of the concepts of autonomy and gender came about in part because of their interactions on the world stage.

International Tensions and National Responses

Following Josef Stalin's death in March 1953, a brief power struggle ensued inside the Kremlin from which Nikita Khrushchev emerged as the new Soviet premier in September. Although Khrushchev and his closest advisors originally intended to assuage the fears of Western European leaders about Soviet intentions, by 1955 they had developed an approach to foreign policy that just barely masked what would become important points of contention among world leaders. The main tenets of the new Soviet foreign policy consisted of creating a buffer zone between the Soviet Union and opposition states, securing relations between the Soviet leadership and the leaders of the "people's democracies" in eastern and central Europe, and establishing some forms of cooperation with the NATO countries. Part of the means for reaching the Kremlin's objectives included the establishment of the Warsaw Treaty Organization in May 1955 to serve as a legitimate reason to station Soviet troops in eastern Europe, much as the United States had done in western Europe through NATO.[4] Khrushchev cemented his authority and new leadership style with his "secret speech" to the Twentieth Congress of the Communist Party of the Soviet Union in February 1956, in which he delivered a blow to Stalin's legacy and initiated the process of de-Stalinization.[5] As historian Vladislav Zubok has noted, "For a while, it seemed that the politics of de-Stalinization and the new foreign policy reinforced each other."[6] However, events in the Middle East and eastern Europe soon turned Khrushchev away from his moderate intentions toward a much more hardline reality. The possibility for détente had never really existed anyway since President Eisenhower did not trust the Soviets and had warned NATO countries to watch for signs of Soviet deceit. According to the Eisenhower administration, the publication of Khrushchev's speech, which had been leaked to the New York Times in June, simply revealed how flawed the communist system was and how far Soviet leaders would go to maintain their hegemony. While a decrease in the intensity of the Cold War characterized the period after Stalin's death, especially between 1953 and 1956, historian Mark Kramer has sustained that "Soviet and US leaders continued to embrace irreconcilable notions of how the world should be configured. These clashing visions, combined with the immense military strength of the United States and the Soviet Union, ensured that the Cold War would continue."[7]

In Italy, leaders of the Italian Communist Party and the Italian Socialist Party followed events in the Soviet Union with great interest. Palmiro Togliatti hoped that Stalin's death might lead the Italian communists back to the strategies that had helped them gain ground in the immediate postwar years. Togliatti therefore threw his full support behind Giorgio Amendola, who had been successful at taking a less rigid stance on communist policies and attracting new supporters in the Italian south. Khrushchev's speech generated numerous questions, however, especially in regard to the continuation of the Popular Front alliance, which had suffered during the 1953 election period. Socialist leader Pietro Nenni and Togliatti read Khrushchev's speech just before the beginning of the Twentieth Congress and initially reacted to it with shock. Nenni, encouraged by other socialists such as Lelio Basso, then began to criticize Stalin and the way the Soviet Union had been run under him.[8] Rapid industrialization, the single-party system, and the dictatorial tendencies of communism, Nenni argued, had allowed Stalin's abuses to reach terrifying levels. The fact that many socialists had viewed Stalin as a peaceful man could be attributed to Stalin's ability to cover up his crimes but also to a corrupt communist system. The Soviet Union, as the socialists now saw it, should not be viewed as the model socialist state. Togliatti interpreted Khrushchev's words differently as he attempted to bridge his loyalty to the USSR and

Stalin with the revelations of the report. As Alexander De Grand has pointed out, "Rather than attack the crimes of Stalin, in which he had some role during the purges of the 1930s, Togliatti took the occasion to reassert the autonomy of the Italian model."[9] Togliatti feared a communist isolation and fought back against Nenni and his supporters.

The buzz from Khrushchev's speech, however, soon died down as Soviet reactions to the Suez crisis and uprisings in Poland and Hungary demonstrated that communist foreign policies would continue on course. The "thaw," as it turned out, was very short lived. In Egypt, war broke out in October 1956 over control of the Suez Canal. Khrushchev backed Egyptian President Gamal Abdel Nasser's nationalization of the Suez and threatened Great Britain, France, and Israel with nuclear war after those countries sent troops into the region. Taking the Kremlin's plans to launch missiles on London, Paris, and Tel Aviv seriously, Eisenhower intervened to try to reach a cease-fire through the United Nations and by using economic pressure. The Suez crisis ended by early 1957, but it left the French weary of NATO and more determined to expand their own nuclear program, and it made the British more aware of their dependence on American aid. The Soviets, in contrast, were emboldened by the reaction their threats generated and came to see themselves as the undisputed rivals to U.S. military power. In October in Poland, Khrushchev and his advisors attempted to abate an upset in the leadership of the Polish Communist Party by heading to Warsaw and bringing Soviet troops into Polish territory. The Kremlin did not ultimately use military force to settle the matter, but only because it had been convinced of first secretary Wladyslaw Gomulka's loyalty.

The situation in Hungary, however, was much more complicated and had direct repercussions in Italy. With events unfolding in Poland and Egypt, the people of Hungary revolted against the hardline pro-Soviet government on October 23, 1956. Pro-reform communist Imre Nagy took control of the Hungarian government and threatened to pull out of the Warsaw Pact and seek help from the United States to establish its neutrality. At first, Khrushchev was reluctant to use force to stop the uprising because of the "new foreign policy" that was helping the Soviets reform their image in the West and because of pressure from Chinese communist leader Mao Zedong. However, Mao changed his position, and Khrushchev garnered support from Yugoslav leader Josip Broz Tito for military intervention.[10]

The Soviets moved forces into Hungary during the first days of November, and despite pleas for help by Nagy to the international community, violently crushed the revolution, killing 2,502 Hungarians and injuring another 19,226, and reestablished a pro-Kremlin government under János Kádár.[11] The reaction in Italy generated a definitive split between the staunchly pro-Soviet communists who viewed the Hungarian revolutionaries as counterinsurgents and members of the left who strongly objected to the Soviets' use of force. Most of the Italian Communist Party leaders, with the exception of Confederazione Generale Italiana del Lavoro head Giuseppe Di Vittorio, supported the Kremlin's intervention, but according to De Grand, the party lost 250,000 members because of events in Hungary.[12] Historian Paul Ginsborg puts that figure at closer to 400,000 and calls 1956 "a watershed year for both parties on the Italian left."[13] Pietro Nenni and his supporters among the socialists used the Hungarian revolution to further build their case for pulling away from the Communist Party and seeking an alliance with Amintore Fanfani and other progressive members of the Christian Democrats.[14] The conservative members of Christian Democracy and the Americans were still weary of Nenni and the socialist platform, however, and a division occurred within the party that would lead to Fanfani's resignation from the party after a disappointing showing in the 1958 elections.

The UDI and CIF forcefully yet cautiously responded to these international events that threatened to lead the world into war. As the Suez crisis began to unfold, the CIF reported on new developments and, in the July–August 1956 issue of Cronache e Opinioni, asserted that Nasser's insistence on the nationalization of the canal would likely lead to an escalation of the conflict.[15] In September, Marisa Rodano and Rosetta Longo of the UDI sent a letter to women's leaders and associations in Egypt, France, and Great Britain, including the Union des Femmes Françaises and the National Assembly of Women, expressing the concerns of Italian women for the safety of the people of the Mediterranean and observing that "world peace cannot but feel itself in danger."[16] According to Rodano and Longo, women's peace efforts could affect the turn of events; they claimed: "It's also because of our own merit that the atomic bomb was not dropped another time; it's also because of our own merit that the bloody conflicts in Korea and Vietnam have been rewritten through diplomatic negotiations." One and half months later, the UDI drafted a resolution on the

Egyptian war and again asserted that "the peace that women made secure through their impassioned actions today appears upset." The women of the CIF scolded Frenchwomen for their "brief nationalist inebriation" and expressed their hope that their "French sisters" would "return to feeling European" after the distance that had been created by their response to the Suez crisis. CIF member Clara Valente, who had won a United Nations grant to study social questions in England, asserted in a letter to *Cronache* that it was time for women to return to a common place in a European spiritual community, now inspired by the suffering, deaths, and losses "of so many heroic women of the people of the great and Christian HUNGARY."[17] Fear of war and a sense that the women's and peace movements were facing a crucial moment characterized the reactions of both the UDI and the CIF to the Suez crisis.

The events of Hungary provoked even sharper and more dramatic responses. For the CIF and the Christian Democrats, the Soviet repression of Hungarian dissidents reconfirmed their fears about communism. CIF members had already expressed doubts that Khrushchev's de-Stalinization speech would result in a change in Soviet policy. In a news column titled "The Month in Review," the *Cronache's* editors commented that "it doesn't seem to us that the principles expressed [by Khrushchev] mutate the communist threat in substance."[18] Paola Gaiotti concurred in her article about the "destruction of the myth of Stalin," stating that "the condemnation of Stalin can be the first step in the political and cultural correction of communism" but only if "we, the non-communists, do not quieten in the face of the condemnation of the man, but force Russia to make fundamental choices and clarifications, demonstrating through facts the superiority of the democratic system."[19] The CIF was also anxious about Soviet atomic power and accused the Soviet leadership of using communism as a pretense to invade Hungary. According to Clara Valente, Hungary "seemed gobbled up in an enormous machine composed of a group of states that only appear independent and that recognize Russia as the supreme guide."[20] In December 1956, the women of the CIF sent a letter to Hungarian women through Catholic Action representative Fr. Geraldo Bakes, which was to be published in the Hungarian magazine *Katolikus Szemle*. Underscoring the Italian and Hungarian women's shared history in Christian traditions, the CIF wrote, "In your great sacrifice at least this demonstrated certainty might comfort you, that by your merit and that of your dear fallen, Christian and civic ideals and free men's souls live brightly in martyred Hungary."[21] In response, the CIF's central president received a clandestine letter from women in Hungarian Catholic Action describing conditions in their country. "We're talking to you about a terrible hell," it read. "There's no more hearth here, the family no longer exists. They deport our husbands and children to Siberia by the thousands. Every family here has a glorious fallen one."[22] The Hungarian women called on the women of the CIF to help them by protesting Soviet actions and letting their voices be heard in the West. The CIF heeded their call by publicizing their plight.

The UDI, like a good part of the Italian left, was deeply affected by the Hungarian crisis, as it shattered the association's belief in the Soviet promise. In its resolution on Egypt, the UDI actually devoted more space to the dramatic situation unfolding in Hungary than to events in Egypt and offered its solidarity to the Hungarian women. "So much warmer and emotional are our wishes for you since we fear that the mobilization of the Magyar army, the presence of Soviet troops, and the eventual intervention of the western countries requested by the conservative forces may give rise to a hotbed of war in the heart of Europe such to put in dramatic terms the problem of peace among peoples."[23] The UDI pleaded with the Italian government to keep Italian forces out of both conflicts and to put pressure on the United Nations to bring an end to them. Anna Matera of the Italian Socialist Party also sent a letter to the Committee of Soviet Women asking its members to unite with Italian women to help to bring Hungary back to normal as quickly as possible.[24] In their letter to women's leaders about Egypt, Rodano and Longo affirmed what would become a central tenet of the UDI's position on the relationship between peace and women's rights from the mid-1950s on: "The age of women's emancipation means also the overcoming of the calamity of war." According to the UDI, without peace women could not really hope to advance their claims to increased civil rights.

The possibility of nuclear war loomed heavily because of the situations in eastern Europe and the Middle East that had led world leaders to use nuclear brinkmanship as part of their military strategies. As a result of such developments, the UDI became especially active in disarmament efforts at the European level and now explicitly tied them to women's rights. As Baldina di Vittorio Berti explained at a meeting of European women in Brunate, Italy (near Como), "Responsibility of Women in the Atomic Age": "It is necessary to explain that our common ideal of the emancipation of woman is subordinate to the safeguarding of peace."[25] Vittorio Berti explained that many Italian women incorrectly believed nuclear war was not really possible and that others had been discouraged from speaking out in favor of peace because of the current Italian political situation. "There's also a certain lack of interest," Vittorio Berti said, "because the defense of peace is not always presented to women as a unifying principle but as a position of political parties that fight among themselves." She argued that women needed to put aside their political differences and act as a part of an independent women's movement. She therefore connected peace, women's emancipation, and autonomous women's movements in a way that carried the UDI in a more theoretically mature direction and signaled the association's attempts to differentiate itself from the Italian Communist Party and later the Women's International Democratic Federation.[26]

At the same time, however, the need for the UDI to reevaluate its positions was motivated by its desire to keep the association together. The repercussions of the invasion of Hungary on the UDI were momentous, not the least because the Italian Communist Party's leaders asked socialist women to leave the UDI after the events of November and December 1956 and the dissolution of the Popular Front. Some important women, such as Rosetta Longo, left the UDI, whereas others, for instance Lina Merlin, did not, which stirred up the UDI's Executive Committee. Moreover, although the majority of communist UDI women continued to be members of the Communist Party, many chose to break away from the party completely, citing both Hungary and the party's failure on women's issues.[27] Of the women who stayed loyal to the party and to the Soviet Union, many nevertheless understood the contentiousness of the political situation and so attempted to take wider perspectives in the ongoing peace movement that did not necessarily include sending messages of support for Soviet actions even when opposing the politics of the leading Western democracies. By the late 1950s, this meant the UDI was taking a more consistently politically neutral tone in international affairs and demanding that the Italian government support nuclear neutrality. In November 1957, for example, the Italian defense minister agreed to the installation of NATO missile launch sites in northern Italy. The UDI protested the decision with large rallies on International Women's Day, March 8, 1958.[28] Several months later, in June 1958, after French President Charles De Gaulle authorized nuclear testing to begin in 1959 in the Algerian part of the Sahara desert, the UDI sent him a telegram pointing out the possible "grave consequences" on the health of all the people of the Mediterranean and noting that such actions contradicted the "atmosphere of détente and the prospect for disarmament following recent international meetings."[29] A small number of UDI women led by socialist Lina Merlin, however, considered the possibility that "the atomic age can become something else: in place of destruction it can offer a new impetus for progress, multiplying the benefits of work and science" and thus opened some debate about the nuclear question inside the UDI although focused on the question of energy dependency rather than on weaponry.[30]

Messages of hope for a lasting peace continued in the August 9, 1959 issue of *Noi Donne*, which recounted the lightheartedness of the Moscow meeting of Vice President Nixon with Khrushchev and both of their wives. Pat Nixon said from the Soviet leader's country home at a press conference, "We were five women present during the meetings. We also agreed on the fact that we have to protect peace for our children whom we love so much."[31] The August 16, 1959 issue of *Noi Donne* included photos of Eisenhower and Khrushchev's historic meeting in the United States. In a short article in the same issue titled "Hope in the Entire World," the editors reported that the Bolshoi Ballet was performing in New York City while an American company was staging *Porgy and Bess* in Moscow.[32] Then, in September 1959, after Khrushchev's return to the Soviet Union, the UDI sent telegrams to both him and Eisenhower to acknowledge the "satisfaction and hope elicited in the hearts of Italian women" by recent events and to express the association's full support for concrete actions taken to establish peace and friendly relations among nations.[33] The UDI's previously polarizing words changed with political developments and no longer granted special license to the Kremlin. The CIF watched these exchanges between the leaders with interest as well. Liliana Piccinini reported on Khrushchev's meeting with Eisenhower, which was to be followed by a non-urgent visit to western Europe, a signal to the CIF that "our old Europe is still the keystone of the international situation: the fate of the community of States will decide the fate of Europe."[34] The future of Europe, in fact, looked promising.

European Integration and Decolonization

On March 25, 1957, Italy, France, Germany, the Netherlands, Belgium, and Luxembourg signed the Treaties of Rome, creating the European Economic Community and the European Atomic Energy Community (Euratom). The major purpose of the European Economic Community was to establish a wider common market based on similar principles to those established by the European Coal and Steel Community in 1951. The objective of the lesser-known Euratom was to develop atomic energy for use in Europe; it was later absorbed into the structure of the European Economic Community. Behind the creation of the European Economic Community was the desire to make Europe's economy stronger by breaking down trade and investment barriers that had existed since before World War II. By allowing for a greater movement of goods, services, and peoples among the major European countries, proponents argued, Europeans would strengthen their diplomatic and personal ties, making reconciliation possible and lessening the likelihood for another war in Europe. The leading Italian supporters of Europeanism and later signatories of the European Economic Community, including Antonio Segni (Christian Democrats) and Gaetano Martino (Italian Liberal Party), argued that an integrated Europe would reinforce and spread democracy. It was also considered a way to "tighten Europe's ties with the USA, which was seen as a crucial element for the economic re-launch and political stabilization of western Europe and for the organization of an effective defense system across the Atlantic."[35] Opponents, however, claimed that the European Economic Community's own modus operandi was undemocratic and even secretive and that a single vision of a united Europe was unrealistic and undesirable. Others preferred to construct a comprehensive Mediterranean policy to guarantee greater Italian autonomy in the region, especially for the agricultural sector in the Italian south.[36] In July 1957, the Italian communists refused to ratify the treaties. The socialists abstained from the parliamentary vote, citing concerns that "certain European monopolistic groups might exercise a predominant influence in the Common Market" but at the same time acknowledging that they "understood the great possibilities of benefit which this project opened up to all Europeans without distinction of class."[37] Political sentiment in favor of the European Economic Community ultimately overshadowed the negative, and the fact that Rome was chosen as the site for the signing of the treaty signaled Italy's key role in integration and its entry into the leading world economies. By 1958, the Italian economic miracle was under way, in large part because of Italian participation in the European Economic Community.[38]

The Italian women's associations discussed the idea of a unified Europe with great interest. A *Cronache* author writing anonymously explained how the notion of "European women" conjured up intriguing images of a historical unity among women in Christianity. According to her, an integrated Europe also appeared to be a necessity given the facts of the Suez and Hungary. The countries, she argued, "have to come together if they want to save themselves, and not just because of atomism; the two mighty coalitions together form a kind of political and economic void and, as we know, nature abhors emptiness . . . ; the reunification of the peoples of Europe appears fated, or it will be made spontaneously so either through the will of the people or conquest. In the latter case, we will see or have to suffer a new empire, no longer sacred and Roman but Muscovite, which will impose its laws on all people without any concessions to the juridical personalization of the Carolingian empire and, above all, without religious tenets."[39] In other words, unifying western Europe was a critical means for saving at least some of the European people from an imperialist, godless Soviet empire and staying true to Europe's historical and religious traditions. *Cronache's* editor, Liliana Piccinini, viewed European integration as a step forward from the intense nationalism of the past, which had led to the wars of the first half of century. Now, she stated hopefully, European nations would look at each other's common elements rather than those that separated them and would therefore be more open to the outside world. For the Italians, this was especially important given the centrality of regional allegiances to the country's history. If the Italians believed that they were part of something larger than a local context, the women of the CIF hoped, they would be able to extend the values of a democratic and Catholic Italy into the rest of Europe.[40] The *Cronache's* editors therefore continued to endorse the European Economic Community and educate CIF women about its purpose and benefits, pointing out, for example, that reductions in trade barriers would benefit consumers by reducing prices. They even hopefully speculated that economic unity could result in greater political unity in the future: "The Common European Market is the road that leads to the political unification of our Continent."[41]

The women of the UDI shared an interest in encouraging the cooperation of peoples across national borders, as they were doing in their European disarmament efforts, but they were not universally enthusiastic supporters of European economic or military integration. According to the main line of the UDI, on one hand, the European Economic Community offered the potential to counter the presence and power of the United States in Europe. On the other hand, the creators of the European Economic Community had also clearly had opposition to the Soviet Union in mind when they drew up the terms of the Treaty of Rome with the capitalist ideals of a free market as the economic centerpiece. UDI women questioned how far integration would extend and were especially weary of any attempts of the western European nations to unite their defensive forces. Military cooperation, they feared, might linger just beneath the surface of economic cooperation or cooperation on atomic energy through Euratom, which most UDI leaders already opposed in principle. Lina Merlin, however, argued that the development of nuclear energy programs would benefit countries such as Italy that had few resources for fuels. Nevertheless, Ada Alessandrini had opened an UDI campaign against the proposed European Defense Community in 1954, arguing that it should be blocked because it "annuls the political independence of our country and dissolves our glorious national army; but also because it divides the nations of the worlds, aggravates contrasts among peoples, especially in the heart of Europe, and especially because it sanctions the legitimacy of atomic, bacteriological, and chemical war."[42] The Italian parliament approved the terms of the European Defense Community, but the French parliament did not; NATO thus remained the primary European defensive force. Nevertheless, a majority of Alessandrini's UDI colleagues echoed her concerns that the codification of common Western political or foreign policies would be the next step in European integration. Given the association's ties to women of the Soviet Union and eastern Europe as well its international socialcommunist rather than supranational capitalist framework, the UDI was at first hesitant to express a positive standpoint on the European Economic Community and Euratom. Moreover, UDI women noted the differences in opinion about the European Economic Community that had accompanied the communists' votes against it and the socialists' abstention.

What quickly became apparent both to supporters and critics of the European Economic Community, including the women's associations, were the effects the new economic community would have on Italian workers. By 1960, Italy was exporting 29.8 percent of its products to European Economic Community countries—up from 23 percent in 1955—and that figure would grow to 40.2 percent by 1965. The manufacture of consumer goods such as washing machines, refrigerators, and cars boomed as demand in Italy and across western Europe burgeoned. At the same time, industrialists found themselves in a commanding position as labor costs decreased over the 1950s, mostly because of the mass migrations of rural southern peasants to northern cities where factories sprang up thanks to supplies of fuels and the region's geographical proximity to the rest of Europe. The industrial triangle of Milan, Turin, and Genoa emerged and became the main site of the so-called economic miracle. New sources of labor, combined with lax government policies on workers' regulations and safety that resulted from a weakening of the trade unions under Christian Democratic governments, guaranteed an ample supply of laborers willing to work long hours for wages that were the lowest in Europe.[43] The new economic conditions had a tremendous influence on the situation of women. By the end of the decade, the UDI and the CIF recognized the effects of the European Economic Community on women workers and housewives in Italy and beyond. Shifts in labor patterns led both women's associations to reevaluate their positions on women's work inside and outside the home and to examine the implications of modernization on Italian family life.

As the European countries began to break down barriers in Europe, they also faced the consequences of postwar decolonization at home and abroad. In the 1950s, former European colonies in Africa and Asia launched independence movements one after the other. Late in the decade the UDI, especially through its work in the Women's International Democratic Federation, took a special interest in developments in Algeria, Indonesia, Vietnam, and the Congo. Of particular concern was how independence movements affected the lives of women and children and the potential of limited conflicts to escalate into full-scale wars. In Algeria, in September 1956, the Front de Libération Nationale unleashed its urban guerrilla fighting tactics in the Battle of Algiers, bringing increased international attention to what had previously been regarded as a small rebellion that would be easily put down by the French. The UDI and the Women's International Democratic Federation supported the Algerian bid for independence. Journalists for the federation's *Women of the Whole World* ran a series of stories about the women of Algeria and published the text of its memorandum on the Algerian conflict as a supplement to the November 1957 issue. In addition to demanding that a "peaceful, just and democratic solution . . . be reached conforming to the interests of the people of Algeria and to the principles of the United Nations Charter," the publication included several reports of the unwarranted arrests, brutal torture, and summary executions of men, women, and children that in many ways recalled the federation's 1951 report on Korea.[44] Later issues featured women fighting for Algerian independence. In the February 1958 issue, for example, Front de Libération Nationale member Djamila Bouhired recounted her dramatic story of capture and torture at the hands of French authorities. At her trial, Djamila boldly declared: "If you kill us, do not forget that you are murdering the traditions of liberty of your own country, it is the honor of your country that you are besmirching, its future which you are endangering, and you will not prevent Algeria from becoming independent."[45] Other stories of defiant women resisting their European colonizers appeared in *Women of the Whole World* as well, including a biography of the founder of the Women's Union of Hanoi, Nguyen Khoa Dieu Hong, who was the leading female member of the Viet Minh during the Vietnamese independence struggle that temporarily ended in 1954.[46] On Africa, the federation published articles about countries such as the Sudan, the Congo, and South Africa, and in December 1958 it ran a four-page color spread about the All-African Peoples' Conference held in Ghana, which had won independence from Great Britain in 1957. American cultural anthropologist Eslanda Goode Robeson covered the event for the Women's International Democratic Federation. She commented that her "only dissatisfaction with the Conference was the lack of women delegates"; only eight women representatives attended the conference, and only two of them spoke at the plenary session.[47] Women's rights and independence converged on the pages of the federation's magazine and reminded European activists of their responsibilities toward women around the world as they all attempted to make progress in their individual national contexts.

Gender, Ideology, and Women's Rights

Just months before the dramatic international events that made 1956 a watershed year, the UDI had already taken steps to redirect the association's future. In July, its executive committee prepared a document proposing to its provincial committees that the organization put women's emancipation at the center of its struggles and make it *"the UDI's reason for being . . .* in other terms *to act on the struggle for emancipation* rather than *continuing to say* we will struggle for emancipation [emphases in original]."[48] To turn words into actions would require that the UDI assert its authority as an autonomous women's association and move away from the political lines established by the political parties and trade unions. The executive committee pointed out, for example, that some UDI women had purposely neglected certain women's issues, such as birth control and prostitution, and compartmentalized others, such as reforms to the family code, because they were afraid to confront male leaders on the left who either did not agree with the women's perspectives or were afraid to upset their constituencies.

Divisions between the socialists and communists on both international and domestic policies had also contributed to disaccord among the UDI's leaders. As the Socialist Party sought greater autonomy from the Communist Party, party leaders asked women to follow their example, which created tension in the UDI. The executive committee, however, recognized the diversity of the UDI's membership and recommended that the association do more to encourage the advancement of women outside the typical socialist-communist orientation of its leaders. "The Executive Committee has noted that already today there are many women of diverse ideological and political orientations. It's true for example, that large currents of women members of the UDI profess the Catholic religion; in the future, it won't even be possible to see the UDI's united politics just as deriving from a gain at the base or certain isolated personalities."[49] By making women's rights the primary focus of the UDI, the association could encourage a healthy debate on the relationship of political orientation to perspectives on women and avoid some conflicts based on political party affiliations. Until now, the report said, the politics of the most visible UDI women "ended up pushing away those women's forces, which although favorable to women's emancipation, do not accept a society, to put it this way, of a socialist type."[50] Even the most loyal communists from the UDI's rank-and-file membership began to privilege gender over the party line and identified first as UDI women. For example, Ermanna Zappaterra of Ferrara, who entered local government in the mid-1950s as a member of the Communist Party, said: "For me the party was something I cared about because it was my ideal, because I followed that road. However, it came after; first came 'the feminine.' 'Oh, no, dear lady comrades,' I said once in City Hall, 'even if you have forgotten that before being members of the party you are women, I have not forgotten it.' I came to the PCI meetings as an UDI woman."[51] The new orientations proposed by the UDI led it to set a focused but inclusive national political agenda while its disarmament efforts continued at the international level.

While the UDI was asserting its autonomy and seeking to appeal to more women through the language of emancipation, the CIF was reconsidering its role among the many Catholic organizations that focused on similar issues and revising its ideology. In her address to the 1957 National Congress, titled "The Organization of the CIF as an Instrument of Democratic Education," Amalia di Valmarana's explanation of the relationship of the CIF to other organizations indicated a shift in focus:

> While we continue working with certain agencies with which we are
> federated in order to clarify and express our overlapping interests in
> the civic-social-assistance camp, that is on problems that threaten the
> rights and interests of the family, women and children and that we
> consider a specific but not exclusive area of activism for the CIF, for
> other problems, especially those that are exclusively religious or of a
> purely political, cultural, or union-based nature, which are not part of
> the activities directed by the CIF, we rely on and, where necessary, call
> on other specific associations whether inside or outside the federation,
> offering though our collaboration in cases when it is required.[52]

In other words, the CIF viewed women's issues as the main focus of the association and would work with other bodies and institutions when their interests overlapped. The CIF would not, however, direct projects with other groups when women and related matters, such as the family and children, were not the main emphasis. On a structural level, Valmarana recommended that the CIF continue operating in a transparent and democratic manner that considered multiple points of view but focus on actions consistent with its focus on bettering women's lives. Valmarana suggested granting more authority to regional CIF offices so they could pursue programs of interest to women in the diverse regions of Italy but without losing the national direction established by the president's office in Rome.[53]

Once the women's associations reaffirmed that their commitment to women was their main priority, they launched a series of campaigns that the political parties, trade unions, other organizations, and the public would debate throughout the end of the 1950s and well into the 1960s. At stake in the legislative proposals was nothing less than a deep consideration of the differences between men and women and whether presumed differences should result in the continuation of policies that justified and codified separate gender roles that kept women in positions of political, economic, and social inferiority. In their approaches to new legislation, however, the Italian women's organizations veered away from the narrow parameters used by Nixon and Khrushchev during the famous Cold War "kitchen debate" in July 1959. The American vice president claimed the suburban housewife was the ideal model of women's emancipation and argued that she best represented the lifestyle that was possible because of capitalist economic growth. The Soviet premier, in contrast, insisted that Russian women factory workers enjoyed full equality with men in the workplace and therefore were more liberated than American women who stayed in the home. As historians such as Elisabetta Bini and Marina Casalini have argued, neither American nor Soviet gender models were uncritically adopted by Italian women.[54] The UDI and the CIF were particularly sensitive to the need to converge ideals with actual conditions and, beginning in the mid-1950s, they introduced and discussed a number of initiatives. Most fall under the categories of work (e.g., equal salaries, access to all careers, protections for women workers), home and family (e.g., pensions for housewives, divorce, adultery laws), and public morality (e.g., prostitution);[55] the lines among these groupings often overlapped, of course, showing that public and private life were not always easy to distinguish. During the debates over woman-centered proposals, the women's associations were forced to reflect on their theoretical and practical approaches to gender. To successfully present their arguments inside and outside the associations, the women had to clarify their thoughts and find avenues to reach the women and men that could help them ensure that their points of view became dominant.

By 1955, more than 6.6 million Italian women worked outside the home, making up 29 percent of the total workforce, and that figure grew as the economic miracle took hold by the end of the 1950s.[56] However, women faced discrimination in the workplace, could not enter into all careers open to men, and, on average, received 16 percent less pay than their male counterparts for the same work. The UDI and the CIF argued that such unequal treatment was neither fair nor legal and began to put several plans into action to change and enforce legislation while attempting to open women and men's minds to a general principle of gender equality. The UDI and the CIF agreed on the necessity of legal equality between women and men, but they often disagreed in their approaches to specific pieces of legislation because of their particular ideological viewpoints. The new orientations suggested by the UDI's leaders in 1956 led the association to attempt again to reach out to Catholic women and to collaborate with the CIF. Marisa Rodano sent the CIF a letter in July 1956 proposing that the two associations unite efforts and noting that "in the past, every improvement in the conditions of women's social, civil, and political life was obtained through actions carried out together: the conquest of the right to vote and the law for the protection of working mothers represent successes obtained by women who demonstrated in some moments and in some cases, unity of purpose and will." Continuing her request for the two associations to work together to put pressure on Parliament to move on new legislation to benefit women, Rodano commented, "Even if they remain distinctive, our organizations will be better able to live up to the trust of Italian women when they learn how to overcome differences and meet on the road that leads to common goals for women's emancipation."[57]

The CIF's Amalia di Valmarana continued to resist opening up to the women of the UDI, even though she expressed the CIF's concurrence with many of their aims for women. In her address at the CIF's Eighth National Congress in 1957, Valmarana stated, "Equal rights, equality before the law, access to careers and to elected and administrative offices, and the administration of justice are common objectives that Catholic women's forces also aim to achieve for real equal rights."[58] The CIF, Valmarana noted, would continue to try to educate members of the government, Catholic organizations, such as Catholic Action, and its own members about the social and cultural benefits of women's equality, but without offending its Catholic base or the tenets of Christianity. Such a position meant that the CIF would persist in seeing the world and the Italian political system as divided into two distinct blocs that made complete cooperation improbable. "While the Marxist position sees women's inclusion in society as a productive force that leads to the construction of the communist state," Valmarana said, "the Catholic conception sees woman, combined with man in life and the progress of society, bringing with her a specific and non-substitutable contribution."[59] The same idea was carried into the rank-and-file membership of the CIF. For example, Irene Rosa Colizzi of Bologna, who joined the CIF in the mid-1950s, said, "I only remember that the main purpose of the CIF was that of putting our values as Catholic women above the moral and religious errors that the UDI and the leftist lay world were spreading."[60] UDI member Rosanna Galli of Modena recalls a lengthy conversation with a childhood friend and member of Catholic Action that exposed the absurdity of their mutual diffidence: "Every two minutes she would say to me, 'I agree with you but I can't because you are materialists.' I didn't really know what 'materialists' meant so I looked for a way out and said 'We're what you say, however, I want the right to work, the right to study, I want the farm workers to own their land, etc., just like you."[61]

The fact that the two women's associations chose not to combine resources and work together could be interpreted as a sign of weakness in the women's movement. However, the fact that the associations continued to operate among their traditional supporters actually broadened their reach. In particular, the CIF's lack of interest in combining forces with women of the left had the unintended consequence of softening the message of gender equality among more conservative political and religious forces. Signs of solidarity with the UDI would have likely earned the CIF the consternation and suspicion of powerful women and men in the political parties and Catholic organizations and made their inroads into Catholic homes more difficult. Acting separately, the UDI and the CIF pushed forward their visions of gender equality and carefully negotiated their points of view with the groups in which they were accustomed to working. Moreover, through debate with each other, the women's associations refined their positions. As the CIF's Anna Maria Pazzagalia recalls, "Given that the 1950s were passing by, the woman question and the resulting recognition of the rights of woman in a democratic lay society that tended toward male chauvinism required assiduous study and frequent participation at meetings and debates with women's associations (especially the UDI) that were particularly experienced and resistant to accepting Christian demands."[62]

With the support of the UDI, the CIF, and the women's sections of the trade unions, women workers began to challenge the government to enforce the equal salaries laws already in existence. Since the early 1950s, in *Cronache e Opinioni* the CIF's Clara Valente had been reporting on women's reluctance to challenge their employers for fear of being demoted or fired.[63] Writers for *Noi Donne* published several stories about women who had experienced just such treatment and recounted their efforts to resist discriminatory practices. For example, in Milan, the Fonderia Metalli Almara fired two female employees when the company decided to restructure certain positions for male workers. Two men replaced the women and earned more for doing the same work the women had done. At the Carlo Erba chemical plant, managers transferred a female employee with twelve years experience to a lower paying position after she asked for the same salary as her male coworkers. Both cases came before the magistrate in Milan, and judges determined that article 37 of the constitution had been violated.[64] Encouraged by the results of these and similar cases, UDI president Maria Maddalena Rossi, along with Luciana Viviani and other UDI and women parliamentarians, took their concerns about the fair application of equal salaries laws to Parliament and received a favorable response. The government agreed to send out letters to employers stating the principles of the law and cautioning that it would be rigorously enforced.[65] The UDI and the CIF participated in a conference in Milan on article 37 with a number of other associations, including the National Nurses Association; the Women's Federation of Arts, Professions, and Business; the Union of Female Attorneys; the Metal Workers Association; the YWCA; and the Women's International Democratic Federation. In addition, representatives of trade unions, universities, and the entertainment world were invited to attend. In an article about equal pay in the federation's *Women of the Whole World*, Ines Pidorni Cerlesi said of the accord reached at the Milan conference: "It is advisable to stress that this unity, of which the Union of Italian Women is the standard bearer, now extends to the traditional feminist movement and with some differences, to the Catholic Women's Movement. The Catholic Association of Italian Working

Women, although the last to declare itself on the question of equal pay, is now active regarding this question."[66] The UDI and the CIF recommended creating a permanent national committee on equal salaries, which they both sat on and that later became the Committee for the Defense of Women's Rights.[67] In each of these activities, both the UDI and the CIF affirmed their commitments to women workers.

So although the women of the CIF did not seek a closer alliance with the women of the UDI, they did begin to modify their positions on women's work outside the home. A survey the CIF conducted in 1957 found that only 50 percent of women were satisfied as housewives—down from 90 percent in 1949.[68] Jolanda Magnani, a twenty-year-old teacher from Reggio Emilia, shared a growing sentiment among the CIF's younger members, "I don't find it right that family life should shut women off from other interests (culture, professional life, politics, religion, apostolic). I think instead that these interests can make her a more complete person and fit to carry out her mission in the world."[69] Without rejecting a long-held perspective that women's primary mission was in the home, the CIF nevertheless began to recognize that a woman may have reasons other than economic necessity for seeking and keeping paid employment. Valmarana wrote that some members saw paid work "as a means that allows for the development of personal qualities and that she feels as a must for solidarity and contribution to the progress of society."[70] As Valmarana reminded participants of the CIF's 1957 congress: "All questions that regard mothers and workers, economic assurances for the defense of the family, equality for women in regards to accessing public offices have always been supported by the CIF."[71] Women's access to all careers thus became a special focus and led the association to put additional pressure on the Christian Democrats to modify existing legislation that kept women out of the judiciary and the highest echelons of public office. In December 1956, Parliament passed law 1441, which allowed women to become judges. Women's full access to all careers would not come until 1963, however.

While the CIF began not only to accept but also to fight for women's right to paid employment outside the home, the UDI reconsidered its position on housewives in line with its developing theories of women's emancipation. Both associations put forward a call for pensions for housewives to recognize the contributions of the more than 10 million Italian women whose primary workplace was the home.[72] In this case, the women's associations agreed that some sort of pension plan was needed to provide for women in their old age and during periods of illness, just as paid women workers received. Women who did not marry but worked in the households of family members did not have any recourse to the pensions of husbands as widows did, which made their lives even more precarious. The UDI and the CIF agreed that women's work inside the home comprised not only household tasks such as cooking and cleaning but also teaching children and providing a safe and tranquil environment for all members of the family. The productive, moral, social, and affective value of women's work inside the home, they argued, deserved recognition. The associations took vastly different stances on how a pension plan should be established and run, however. They also viewed women's work inside the home from their different ideological perspectives, with the UDI emphasizing the state's role and the CIF looking to the private and religious world for their framework.

The UDI tended to see housework as a particularly challenging category of work that was made even more difficult because of conditions in Italy, especially in the poorest regions of the country. As Nilde Jotti pointed out, "We can nevertheless say that the work of housewives in Italy is particularly difficult in and of itself and is made even more so because the living conditions of the Italian people are among the lowest in all of Europe. . . . In the poorest regions women who dedicate themselves to working in the home for years and years of their lives never have even a single hour of time for fun or distraction."[73] Jotti and the UDI noted that many capitalist countries, such as France, had begun to offer more social services to benefit the economic and social organization of the family and the state, but that Italy fell behind in this area. If the Italian state was not able or not willing to provide such services, it was time that it at least recognize and compensate the social value of housewives. Without these women's contributions in the home, the entire economic life of the country would fall apart. As Anna Matera put it, "Housewives are workers: that is the point. In the same way as other non-payrolled workers, they are advancing their right to pension coverage."[74] For the UDI, the question of a pension for housewives went hand-in-hand with the association's agenda of women's emancipation. The UDI "sees in the right to work the central point of women's emancipation and hopes for an economic development that allows all citizens, men and women, to have a job that is worthily compensated, with hours and working conditions that respect personal rights, together with a social organization that creates a network of help and solidarity around the family."[75] Given its socialist principles based on the right to work and the responsibility of the state toward its citizens, the UDI proposed a universal pension plan to be established and paid for by the government.

The CIF, in contrast, saw the housewife as the ideal Christian woman all women should emulate. The UDI's position on housework appeared to Valmarana to suggest that it amounted to little more than drudgery. As she commented, "The women Marxists see the family, or at least female work on behalf of the family, as a form of slavery, as a chain to break to advance from the past. We instead think that it is above all in a family founded on Christianity, and in which the work of women is irreplaceable, that foundations are laid that put the individual—man or woman—in conditions to be able to make choices to bring their own contributions to construct a renewed world in continuous civil ascent."[76] Valmarana and the CIF nevertheless acknowledged the most challenging aspects of housework and recommended offering women who worked inside the home more social services while establishing pension and health care plans for them. The CIF and other Catholic organizations proposed to do more to assist mothers by taking care of their children in additional privately run daycare centers, after-school programs, and summer camps and to reach out to teenage girls to teach them about running a household.

The World Movement of Mothers intervened on behalf of the women's organizations at the United Nations, which Italy had joined in December 1955, and pointed out that the value of the economic and affective roles played by housewives would be incalculable. The organization asked the UN's Commission on the Status of Women for support in helping form public opinion to support housewives but stopped short of suggesting that states pay for it.[77] Information about the various legislative proposals ran in issues of *Cronache e Opinioni* during the spring and summer of 1957 alongside interviews with CIF members who discussed their opinions on the matter. Two Roman women, for example—Rosa Maugeri, a forty-four-year-old housewife married to a bartender, and Marianna Pelliccia, a sixty-year-old widow and grandmother—both affirmed that they would be happy to contribute to and to receive a pension even if they did not quite understand how the mechanism would work.[78] As in the case of opening careers to women, the matter of pensions to housewives would still take several years to work out in the legislature; a law passed in 1963 would create private voluntary pension plans.

In addition to women's work inside and outside the home, questions of tradition and family morality entered into public discussions and legislative proposals. During the late 1950s, the women's associations and the political parties revisited divorce laws, though the final word on divorce in Italy would not come until a referendum in 1974.[79] In October 1954, Senator Luigi Renato Sansone, a socialist, introduced legislation allowing divorce in certain limited cases. His proposal received little attention in Parliament and was not taken to a vote. With Senator Giuliana Nenni, a socialist and UDI member, Sansone redrafted the bill. Discussions about the indissolubility of marriage reentered the public arena prior to the proposal being again taken to Parliament in June 1958. Nicknamed the *piccolo divorzio*, or little divorce, the socialist proposal called for divorce to be permitted if one partner had been sentenced to fifteen years or more in prison; one spouse had attempted to murder the other one; a couple had been separated for fifteen years with no signs of reconciliation; there was a proven case of prolonged mental illness; or, in cases of international marriage, the country of one spouse permitted divorce. The *piccolo divorzio* proposal generated anything but a small response. The Christian Democrats and the Italian Communist Party opposed it vehemently—the former because of its position that marriage was a Catholic sacrament, and the latter because of its fear of being seen as wanting to break up the Italian family. The CIF shared the Christian Democratic Party's sentiments but emphasized the importance of the family as the basis of society even more than the party did and argued that the traditional vows of marriage meant that spouses were committed to each other despite mental illness or incarceration. In cases of separation, the CIF recommended seeking assistance from parish priests or trusted members of the community to work out differences, and in cases of international marriage, the CIF noted that the laws of both countries had to be respected and so that foreigners marrying Italians needed to be aware of the legislation.[80]

The UDI found itself in a difficult position. Many socialists supported the Sansone-Nenni proposal, but the communists did not. At the same time, the UDI's stronger emphasis on women's emancipation made issues such as divorce critical to the association's development. Writers for *Noi*

Donne therefore took the matter to Italian women and asked for their opinions. A series of articles in January and February 1957 explored such matters as the consequences of the indissolubility of marriage, divorce laws in other countries, and public opinion. The UDI leaders largely supported divorce in certain circumstances and argued that working-class women often had a much harder time surviving in cases of prolonged separations. Women's subordination made their circumstances particularly insecure, however. As one unnamed author commented, "The Italian Constitution, as noted, recognizes equal rights between the sexes. But according to Italian marriage law, the husband is the master of everything, and if one day the two spouses split up, the wife has to leave the house empty handed, except for, in the best cases, when she has the right to alimony."[81] Most of the UDI's members, however, expressed concerns similar to those of the CIF over the possibility of legalizing even some divorces, and stated in letters to *Noi Donne* that marriage required sacrifice and commitment from both spouses; there should not be an easy out in difficult moments. A fifty-year-old woman identified only as an obstetrician from Biella underscored the precariousness of women's position in marriage and expressed concern that granting divorce would allow men to more easily leave their aging wives for younger women. "If the man knows marriage is indissoluble he'll think twice before making a move on another woman."[82]

Without unity among women, the Sansone-Nenni bill could not survive. The proposal was not taken to a vote, and not until the mid-1960s would the Italian public be ready to revisit the matter. Nevertheless, the *piccolo divorzio* question did result in a reexamination of marriage and family and the roles of women and children in the private sphere. A *Noi Donne* article provocatively titled "Is Marriage the Tomb of Love?" featured five married couples' responses to personal questions about marriage and family. The couples interviewed identified what they saw as the sources of most disagreements in the household—money and raising children—and discussed how they had worked through their problems. The couples also noted international models alternative to the Italian situation; in Italy, they said, women took on most of the responsibilities in the household regardless of whether they worked outside the home. One wife, Eda, mentioned with some surprise the young American couples who lived near her home. The husband, she said, studies medicine during the day and then "returns home, helps the wife wash up the kitchen, cleans the floors, and attends to the baby; and it's common to see the American woman sitting down listening to the radio or reading." Eda's husband had suggested hiring another woman to help her with household chores, to which Eda responded that she did not want to turn all her money over to someone else and that she had "heard that in the Soviet Union there are organizations that have a function like this."[83] In other words, whether helped by husbands or by organizations, American and Soviet women did not seem to have the same burdens in the home as did women in Italy and even had opportunities for rest and enjoyment. According to some women, women's emancipation, in addition to legal equality, also meant freeing women's time for leisure, hobbies, and politics. The CIF agreed that families needed more social services to help them balance the many demands on their time but in part to allow them to more actively participate in their communities: "If the family performs its duties, we will see lasting development in our society; a mutually, well-ordered society benefits the family since national interests are always tightly connected to family interests."[84] CIF women regarded a clear separation of gender roles with legal equality as the best way to retain harmony in the family and did not suggest moving toward either "unnatural" Soviet models or "selfish" American ones.

Conclusion

The hopes for détente ushered in by Khrushchev's de-Stalinization speech were shattered in 1956 when Soviet tanks rolled into Hungary. As a crucial turning point in the Cold War, the failed Hungarian revolution left socialists and communists confused about the future of international communism and confirmed the deepest suspicions of anticommunists about Soviet power and intentions. The western European nations looked to integration to help solidify their connections to each other and distance themselves from the Soviet bloc. As a stronghold of the far left, Italy was key to both the future of socialism in Europe and to European integration, but the rift between the Italian socialists and communists caused by international events made national politics especially awkward and challenged the unity of the UDI. Meanwhile, though the Christian Democrats benefited from problems on the left, disaccord on the right among them and the Republicans and Social Democrats led to two changes in

government in the late 1950s and to an uninspired "progress without adventures" campaign that Christian Democrats won in 1958. By the end of
the decade, little had changed in terms of the country's electorate, but
important changes in perspective led to new developments for the wom-
en's associations.[85]

In the second half of the 1950s, the UDI and CIF observed and responded
to conflicts abroad that resulted from the Cold War and decolonization.
Both associations reevaluated their central objectives and methods for
achieving them and arrived at the conclusion that they must put women
at the center of their struggles and not be distracted or misled by purely
political pressures. As a result, the UDI and the CIF participated in the
drafting of new legislation on women's work inside and outside the home
and engaged in public discussions with their members, political party and
trade union leaders, and other social service and special interest organizations. As had been the case in the past, the leaders of the UDI and the CIF
engaged each other in debates about women's rights, roles, and responsibilities, and, as before, they found little common ground. Nevertheless,
the separate worlds of the women's associations led them to take women's
issues into the most disparate sectors of Italian political and social life.
Not every initiative found its resolution by the end of the decade, but the
women's associations laid the groundwork for women's full legal equality.
In 1958, the Italians entered into a period known as the economic miracle, which had direct consequences for Italian workers and urban and
rural life into the 1960s and beyond. Women's roles again became public
contested terrain as domestic duties appeared to become easier and
women's time freer, but as will be seen in the next chapter, contemporary
life opened a new series of challenges for the national and international
women's movements.

5   Opening to the Center, 1960–1963

In the April 1963 issue of *Cronache e Opinioni*, Amalia di Valmarana asked CIF members to contribute to the World Movement of Mothers to help sustain the organization, which at that time was facing a financial crisis. In her plea to the *Cronache*'s readers, Valmarana acknowledged that "maybe it is difficult to persuade all of our readers, already pestered by thousands of requests, of the great utility of the World Movement of Mothers, but it would be enough to read all the letters that come to us from all over the world; it would be enough to hear the stories that experts, missionaries, and holy mothers from all countries tell us, to realize the great magnificence and the grand possibilities of this institution . . . that is among the most important instruments for the solution to problems that do, and that must, lie at the hearts of the women of all the world."[1] Valmarana assured executive committee representative Maria Penco, who had recently attended a World Movement of Mothers meeting at which Irène Mancaux told her the organization would likely have to shut down, that she would ask the Vatican's secretary of state and the Italian cabinet for money to save the organization.[2] Meanwhile, following the dramatic exit of the Italian delegation from the Women's International Democratic Federation's June 1963 Congress in Moscow over political differences and organizational priorities, members of the UDI pondered whether to remain a full member or become an associate member of the international organization, a decision that could have important economic and leadership consequences for the federation and could redirect the UDI's participation in international politics. In 1963, both international women's organizations, now active for nearly twenty years, faced serious threats to their futures that directly involved the Italian women's associations.

What happened to bring them to this point? The answer to that question is the subject of this chapter. In the early 1960s, the CIF renewed its commitment to women's international cooperation through its support of the World Movement of Mothers. The UDI, meanwhile, modified its course and questioned the very mission of the Women's International Democratic Federation. Those decisions and their repercussions resulted in making 1963 a watershed moment for all of these organizations.

This chapter explores the important transitional years that ended in 1963 in an attempt to account for the battle for survival waged by the international women's organizations in a period of continued economic growth and monumental political changes. By the end of the year, people around the world were grappling with, among many other episodes of global consequence, the assassination of the U.S. president, the meeting of the Second Vatican Council and the death the pope who convened it, the expansion of the European Economic Community, the Sino-Soviet split, and the reheating of conflicts in Vietnam. As the international women's organizations lived through these events, they also confronted their own economic and political problems. And the UDI and the CIF reevaluated their positions and roles in relation to the international women's organizations and resituated themselves in both the national and global contexts. The UDI challenged the Women's International Democratic Federation to back away from Cold War entanglements and reemphasize its commitment to women's emancipation. The UDI's desire to depoliticize the international women's movement, however, was motivated not only by explicitly stated objectives to advance women's rights but also by a need to maintain unity in the Italian association and deal with national political pressures that resulted from the socialists' cooperation with the Christian Democrats, a move that now threatened to upset the alliance of women on the left. The CIF, in contrast, used the moment ushered in by Vatican II to reexamine women's spiritual lives in the face of economic and technological progress. To guarantee that Catholic women's voices would be heard in national, European, and global matters, especially those of great social and economic consequence, the CIF encouraged Italian women to take a more comprehensive view of the political world and see it not as something of concern mainly to a small class of men. Saving the World Movement of Mothers meant holding on to women's important roles across multiple milieus.

Italian Politics and the Vatican

As historian Paul Ginsborg has noted, two major changes in Italian Cold War politics occurred in the early 1960s—the election of American president John F. Kennedy and reforms to Vatican foreign policy initiated by Pope John XXIII. Kennedy's presidency, which began in 1961, altered American positions on Italy and opened the door to an Italian center-left coalition. Following an official state visit with Kennedy in June 1961, Amintore Fanfani and Antonio Segni of the Christian Democrats began to "open to the left," a policy continued by Christian Democratic leader Aldo Moro, who sought an alliance with the socialists. Although Kennedy did not push a coalition between the Christian Democrats and the socialists, he seemed to think such a partnership would "provide Italy with a government more committed to reform and justice."[3] Historian Leopoldo Nuti has remarked that Kennedy's European policy was driven more by pragmatism than by ideology: "He took as his main tasks the prevention of a nuclear catastrophe and the reorientation of the Cold War towards a different, less conventional kind of confrontation."[4] He was therefore less interested in sustaining the dogmatic conflicts that had been characteristic of previous Cold War presidents. In the same year Kennedy was elected, Pope John XXIII expressed favor for the Christian Democrats' new openness and vowed to step away from the direct intervention in national politics that had characterized his predecessor's papacy. As a result, the Vatican modified its position condemning dialogue between the Christian Democrats and the socialists, a position it took in articles in l'Osservatore Romano throughout 1960.[5] Socialist leader Pietro Nenni's subsequent public expressions of support for NATO, which moved the socialists away from their traditional position of neutrality in foreign affairs, strengthened ties between the Christian Democrats and the socialists and eventually contributed to the socialists' entry into a center-left coalition government in May 1963 led by Moro. A private conversation between Nenni and Kennedy in Rome in the summer of 1963 was seen as further confirmation of the U.S. president's approval of the new center-left government.[6]

The political parties carefully evaluated this new territory in which the reform-minded socialists moved away from their historical cooperation with the more ideologically similar communists and toward the pro-American and pro-consumerist Christian Democrats.[7] As a result, the CIF and the UDI were forced to evaluate the consequences of these important national political shifts to their own constituencies. The CIF's Cronache e Opinioni editor Liliana Piccinini first reported on the "opening to the left" after the Italian Socialist Party's congress in March 1961, mainly highlighting the party's internal problems and the obvious tensions between it and the Italian Communist Party but also criticizing Nenni for appearing to challenge Italian foreign policy decisions in Asia and Africa in the interests of maintaining neutrality.[8] According to Piccinini, the socialists' ideology was still ultimately based on the principles of Marxism and thus incompatible with Catholicism. It appeared that the CIF preferred to see that the door to the left remain closed. However, as the relationship between the Christian Democrats and the socialists deepened, and the reality of the center-left coalition loomed in advance of the 1963 national elections, the CIF backed away from its criticisms of the Socialist Party in the interests of not scaring away Christian Democratic Party voters. Elisa Bianchi, writing in *Cronache e Opinioni*, reassured CIF women that "it is unthinkable that the leaders of a party, which has always remained loyal to the principles of Christian social doctrine, have not evaluated the dangers that could arise from a collaboration with a party like the PSI [Italian Socialist Party] that has such a diverse ideological orientation and that their choices are not the result of their thoughtful sense of responsibility and their conscious enterprise."[9] The CIF guaranteed its members that the alliance of the two parties would be based on specific actions rather than on common ideology and that it could very well serve to completely fracture the socialists' ties to the communists. It was now important to "give its support to the [Christian Democratic] party, if it is able to express in political terms the deepest demands from the women's world that the CIF represents" and support its women candidates.[10] When the Christian Democrats saw a drop in its share of the votes from 42.4 percent in 1958 to 38.3 percent in 1963, the CIF could not help but wonder if women voters had become generally uninterested in politics or if they had instead questioned the Christian Democrats' new stance on the socialists. Don Leone Bentivoglio, the CIF's ecclesiastical consultant, asked members to work extra hard to educate young people about politics in summer camps and daycare programs, claiming that, "the principle cause (not the only one) of the communist advance in Italy—a very dangerous and humiliating phenomenon in a Catholic country—is the grave lack of a cultural, moral, and religious education of the people."[11] According to Bentivoglio, the CIF needed to do more to correct this.

The alliance between the Christian Democrats and the socialists was also troubling to the UDI, which was seeking to hold together a fragile unity across party lines. Continuing as it had after the events in Hungary in 1956, the UDI attempted to appear as *super partes* as possible and stress the importance of women's emancipation above the internal disagreements of the political parties. Anna Matera, a member of the Central Committee of the Socialist Party and the UDI Executive Committee, explained the different political needs and roles of the parties versus those of the women's associations. "The function and placement of the women's associations is different," she wrote. "The latter find their reason for being in the necessity of overcoming political and ideological boundaries, in order to call all women to an autonomous battle for their emancipation within the framework of existing structures, even if it is evident that women's emancipation is itself a strong force that sooner or later will push society to modify its own structures."[12] The feminine forces of the left were nonetheless forced to carefully navigate the contentious national political situation to continue to work together, which generally meant that communist women looked to reach agreements with the socialists and to offer an ideological perspective that better matched their own, or at least one that fit better than the ideological framework offered by the women of the Christian Democrats. Because of these external pressures, UDI members who were socialists often found common ground on foreign policy with members who were communists and took little action on national politics.[13] In fact, it was difficult for the UDI to make sweeping public statements supporting one political party in advance of the 1963 elections, so it focused instead on women's issues and women candidates to maintain a sense of a common purpose. When the votes were cast, the parties of the left held on to most of their supporters, with the communists growing even stronger and obtaining 25.3 percent of the votes, up from 22.7 in 1958, and the socialists losing just a fraction of voters, declining from 14.2 percent in 1958 to 13.8 percent in 1963. The center-left coalition took charge of the government but it appeared the socialists and the Christian Democrats had been affected by women's lack of confidence in the new arrangement.

Kennedy's election and John XXIII's papacy had more far reaching consequences, however, than the Italian elections, particularly in regard to the Italian and international women's organizations. Kennedy's influence and John XXIII's major reforms brought Catholicism to the center of international discussions and received a welcome boost from Catholics worldwide. As the first Catholic to win the U.S. presidency, Kennedy demonstrated how to be a modern Catholic who supported such values as social justice and equality but did not take orders from the Vatican.[14] When Liliana Piccinini reported on Kennedy's inauguration speech, particularly his statement that he was guided by God, she noted, "This phrase was not intended as the traditional invocation to God that every president makes at his inauguration. It is something more that deserves to be underscored. It is certainly a profession of faith made without ostentation by a man who feels Catholic before anything else: the work of God must be our own: it is thy kingdom come."[15] The CIF's admiration of Kennedy and its hopes that under his leadership Catholic women worldwide could extend their appreciation for the American lifestyle beyond its economic aspects and into the spiritual realm continued throughout Kennedy's presidency until his assassination in November 1963. After Kennedy's death, Piccinini expressed the sentiments of the CIF and Catholic women throughout Europe: "As the fervent Christian that he was, Kennedy aspired to an ever more conscious and vital community among free peoples, a community that had trust in the power of liberty, the rights of the individual, the capacity of democracy to renew and resolve all the problems of human beings."[16] In Kennedy, the CIF and the Catholic women's movement had found and lost an important model of lay Catholic civilization.

The UDI's reaction to John F. Kennedy was mixed. On one hand, his youth, vibrancy, and progressive ideals had promised reconciliation and international cooperation. On the other hand, Kennedy had remained a fervent anticommunist, whose nuclear brinkmanship during the Cuban Missile Crisis threatened the lives of millions of people. The UDI and the Women's International Democratic Federation viewed Kennedy's policies in Germany as inconsistent and saw his relationship with Khrushchev as highly unstable and thus likely to lead to escalation over even minor matters. Behind the scenes, however, the federation's president, Eugénie Cotton, "was frequently heard [making] nauseating praises of Kennedy."[17] According to some UDI women, the violence that ended Kennedy's life was endemic to the United States and supported by the capitalist system.[18] Although certainly not heartened by Kennedy's passing, the UDI did not so much mourn the man as use the opportunity to comment on the society that had produced and destroyed him.

The last years of the papacy of John XXIII elicited a different sort of response from the women's associations. Political scientist Cecelia Dau Novelli has argued that despite the "good Pope's" highly regarded encyclicals, *Mater et Magistra* (1961) and *Pacem in terris* (1963), and his overall enthusiasm for women's emancipation, the CIF's relationship with Pius XII had been steadier.[19] Certainly, John XXIII's preference to stay out of national politics and to neutralize the Cold War discourse of his predecessor had immediate political implications. In fact, some Italian Catholics blamed the Christian Democrats' weaker showing in the 1963 elections not on the party's "opening to the left" but on the timing of the release of *Pacem in terris*. Although the CIF took issue with this interpretation of events and defended the encyclical as "the new document the Pope has given to us so that we can look at the Christian world around us and live accordingly," it was clear that the pope's openness had, in fact, led to the possibility of a grayer area in the once black-and-white battle between Marxism and Catholicism.[20] The opening of Vatican II in October 1962 also confused and concerned many CIF women, who had to be reassured that the ecumenical council intended to help them to renew rather than question their spiritual beliefs. In the months before the Second Vatican Council was convened as well as during its meetings, *Cronache e Opinioni* ran articles to explain what it was, how it worked, and what consequences it would have on Catholics worldwide.[21]

Leadership changes in the CIF are perhaps of more direct relevance to the different dynamics in the CIF-Vatican relationship in the early 1960s, however. In 1962, Alda Miceli became president of the CIF and set an example of Italian Catholic womanhood very different from that of her predecessor, Amalia di Valmarana. Valmarana was a married mother of two from an aristocratic family, whereas Miceli was from a bourgeois family and never married or had children. She was not, however, interested in becoming a nun, a choice that was more typical of devoutly religious single women in her day. Miceli's personal choices made her an important spokeswoman for women's emancipation. Although Valmarana continued to have a large role in the CIF as its vice president and most active officer in the international arena, Miceli's life experiences made her the ideal agent of a modernizing vision of women's associations and their connections to other lay Catholic and non-Catholic organizations. John XXIII's reluctance to intervene in national politics resulted also in Catholic Action's diminished role as a political force and allowed the CIF to have an even larger voice in its dealings with the Women's Union of Catholic Action, which Miceli used to challenge some of Catholic Action's more conservative positions on women.[22]

Ultimately, Miceli's own vision of Catholic women's roles in contemporary society corresponded with those of John XXIII much as Valmarana's had with those of Pius XII. Pius XII and Valmarana had viewed women primarily as wives and mothers whose employment outside the home was an unfortunate necessity for some. Even if Valmarana had modified her official position by 1960 and pointed to a need for a balance between work and family, her comments frequently revealed her fears about women abandoning the home in favor of material pursuits.[23] Miceli and John XXIII, in contrast, argued that women's work outside the home did not inevitably lead to morally and spiritually bankrupt families. John XXIII remarked on this point in a speech to the women of the CIF, saying "it is necessary to look at the reality of the facts that demonstrate how the advancement of woman toward new sources of activity and work is always vaster, and her aspiration for an activity that can make her economically independent and free from poverty is always more diffuse."[24] *Pacem in terris* underscored the importance of providing the conditions needed to allow women to work outside the home and still fulfill their roles as wives and mothers. Moreover, the encyclical recognized women's active roles in political life, stating that "far from being content with a purely passive role or allowing themselves to be regarded as a kind of instrument, they are demanding both in domestic and in public life the rights and duties which belong to them as human persons."[25] Miceli's leadership of the CIF was instrumental in the association's development of additional programs that would advance women's career opportunities and political lives while seeking more effective means of delivering the sorts of social services they needed to achieve a personal and professional balance.[26] Other CIF supporters, such as ecclesiastic consultant Monsignor Bentivoglio, noted the CIF's special role in transforming the pope's words into concrete actions on behalf of women and peace, "for the CIF the call from the Pope and the action of women for tranquility is particularly precious and urgent . . . true pacifists have never been passive!"[27]

The CIF did not retain an exclusive relationship with the "good pope," however. Under the leadership of devout progressive Catholic Ada Alessandrini, the UDI and the Women's International Democratic Federation both responded favorably to the new tone in the Vatican. On June 15, 1963, UDI women marched in a memorial peace demonstration in Rome with representatives of several labor, Catholic, and communist organizations holding banners with images of the pope, Spanish revolutionary Julián Grimau, Greek dissident Grigoris Lambrakis, African American civil rights activist Medgar Evers, and excerpts from *Pacem in terris*.[28] Contemporaneously and in preparation for the WIDF's 1963 Congress in Moscow, Alessandrini prepared a speech about the encyclical calling it "an affirmation of women's rights and peaceful coexistence."[29] In her analysis of the meaning of *Pacem in terris* for women and other oppressed peoples, Alessandrini emphasized the encyclical's sections on the rights of women and the working class and the struggles of people still living under colonial rule. According to Alessandrini, the pope had effectively and movingly reaffirmed that all people are guaranteed the same natural rights and that it was not moral to suggest that there was a "naturalness in inferiority" or to take an attitude of superiority because of sex, race, class, or political position. In recognition of John XXIII's importance to the women coming together for the federation's congress, Alessandrini remarked, "This is not the first time a delegation of Catholic and non-Catholic women has made presentations at the WIDF conference united in intentions and in friendly agreement, but it is the first time that we have come united together because of the words of and appreciation for a pope—words for some that come from a father who has power from above but for others those of a man at the head of a powerful international organization."[30] In other words, whether Catholic or not, Alessandrini wanted the women of the federation to regard the pope's message as conciliatory and use the opportunity his papacy presented to advance women's emancipation worldwide. After quoting some of the pope's own words in her opening address at the Moscow Congress, Eugénie Cotton, in fact, commented, "Isn't it remarkable that Pope John XXIII spoke the same language as the World Peace Movement?"[31] The brief tenures of John F. Kennedy and Pope John XXIII had far-reaching effects on the development of international politics and women's movements, especially because they allowed new opportunities for dialogue.

The Soviets, the Americans, and Cold War Escalations

John XXIII's proclamations for global peace in many ways echoed the ongoing efforts of the Italian and international women's organizations to work for disarmament and continue to pressure the United Nations and the European community to seek new accords to mitigate potentially dangerous tensions, particularly those looming between the United States and the Soviet Union. As historian Mark Kramer has remarked, despite the Sino-Soviet split and subsequent competition between the Soviets and the Chinese during the early 1960s, "the US-Soviet divide remained the primary basis of world politics."[32] In fact, between 1961 and 1962 the Cold War escalated because of the construction of the Berlin Wall and Cuba's entry into the Soviet sphere and veered toward possible armed conflict involving nuclear weapons. Faced with failed negotiations between socialist and capitalist countries and the continued mass exodus of East Germans through Berlin, on the morning of August 13, 1961, East Berliners awoke to find barbed wire barriers being erected along the border with West Berlin. While the Soviet-backed East German government claimed such measures were necessary to prevent the West's corrupting forces from seeping into the communist society, the Americans and their Western allies decried the move as an affront to human liberty. American forces put on a show of military strength near the German border, but they did not take direct action to intervene against the new physical boundary, and a face-off involving Soviet and U.S. tanks at Checkpoint Charlie ended without incident. Nearly two years later, on June 26, 1963, the West enthusiastically applauded Kennedy's famous "Ich bin ein Berliner" speech. Yet, the president's rhetoric ultimately underscored the permanence of a divided Germany and in some ways lessened tensions over the German question. The Cuban missile crisis of October 1962 also concluded without an eruption of fire between the two blocs, but came much closer to a dangerous confrontation, especially given existing tensions between the Kremlin and the White House that had been exacerbated by the Bay of Pigs invasion in April 1961. In an impassioned television address to the American public on October 22, 1962, Kennedy announced that the Soviets had installed midrange nuclear missiles in Cuba, and he demanded their immediate withdrawal. Over the following days, Khrushchev and Kennedy reached an agreement without directly involving Cuban leader Fidel Castro and avoided nuclear war, much to the relief of the women and men around the world who had been watching events with great trepidation.[33]

The possibility of war reanimated the women's associations' focus on peace but brought to light new questions about how to approach its achievement. As I emphasized in earlier chapters, the CIF had long before come to see the UDI's use of the term "peace" as trapped in the same communist wrappings used by political parties and other organizations of the left. However, since the pope had reclaimed peace for Catholics and placed it in a framework that was connected to real world political developments, the CIF, too, was able to focus on events that threatened to erupt in conflict. The CIF's leaders, however, did not back away from their anticommunist positions and continued to view the Soviet Union with great suspicion. In articles in *Cronache e Opinioni*, Liliana Piccinini kept CIF women informed about Soviet actions and helped direct responses from the Catholic women's associations. For example, in January 1960 she reported on Khrushchev's promise to reduce troops and arms but remarked incredulously, "On the other hand he announced that Russia is proposing to multiply its nuclear reserves and create new and more terrible arms capable of 'eliminating from the face of the earth' all powers with which it might find itself at war. We should thus ask ourselves if what Khrushchev has announced is really disarmament or actually rearmament."[34] In fact, not long afterward, at the Soviet Communist Party Congress in October 1961, Khrushchev announced plans to test the most powerful hydrogen bomb yet, the so-called Tsar-Bomb, with the intent of protecting the USSR and the rest of the communist bloc from "any sort of aggression." In response to the nuclear tests, the CIF's presidency drafted a motion condemning them: "The CIF, in the name of all Catholic women's associations, uniting the voice of the women of Italy, heartily deplores the continued atomic explosions that constitute a grave assault to the physical health and to the security and tranquility of all the populations of the world, expresses its most fervent vote that these be stopped immediately, and hopes for the implementation of more valid initiatives to guarantee everyone's peace."[35] The CIF presidency also used the opportunity presented by the PCI's defense of the Soviet experiments to point out that little had ultimately changed in the Soviet Union where "we are still dealing with a system that is as condemnable today as in Stalin's time."[36]

Soviet support for the Cuban Revolution, Khrushchev's subsequent decision to send nuclear missiles there, and the construction of the Berlin Wall served as further evidence that the Soviets could not be trusted. Furthermore, CIF political consultant Ivo Murgia suggested that the Italian communists were perhaps even more deplorable than the Soviet leaders: "Still today, Italian communism is by duty and by trade less conciliatory than the Soviet government appears to be; in the face of great crises (example: Cuba), it arrives first and zealously with respect to the Kremlin, which acknowledges only a few hours later whatever *l'Unità* has negated."[37] Peace and reconciliation with the Soviets appeared unlikely from the perspective of the Catholic women's associations so long as they saw few concessions being made to bring about meaningful changes.

For the UDI, the question of peace and Soviet foreign policy was much more complicated and had lasting repercussions on the Italian women's relationship with the Women's International Democratic Federation. The UDI and the federation had long connected the struggle for women's emancipation to the struggle for disarmament and had generally seen the United States as the aggressor against the Soviet Union. As recently as 1959 at a peace conference held in Brunate (Como), Italy, Baldina di Vittorio Berti of the UDI executive committee stated that "our common idea of women's emancipation is subordinated to the preservation of peace."[38] As the women's organizations had always argued, without lasting peace, women could not really achieve other objectives. However, as the UDI began to question several of the federation's positions on Soviet foreign policy, the two women's associations entered into heated discussions that would erupt in a direct confrontation at the international association's 1963 Moscow congress. In 1960 and 1962 in Austria and in 1961 in Germany, the UDI participated in several peace and disarmament conferences organized by European women outside the auspices of the Women's International Democratic Federation in the hopes of expanding the peace movement beyond its traditional socialist and communist base. Vittorio Berti pointed out in 1959 that "the defense of peace is not always presented to women as a unifying principle but as a position of political parties that fight amongst themselves."[39] In several articles in the federation's *Women of the Whole World*, the UDI reported on its peace initiatives in Italy that had crossed party lines and brought together tens of thousands of demonstrators in a single protest.[40] Although the UDI had long

attempted to unite women from various political parties, and had sometimes been successful at doing so, by the early 1960s national and international events forced the UDI to rethink whether it was primarily a
women's association that supported communist parties or one that used
Marxist principles to devise an agenda for women's rights.

The Soviet repression of Hungarian dissidents in 1956 had already provoked criticism by the UDI and generated internal tensions, and new Soviet actions now threatened to deepen differences of opinion among the
UDI's communist and noncommunist members and weaken the Italian
women's movement. Inconsistent political messages, the UDI argued, also
jeopardized worldwide women's movements, and, as a result, the association avoided making public perfunctory statements on the most recent
Cold War developments. In fact, the UDI remained strangely silent on the
Berlin Wall—there was no mention of it at all in the issues of Noi Donne
that followed its erection—and made a general nonpartisan appeal to the
Italian government and the United Nations for a peaceful resolution in
Cuba.[41] Nevertheless, the UDI did not suggest that the Women's International Democratic Federation back away from taking political positions,
advising only that it deliver a unified platform. As the UDI explained to
the federation's Bureau in 1962, "It is therefore correct and necessary that
our Federation express its positions on the fundamental questions of the
struggle against colonialism, Nazifascism, and international problems of
vital importance, for example, the nuclear truce and disarmament, but it
must do so positioning itself above partial judgments and sustaining ideals and principles capable of uniting women and, therefore, of extending
the women's movement for the defense of peace."[42] Therefore, when the
federation opted to defend the Soviets rather than to defend peace, the
UDI was compelled to point out its contradiction. On the Soviet Union's
nuclear experiments, for example, the UDI's Serenna Madonna commented that it was not helpful to discuss the validity of the Kremlin's argument that new weapons were needed to maintain equilibrium with the
United States, but instead that the federation had an obligation to "ask
that the experiments, regardless of their strategic value, be suspended
immediately because of their negative effect on the health of human beings and because they are anyway an expression of force and as such do
not come together to create an atmosphere of détente that women of all
the world cry out for."[43] As the UDI insisted, the federation's purpose had

been undermined by its inability to separate its guiding principles from the particularities of the merits of individual political questions and its subsequent refusal to criticize Soviet actions. The UDI's disillusionment with Soviet foreign policy now generated critiques similar to those long sustained by the CIF.

Internal and International Struggles

In the early 1960s, Amalia di Valmarana strengthened the CIF's interactions on the international stage, first as the association's president and then as its primary external affairs representative. Valmarana had long recognized the importance of the multiple dimensions of women's activities and political engagement: "The concerns and the presence of the CIF are not limited to the consideration and solution of problems on the national level but extend to the international level. In this historical moment in which every problem assumes global dimensions, it is necessary to enhance the presence of the CIF in international bodies and meetings not only to share the contribution of our research and experiences and enrich the contributions of others, but also because the extension of relationships is a means for social education and its expression."[44] Getting more Italian women involved in solving certain problems, however, was not an easy task. In a 1962 article in *Cronache e Opinioni*, several people who were interviewed speculated on why women were stepping away from all forms of politics at just the time when their contributions were especially needed. Taking a national perspective, CIF member Matilde Canestrelli explained that historically, Italian women had become politically engaged only in key national moments of great change, such as during the Risorgimento and the Resistance, but otherwise mainly stuck to charitable work. In the absence of a unifying righteous cause, she argued, women did not feel called upon to take part in politics. Maria Pia Flick, an educator and author of children's textbooks, viewed politics as a personal interest that women developed mainly if encouraged to do so. This had, at least, been her experience. "I started to read one, two, three newspapers daily," she said. "One on the right, one on the left, and one Catholic; I asked for explanations, reached conclusions, and became one of those students, who sometimes gives a little satisfaction to her teachers, and in the meantime, I began to understand for myself." Raniero la Valle, a journalist who covered Vatican II extensively, presented another explanation, namely, that women and men alike had come to feel disconnected from a political class that rarely took ordinary people's needs into consideration. The juxtaposition of comments from the interviews with photos of women in international politics—Sirimavo Bandaranaike, president of Ceylon; Maria Badaloni, Italian undersecretary of education; Clare Boothe Luce, former U.S. ambassador to Italy; and Golda Meier, Israeli minister of foreign affairs—highlighted the conundrum. On one hand, such women proved that women were cut out for high-level politics and could effect change in world affairs. On the other hand, these figures appeared to be truly exceptional, not ordinary, women. Valmarana attempted to overcome the political impasse of exceptionality by asserting that women could have a strong political voice and be sure that their values entered into national and international political decisions "with the awareness and the support of laws and provisions that these values can defend and with influential actions on public opinion that can help politicians in a way that is not always simple and easy, even if is it is valid and important for us."[45]

The CIF continued to work closely with the World Movement of Mothers and expanded its involvement in the Food and Agricultural Organization of the United Nations and the International Union of Women's Catholic Organizations, an organization founded in 1910 dedicated to ending worldwide poverty. The three organizations coordinated activities to help increase global agricultural production and improve distribution, and the CIF collected money to start a new food program in Uganda.[46] World hunger and poverty became special foci of the women's organizations, but the CIF and the World Movement of Mothers did not limit themselves to traditional Catholic charitable programs. In 1961, the World Movement of Mothers held a special congress in Abidjan, in the Ivory Coast, dedicated to the women and mothers of Africa. Although Valmarana could not attend the congress, she sent a letter to the organization's Paris offices in which she expressed her support for expanding a dialogue with the women of Africa and noted several important changes, especially decolonization and modernization, taking place there. African mothers, she hoped, would have new opportunities to expand their influence in a cultural environment in which they already enjoyed an influential role.[47] The two organizations also planned events for celebrations of International Christian Women's Day, and they dedicated related festivities in 1961 to mothers with jobs outside the home, thus again highlighting the critical relationship between women's employment and family life.[48]

The CIF and the World Movement of Mothers enjoyed a close working relationship and managed to coordinate major aspects of their planning to allow for continuity across multiple contexts. Threats to the World Movement of Mothers thus ultimately had less to do with political disagreements among the organizations' national members than with internal budgetary questions and personal conflicts. In 1963, the World Movement of Mothers' Mancaux went to Rome where she met with Valmarana and Lea Ermini, its official Italian representative, about the organization's troubling economic situation. A founding member and major benefactor of the World Movement of Mothers had asked to see the organization's annual budgets and requested interest payments owed her before she would consider giving more money. As Maria Penco reported to Valmarana following a meeting with the World Movement of Mothers' council in Holland, the situation required immediate action if the organization was to survive. Penco and the other representatives reached the conclusion that, "Letting the WMM die would be much too painful, especially now that the diffusion of the *Charte de la Mére* has generated consensus and lively popularity, and gives us the possibility to measure world opinion" and decided to do whatever was necessary to save it.[49] Valmarana immediately offered the CIF's full support and promised to come up with a large donation. In addition to her pledge to attempt to secure money from the Vatican and the Italian government, Valmarana asked the regional CIF offices for contributions and requested 100 lire donations from the National Organization for Maternity and Infancy, the Italian Mother's Movement, and the Women's Union of Catholic Action. The Catholic women's organizations rallied and, with the additional support of the French Ministries of Foreign Affairs and Health, Hygiene and Family, the World Movement of Mothers survived.[50] Air France contributed to the cause as well, donating two international round-trip airline tickets for travel to World Movement of Mothers events. To Valmarana's dismay, the Italian Ministry of Foreign Affairs would not allot funds to the organization, but the former CIF president said she would continue to try other government offices.[51]

The CIF's leadership in helping to save the World Movement of Mothers had mixed consequences. On one hand, the Italian association now enjoyed greater power within the international one. In 1966, members elected Maria Penco to vice president while Lea Ermini lost her post, thus making it clear that the World Movement of Mothers had recognized the CIF's contributions over those of some of its other Italian members.[52] On the other hand, the CIF was left with significant financial and administrative burdens. Penco and Valmarana worked tirelessly to persuade Catholic and women's associations to join the World Movement of Mothers because "it would be of great importance for the WMM from the point of view of morale as well as for its small financial assistance."[53] The CIF's leaders also preserved ties with the organization's other institutional members and put pressure on them to participate in its activities and utilize their votes effectively. When the longstanding social assistance organization for women and children, the Opera Nazionale Maternità e Infanzia, which, like the CIF, had the right to three votes in the World Movement of Mothers organizational matters, failed to use them, Penco complained that only the CIF seemed to be committed to international cooperation. Penco soon told the World Movement of Mothers presidential board members that the CIF would not be able to sustain the international organization indefinitely and even made clear that she could not attend more than two Bureau meetings a year since the CIF assumed the cost of her travel.[54] Nevertheless, Penco continued to see value in working with the World Movement of Mothers, and following its 1966 international conference concluded, "I retain that these international contacts are extremely useful and important, also to be able to have a wider view and better knowledge of the most current and urgent problems."[55] In the end, the crisis at the World Movement of Mothers improved the organization by making it more financially secure and transparent, and it extended the CIF's international influence by demonstrating that the Italian association could help resolve a major challenge.

The same dynamic did not emerge in the UDI's relationship with the Women's International Democratic Federation in the same period, however. In addition to the aforementioned political disagreements between the two organizations, the UDI began to call the organization's structure and voting procedures into question and, more important, expressed reservations about the federation's priorities and ability to coordinate an international democratic women's movement. First, the UDI wondered if the federation's claims of functioning democratically were matched by its actual operations. In terms of voting, delegations representing larger populations received more ballots at the triennial international congresses, even if actual participation was uneven. Under such an arrangement, countries such as the Soviet Union would always be allotted more votes and decision-making power, while very active but smaller delegations, like that of the Italians, would remain on par with member countries that contributed very little. Instead, the UDI proposed voting by delegation because under such a form "that which counts is the opinion of the member organizations and not that of single persons."[56] Second, the UDI accused the federation's leaders of operating the organization as a super-association rather than as a federation. According to a motion presented by the UDI, members of both the Secretary General and Executive Committee had been overstepping their boundaries and managing the organization as a unified body, whereas in reality it "doesn't have the task of directing a worldwide movement but that of studying real situations, coordinating experiences, promoting exchanges, and suggesting and organizing common initiatives."[57] Too much centralization had resulted in the secretariat's speaking on behalf of the international organization's members without asking them if it was all right to do so. In other words, in its current form, the UDI claimed the federation represented the interests of a few likeminded women at the expense of opening discussions and debates that could have produced more fruitful results and a "greater prospective for enlargement, greater prestige, and more secure operating efficiency."[58]

The UDI's main challenge to the Women's International Democratic Federation, however, regarded its priorities. According to the UDI, the federation had lost sight of its mission to put women's emancipation at the center of its activities while it had been drawn further into the political battles of the Cold War.[59] The UDI now applied its principle of seeking greater reconciliation among women of different Italian political parties to the federation. The UDI's leaders feared that additional politicization of the women's organizations would cause them to lose sight of their efforts to extend women's rights globally and result in useless distractions. As stated in an UDI letter to the organization's Bureau in May 1962, "We have to observe that while the themes of peace and disarmament constitute a permanent and dominant cause in the activities of the WIDF, those that are more specific and pertain to the condition of woman and her necessary emancipation, take on secondary and episodic importance. . . . It is indeed apparent that in the plans and initiatives taken on by the WIDF that the theme of women's emancipation has not had a strong enough place."[60] Despite its repeated calls to the international group's leaders to address the conflict between politics and women's emancipation, the UDI made little headway. Eugénie Cotton and the secretariat responded negatively to the UDI's request to raise their concerns to the full International Congress of Women to be held in Moscow. Cotton suggested instead that the UDI contact other national delegations to see if they shared the Italian women's perspective before taking the UDI's document to the Women's International Democratic Federation's Bureau that would meet just prior to the congress.

Tensions mounted and came to a head in Moscow. Before the conference, the UDI had objected to the WIDF's political partiality, its undemocratic procedures, and its failure to put women first. During the International Congress of Women, the UDI saw the federation continue these same practices. For example, the federation allowed a discussion of a border disagreement between the Indian and Chinese delegations to divert attention away from other matters. As a result, the UDI's Maria Maddalena Rossi, executive chairman of the congress, prevented the Chinese delegation from completing its speech."[61] Friction between the Chinese and Soviet delegations provoked further dissent among those at the congress and threatened to divide the women along the lines of the Sino-Soviet split. Furthermore, the Bureau altered the reports of the Cuban and Japanese delegations to conform to the federation's pro-Soviet, anti-American political line. The UDI objected. When Japanese delegate Fuki Kushida presented a rewritten report, the UDI delegation exited the conference hall as she was speaking. The UDI did not return to hear the Cuban delegation's report the next day. Although members of the press, as well as some of the delegates, interpreted the UDI's actions as an attack on the Japanese and Cuban women and their reports, the UDI attempted to assure them that this was not the case.[62] The UDI insisted, in fact, that its objections were not based on any specific political debates. As Serena Madonna explained at the UDI's press conference in Rome that followed the women's return from Moscow, "we are opposed to any politics that divides the world into two blocs, to any politics that signals a return to the spirit of the Cold War. Because of this we cannot accept that reports clearly written in this way be presented in the name of the entire Women's International Democratic Federation."[63] The conversation about the future of the relationship between the UDI and the federation did not end at the press conference. Some UDI women, mostly communists led by Nora Federici, who was not affiliated with the party, wanted to take an open, conciliatory approach to the federation, whereas others, especially socialists led by Maria Piccone Stella (herself not a socialist) called for a direct confrontation with the federation's leaders and an immediate decision on the UDI's membership.[64] In the meantime, Carmen Zanti left the federation's offices in Berlin and returned to Italy upon being elected to the Italian parliament. Following a period of debate, the UDI voted at its 1964 national congress to move from being a full member to an associate member of the Women's International Democratic Federation, delivering a serious blow to the historic international women's organization.[65]

Work, Family, and the European Economic Community

Despite the difficulties that surfaced in the international women's associations, the UDI and the CIF continued to work on women's issues that had long characterized the central missions of their associations. In 1960, both associations dedicated their national congresses to women, work, and the family and stuck with these themes throughout the 1960s.[66] Related national legislation on pensions for housewives and women's access to all careers continued to be a source of debate among the women's associations and the political parties through 1963, but the UDI and the CIF expanded their discussions beyond the legal context and explored the psychological dimensions of women's work in much more depth. Their studies also added an international dimension as women's leaders took a closer look at women's work and family lives throughout Europe and the United States. The lives of American families held particular interest for Italian women, in part because of their fascination with the Kennedy family, and a number of experts made comparisons between the organization of Latin and Anglo-American households. Clelia d'Inzillo, a deputy for the Christian Democrats, for example, observed that American families lived democratically, which allowed democracy to flourish throughout American society. However, she also noted that since Americans were so independent, they spent little time together: children often vacationed with friends rather than family; mothers busied themselves with work and social activities; and fathers just wanted to be left alone at the end of the work day to relax.[67] Psychologist Mara Selvini Palazzolo even argued that the "crisis of the American family" owed more to the emotional absence of the father than to the physical absence of employed mothers, who suffered from a lack of intimacy in their family lives. "The Italian woman," Palazzolo claimed, "notwithstanding her many difficulties, appears to fall in the middle, psychologically more sane than in other countries."[68] The UDI largely concurred with the CIF's assessments of American families, but continued to regard communist models of family organization as healthier for women and their families as they looked across western and eastern Europe for comparisons.[69]

The question of European women's identities and roles as workers and mothers particularly interested the Italian women's associations. Since the signing of the Treaty of Rome in 1957, they had become increasingly involved in aspects of European economic affairs and policy making that were likely to affect women. The CIF's emphasis on women as mothers and consumers and the UDI's focus on labor continued to distinguish the different vantage points of the associations as they discussed supranational cooperation and lobbied for women's rights. Overall, the women of the CIF continued to have a favorable viewpoint of the European Economic Community. They did not, however, simply wait passively as men in Brussels made decisions that affected women's economic lives. Instead, in their historical role as educators, CIF women gathered and distributed information to the associations' members and affiliates and sought institutional membership of related representative bodies. At several meetings of women from countries in the European Economic Community, CIF delegates discussed women's rights as consumers and their roles in forging cooperative relationships among member states. In 1960, in Luxembourg, for example, CIF women worked with women from numerous countries to draw up a list of demands to include clearer product labeling; accurate and inoffensive advertising; and special education for women and young people about consumer products. They also requested special representation on consumer rights commissions.[70] At another meeting in Paris in 1961, representatives discussed women's roles in bringing down trade barriers and vowed to continue their work. "The dialogue that opened in Paris among one hundred European women has not concluded.

Each woman has returned to her daily activities with the intention to delve into the questions raised, for herself and for other women, in view of taking constructive, concrete actions."[71] To assist women consumers in Italy, Valmarana proposed taking advantage of new media and producing radio and television home economics programs to complement home economics courses being taught in schools and in the CIF's branch offices.[72] As long as women were informed and represented, the CIF was pleased to see European economic cooperation extended.

The UDI had generally been more critical of the European Economic Community, particularly because of its capitalist guiding principles. However, by the late 1950s and early 1960s, the UDI did less to oppose the European Economic Community than to attempt to focus it on issues related to women and work. As it had been doing on the national level, the UDI now took the lead among Italian women's associations in devising European policies to guarantee women access to professional training, protection from unjust firing practices, and equal pay for equal work. In December 1961, the member states of the European Economic Community passed a resolution on equal pay to be implemented by the end of December 1964. An Italian committee formed in 1957 and made up of representatives from the UDI and several other women's organizations with international ties, such as the Alleanza Femminile Italiana (International Alliance of Women), the Consiglio Nazionale delle Donne Italiane (International Council of Women), and the Unione Cristiana delle Giovani d'Italia (YWCA), "deemed it urgent and necessary to call an international Study Commission to allow for an exchange of information and experience, and consequently, to contribute to an acceleration of the fulfillment of equal pay policies in the European Economic Community." The committee called a meeting in Milan in October 1963.[73] Experts and representatives from trade unions, universities, and government offices offered an overview of the European economy and key provisions of the Treaty of Rome. The UDI's Nora Federici, a researcher at the University of Palermo, prepared a comprehensive report on women and work in the European Economic Community to present at the committee's meeting. She pointed out that the growth of the European economy was outpacing women's presence within it and, with the other delegates, recommended a course of action to implement gender equality in the member states. The Italians urged women in all the member states to establish committees like theirs and asked that the European Economic Community create an internal office dedicated solely to women and work. The committee stated that it "particularly hopes that it can open and put in the hands of the women's associations a permanent liaison through exchanges of information and periodic formal and informal meetings, so that on the national and international level each initiative directed toward ensuring that the role of women in the economy and in social life better responds to their requirements, and at the same time, to the needs of an evolving world, receives harmonic and effective support."[74] The activities of the women's associations would continue to grow at the European level. Their extensive involvement in multiple forms of activism drew attention to their intention to collaborate with women across the continent and seek forums that transcended traditional divides.

The CIF, too, continued to participate in conferences and study groups connected to the expansion of the European Economic Community throughout the 1960s. In June 1966, two representatives from the home office in Rome attended a convention in Brussels, organized by the Union Féminine Civique et Sociale in cooperation with the European Economic Community, at which participants discussed Europe's economic relations with the countries of Latin America and Africa and examined the general objectives of the European community. Since most of the participants were from women's associations, they also "wanted to take a look at some aspects of women's work—professional training, working mothers, equal salaries—in the countries of the Community, on the basis of decisions and recommendations of the Council of Europe and the Commissions of the EEC."[75] The CIF's delegates considered the meeting a success, not only because of the themes they examined in Brussels but also because it gave the Italian women an opportunity to deepen their relationship with the women of the Union Féminine Civique et Sociale, which they described as "without a doubt among the bodies known at the international level that has the most affinity with the goals of the CIF."[76] In 1967, the CIF sent representatives to another European Economic Community conference in Brussels, this time to celebrate the tenth anniversary of the signing of the Treaty of Rome. As Piccinini reported, "we are in Brussels for an 'informative' visit: a group of twenty-five women involved in one way or another in political and social life, invited by the European Community to be utilized, they told us, as 'antenna towers,' or in other words, as supporters and disseminators of the goals of the Community."[77]

The CIF's support of the European Economic Community remained strong, even on its controversial energy policy, which included the development of nuclear energy through Euratom. Shortly after the Brussels conference, the CIF sent representatives to Luxembourg to learn more about the history and future of Euratom in sessions led by one of its spokespersons, Fulvio Paolini. Although concerned about the safety of nuclear energy, Piccinini concluded her summary of the conference by expressing her agreement with the aims of Euratom, "that represents one of the most sensitive areas for the development of countries from which it is possible to establish in a concrete way the common will to construct Europe."[78] While the CIF remained one of the European Economic Community's most fervent backers, the UDI retained less direct contact with the commission. Although individual UDI members favored development of nuclear energy, overall the association remained opposed to it and continued to send representatives to peace conferences, such as one in Helsinki in July 1965, where they linked the potential harm of nuclear weapons to nuclear energy technology.[79]

Conclusion

The political climate of the early 1960s was fraught with moments of great tension, such as in Cuba and Berlin, but also with moments of hope and optimism, as was embodied in the figures of John F. Kennedy and Pope John XXIII. Amid great political, economic, and religious change, the women of the UDI and the CIF stayed current in world affairs and engaged in the most important questions of the day. Both women's associations made sure Italian women were represented in Europe and followed new developments in the European Economic Community with great interest. The themes of peace and women's rights gained new momentum thanks to the support of the Vatican and the desire of the women's associations to overcome some of the constraints of traditional politics. The UDI and the CIF, however, continued to work separately and saw more disruptions than opportunities result from the Christian Democratic Party's "opening to left." The UDI especially found itself struggling to try to hold together women whose political parties found themselves at odds, and it used the occasion to reinforce its principle of putting women emancipation at the center of its reason for being. Transcending the Cold War in Italy, however, had repercussions for the UDI's relationship with the Women's International Democratic Federation. To place women's rights at the center of an international women's movement unified in its fight against fascism and its objective of obtaining world-wide peace and democracy, the UDI was compelled to challenge the federation's leadership on its politics. As a result, the UDI called into question the basic operating structure and priorities of the federation and ended up loosening its ties to an organization that had been at the center of its international activities for nearly two decades. The CIF, in contrast, concluded its period of intense efforts to save the World Movement of Mothers by assuming a bigger role in that organization and carrying larger responsibilities to keep it financed. Consequently, the CIF acquired greater status among Italian Catholic organizations and succeeded in keeping channels open from the regional to the international level.

In 1962, *Cronache e Opinioni* ran several articles about changing values in contemporary society. One asked whether female purity was still in fashion, and another questioned what femininity meant. Still another pondered the influence of the spread of new forms of mass communication.[80] In addition to the key political and economic questions of the day, Italian women showed they were keenly aware of generational transformations taking place before them. The women of the Resistance found themselves having to respond to questions being posed by two new generations of young women—women born before the Resistance but too young to experience it themselves and women born after the war who were now coming of age in the 1960s. Sociologist Simonetta Piccone Stella has argued that "the exceptional women of the Resistance—who had done it all: work, politics, children, partnerships with a political leader, clandestinity, war, hunger, partisan adventures" now found themselves being challenged both by traditional models of femininity that had been sustained by Italy's economic prosperity and by young women who wanted to push their demands further.[81] The older generation now had to confront an even larger range of issues. Was female chastity a virtue or part of an old bourgeois culture whose values no longer served a purpose? What did it mean that young people knew the tune to Verdi's *I Lombardi* not from the orchestra hall but from a popular television show? Would feminism put an end to femininity? Although the older members of the UDI and the CIF were not necessarily unified in answering these questions, they did begin to open up discussion and debate about them. They began studying the effect of their successes in making women equal to men before the law and would again place the Italian woman in a broader framework to understand where she stood in relation to the Soviet and the American woman as well as to her European counterparts. The early 1960s thus offered only a glimpse of changes under way that would soon shake the world. A "crisis" in values would soon join a series of other crises for now just mentioned in passing, as in Piccinini's September 1963 article titled "The Crisis in Vietnam."[82]

6   Confronting the Youth Generation, 1964–1968

The end-of-the-year issues of the CIF's monthly magazine, *Cronache e Opinioni*, and the UDI's weekly, *Noi Donne*, poignantly encapsulate the turmoil and violence that characterized 1968: the assassinations of Martin Luther King, Jr., and Robert Kennedy; the repression of dissidents in Prague; student protests throughout Europe and the United States; and the war in Vietnam. Each incident recounted in the magazines reminded readers of the fragility of peace and of the women's associations' key messages. In its feature article, the CIF noted the words of Paul VI, who was elected pope in 1963 following John XXIII's death: "This very sad case of Vietnam is enough to show how difficult peace is even when it can be achieved. Peace is difficult when disputes become ideological. In these situations, the confusion of judgments and opinions aggravates the situation. The world watches, gets excited, comments and condemns, looking to understand where justice lies."[1] *Noi Donne's* selection of its "women of the year" left little ambiguity as to where peace and justice were situated for the UDI. South Vietnamese Viet Cong resistance leader Nguyen Thi Binh and anti–Vietnam War protestor and actress Vanessa Redgrave appeared alongside Ethel Kennedy, Robert Kennedy's widow, and Oriana Fallaci, a pioneering Italian journalist wounded while covering the revolutions in Latin America. *Noi Donne's* inclusion of a generalized militant university student, perhaps best highlights the generational crisis so apparent in Italy and beyond from the mid- to late 1960s. The UDI's journalists described her as "young, beautiful—of a beauty that confers political passion and ideals—decisive, hard to frighten, impossible to stop . . . She doesn't have a name, or better, she has the name of thousands of girls, students or workers, who in the course of the last year have been magnificent protagonists of one of the many struggles that shook the world, from the factories to the universities, in offices, and in the squares."[2] New young women protagonists came to epitomize the crises of their day, crises defined as much by their promise for change as by their disruptive forces.

This chapter grapples with the profound Italian and global transformations that occurred between 1964 and 1968 and the ways in which the UDI and the CIF participated in them. On one hand, the women's associations remained true to their core values and reacted in ways that were consistent with their ideas and actions during the Cold War era. Some of the national battles waged between the women of the UDI and the CIF over women's rights and responsibilities in the family continued to be fought along the same lines as many of their confrontations of the past, namely in regard to their perceptions of women as primarily productive or reproductive. On the other hand, the new and often dramatic challenges of the 1960s revealed some of the associations' weaknesses in confronting new generations of women whose preoccupations differed from their own. Young women now had options that had not been open to their mothers, but they did not always acknowledge the women who made these options possible or recognize continuity in the struggle for women's rights. Moreover, updated models of traditional femininity constructed during the late 1950s and early 1960s and embraced especially by the generation of women that came of age during those years created further disruptions for the politically active women of the Resistance generation. The leaders of the women's associations were not always certain the women born during and after World War II really understood the struggles they had undertaken and sometimes questioned the priorities of the newer generations, even as they tried to relate their experiences in the Resistance to events of the day. As a result, multiple meanings of the term "crisis," defined either as a fracture with the past or promise for the future, came to inform the key conflicts of the mid- to late 1960s.

International political events captured the attention of the women's associations on numerous levels, further revealing generational crises. Despite the loosening of its bonds with the Women's International Democratic Federation, the UDI continued to work with the international organization in select areas. Perhaps with some irony, however, the UDI's commitment to international peace and disarmament efforts again was compromised when the association became a fervent supporter of the Viet Cong and offered harsh criticisms of American policies in Vietnam.

The UDI did not stop by taking sides in this conflict, however, and continued to deliver stinging messages about American society and culture while downplaying Soviet aggressions committed under Premier Leonid Brezhnev. While the UDI forged a new international path outside the Women's International Democratic Federation's framework, the CIF's work in the World Movement of Mothers accelerated. The CIF's commitment to the World Movement of Mothers intensified after the CIF helped to save it and the international organization in return gave the Italian women more influence in its policy making. For example, debates over the need for more attention to spirituality in the *Mother's Charter* ultimately ended to the CIF's satisfaction. Nonetheless, many traditional modes of operating faced new tests, such as when the future of missionary work in a decolonizing world challenged some of the Catholic women's fundamental ideas about service. More than ever, international events appeared to connect women around the world and demand they take action; the framework and the results, however, were perhaps more ambiguous than in the first decades of the Cold War.

Peace Movements and Conflicts in the Third World

In the 1960s, many proponents of Italian and international Catholicism and Marxism made critical modifications to their deeply rooted traditions and ideologies that would have important implications for Italian and international women's peace movements and mark pivotal generational transformations. A renewed commitment to social justice from leaders of both the new left and radical Catholics inspired greater solidarity and enthusiasm for collective action. Although motivated by disparate influences, neo-Marxists and Catholics shared a desire to overcome the global imbalances caused by liberal capitalism and ensure worldwide peace. When conflicts in the third world revealed some of the worst excesses of the Cold War and threatened to upset peace in the West, the women's organizations reacted forcefully, at times in concert with reformers and at times at odds with or even ahead of them. The lives of women in Latin America, Africa, and Southeast Asia particularly interested the leaders of the women's organizations, and they launched their own reforms and projects to better address some of the hardships created by decolonization, ethnic conflicts, and war.

The transformative measures initiated by Pope John XXIII continued and intensified under his successor, Pope Paul VI (1963–78). In addition to bringing the ecumenical meetings of Vatican II to a conclusion in 1965, Paul VI focused intently on "opening a dialogue with the world," an objective that took him to six continents and earned him the nickname of "the pilgrim pope." Paul VI's travels, which began even before he assumed the papacy, exposed him firsthand to the poverty and suffering of people worldwide and led him to seek new avenues for Catholic social justice, especially in the third world.[3] In his historic speech to the United Nations on October 4, 1965, the day of the feast of St. Francis of Assisi, Paul VI outlined his plan to alleviate hunger in the world by calling on industrialized nations to disarm and put their defense budgets toward aid for developing nations, an idea later called the "peace dividend."[4] Paul VI's 1967 encyclical "Populorum Progressio: On the Development of Peoples" explored his idea in greater detail. The encyclical acknowledged some of the harm caused by colonialism and unbridled liberalism and called for a new approach to helping developing nations through prayer, social justice, and the preservation of peace. In recognition of the clashes between old and new that characterized development in many newly liberated nations, the pope cautioned the peoples of the third world not to move too quickly in their desire to industrialize. "The conflict between generations," he wrote, "leads to a tragic dilemma: either to preserve traditional beliefs and structures and reject social progress; or to embrace foreign technology and foreign culture, and reject ancestral traditions with their wealth of humanism. The sad fact is that we often see the older moral, spiritual and religious values give way without finding any place in the new scheme of things."[5] At the same time, Paul VI praised young people in the industrialized world working in private and public organizations that aided developing countries and encouraged more youths to offer their service to their fellow human beings.

Even before the Vatican released "Populorum Progressio," the women of the CIF and the World Movement of Mothers had begun to reevaluate their approaches to helping the women and men of former Western colonies. Missionary work, they retained, was not to be undertaken with the eyes of the colonizer but with an emphasis on shedding ignorance and providing the tools and skills people needed to create their own economic security.[6] Their collaborations with UNESCO and the UN's Food

and Agricultural Organization had encouraged the women's organizations to seek less paternalistic approaches to the problems of hunger and
poverty in Africa and Latin America, and the work initiated during the
World Movement of Mothers' 1961 Abidjan conference continued to inform the organization's approach to cooperation with African women. At
the organization's 1966 international congress in Paris, World Movement
of Mothers President Irène Mancaux underscored the important contributions African women's associations had made both to the enrichment
of the international association and to the education of African women
against illiteracy and in favor of improved health and hygiene, childcare,
home economics, job training, and formal entry into civil and economic
life.[7] Mancaux's presentation mirrored the new directions emerging in the
Vatican with her pronouncement that the congress participants "recognize the traditional values of African societies; denounce the distortions,
excesses and insufficiencies that undermine the dignity of women; rejoice
in the progress and changes brought by the changing social, economic
and political development of nations, but note that these rapid changes
sometimes neglect and maim certain human values that characterize the
Africans, especially the values of women."[8] In many ways, the World Movement of Mothers embodied the better practices called for by Paul VI.

The pope's encyclical "Christi Matri" and the speech he delivered to
100,000 people in St. Peter's Square on October 4, 1966 for the Day of the
Universal Dissemination of Peace in the World also inspired the Catholic
women's organizations to take a broader view of international political
developments and a uniform stance on conflicts in the third world, especially in Vietnam. In the words of the pope, "For the danger of a more
serious and extensive calamity hangs over the human family and has increased, especially in parts of eastern Asia where a bloody and hard-
fought war is raging. So We feel most urgently that We must once again
do what We can to safeguard peace. We are also disturbed by what We
know to be going on in other areas, such as the growing nuclear arma-
ments race, the senseless nationalism, the racism, the obsession for revolution, the separations imposed upon citizens, the nefarious plots, the
slaughter of innocent people. All of these can furnish material for the
greatest calamity."[9] The women of the CIF welcomed Paul VI's message
that peace was the right of all women and men and that everyone had a
duty to seek and protect it. Using language similar to that recently adopted

by the UDI, which called on women to move beyond the rigid dichoto-mies of the Cold War, the CIF presidency wrote in *Cronache e Opinioni*, "Beyond strictly necessary political relations and in harmony among the great powers, we all must work with good will and faithfulness to reduce and eliminate the psychological poisoning that stiffens human relations between men and inevitably sends them to the zone of incomprehension and hate."[10] Being serious about creating peace, the CIF explained, meant accepting that the road that led to it was filled with obstacles and bitter-ness but that "it is a task no one should remove herself from; a task the CIF makes its own."[11]

The Vietnam War presented a major challenge to the efforts of Catho-lics and others to achieve peace in the world and it disillusioned many Italians and other Europeans who had believed in the American Dream of the 1950s. In the 1960s, that dream "was shattered by the newsreels of the napalming of Vietnamese villages . . . and by the example of peasant resistance to the American war machine."[12] U.S. involvement in Vietnam had begun as early as 1950, when American military advisors entered the region to support France's continued claims to its colonial possession and to carry out the American policy of containment by preventing the spread of communism to South Vietnam. Escalation in the Cold War conflict began in the early 1960s with the arrival of American troops. The deploy-ment of combat units in 1965 led to a change in military strategy and initi-ated a new kind of response to the guerrilla warfare tactics used by the Viet Cong in South Vietnam. The Vietnam War incited negative public opinion worldwide, especially because the brutality associated with non-conventional fighting was blamed on the Americans, who had the strength of a powerful military industrial complex behind them, whereas the Viet Cong were lightly armed and informally trained by comparison. Moreover, the response of the European governments to the intensifica-tion of American involvement in Indochina was lukewarm at best. Even the British regarded the Vietnamese conflict as a nationalist struggle rather than an ideological battle over communism.[13] In Italy, Vietnam resulted in heated internal debates among and inside the political parties. In the context of the center-left coalition, the government was torn be-tween its loyalty and commitment to an Atlantic Policy and cooperation with the United States. Minister of Foreign Affairs Amintore Fanfani and the Italian ambassador to the United States both resigned in protest of the government's handling of diplomacy with the Americans.[14] Moreover, U.S. actions in Vietnam radicalized Italian youths who saw Vietnam as another example of "Italy's subservience to the United States."[15]

Vietnam also brought the UDI back to the center of the international peace movement. Following its decision to become an associate member of the Women's International Democratic Federation, the Italian association was forced to rethink its international alliances and redirect its peace activities. The UDI wanted to continue to have a role in the federation in those cases in which the two organizations shared common objectives, and it expressed an interest to returning to its full status if and when the federation's leaders put women's emancipation at the center of their planning and shed their Cold War discourse. Matilde Di Pietrantonio, a former Resistance partisan and member of the city government in Turin, commented that the UDI's loosening of its ties to the Women's International Democratic Federation "is not the beginning of an 'unhooking operation' but a contribution to the search for an international politics."[16] The conflict in Vietnam, however, once again immersed the UDI in the Cold War and became the main focus of its international activities in the mid- to late 1960s. It was also a subject on which the UDI and the Women's International Democratic Federation shared a political point of view. In her obituary of Eugénie Cotton (1881–1967), the UDI's Carmen Zanti wrote that Cotton's "last act, just hours before dying," was "participating in Paris in a large demonstration for peace in Vietnam."[17]

Beginning in 1965, the UDI began assiduously reporting on the crisis in Vietnam, with articles in appearing in every few issues of *Noi Donne* during the entirety of the conflict. In the beginning, the articles served to educate and inform Italian readers about the history of Vietnam, its colonial struggles, and the interests of the West in the region.[18] UDI journalists then began to cover the American side of the war, first highlighting the ignorance of the American public about the war and the brutality of U.S. Marines against the Vietnamese people and, later, focusing on the development of the antiwar movement in American university towns.[19] Like the CIF, the UDI made frequent reference to the words and actions of Pope Paul VI, noting his expressions of anguish and hope for those who were suffering. Unlike the women of the CIF, however, who preferred to see the pope as a purely religious figure, the women of the UDI and *Noi Donne*'s reporters commented on the pope's political actions. For example, in an article about the pope's visit to the United Nations, Ugo D'Ascia, a longtime Vatican correspondent, reported that the Holy See had turned down some expressions of affinity with the U.S. government, rejecting, for example, the use of an official government plane for internal travels in the United States during the pope's visit, and speculated that the U.S.–Vatican relationship had likely been made more difficult by the fact that Paul VI had not expressed any favor for the American side in the war in Vietnam.[20]

The UDI moved far beyond just covering the events in Indochina by taking an activist role in the conflict that traversed the association's history and connected its oldest and youngest members. The women of the UDI saw their own struggles during the Resistance reflected in the conflict in Vietnam, and in the antiwar movement they perceived an opportunity to pass their knowledge of organizing to young women activists. In 1965, the UDI dedicated its celebration of International Women's Day to the women of Vietnam and invoked the women's shared experiences of resistance to a foreign aggressor: "We are living your tragedy and we put out an appeal for you to have what is the right of every human: the right to decide your own future for yourselves, to chose your own path in peace, and to build the kind of world you deem best."[21] The UDI's former Resistance fighters thus constructed a bond between the Italian and Vietnamese women that intensified their commitment to peace in Vietnam and led them to take several concrete actions to achieve it. The December 11, 1965 issue of Noi Donne, for example, included a postcard that readers could detach and mail to the United Nations with the following plea: "To U-Thant, Secretary General of the United Nations, In the moment in which we are celebrating the Christmas and New Year's holidays deeply moved and disturbed by the continuing hostilities in Vietnam, I ask that the United Nations intervene to stop the bombings in Vietnam and to initiate negotiations in accordance with the Geneva Accords."[22] In July 1966, the UDI sent a delegation to Geneva to participate in disarmament talks with women from eighteen other countries where they communicated "the disdain of Italian women for the recent bombing in the suburbs of Hanoi and Haiphong and called for the immediate cessation of bombing, the end of hostilities and the beginning of negotiations, in accordance with the Geneva Accords, with the participation of all parties and forces involved."[23] In 1967, UDI members led peace demonstrations in several Italian cities, and Gisella Floreanini, of the Milan chapter, met with the undersecretary of foreign affairs, Mario Zagari, to deliver a petition signed by ten thousand people calling for an end to the war in Vietnam.

Late in the year, the UDI's Rome chapter held a reunion where women could tell of their antiwar efforts, which emphasized the connections between Resistance women, the women of Vietnam, and the generation coming of age in an era of new conflicts. During the meeting, Carla Capponi, who had been awarded the Gold Medal of Honor for her contributions to the Resistance gave a collection of images titled "Homage to the Resistance" to a young Vietnamese guest named Vo Van Ai with the following message: "We must remember that the UDI rose from the Women's Defense Groups, that is, the nuclei of women who fought Nazi-fascist oppression for the freedom of our country. It is we, women of the UDI, who want to fully commit ourselves to helping your country achieve peace as soon as possible."[24] The UDI's youngest members also recounted their experiences in the peace marches and talked about their desire to continue to tell their peers about what was happening in Vietnam. As an eighteen-year-old student named Renata explained, "Young people today are covered by the veil of wellbeing and don't know what's underneath it. We have to wake them up."[25] During the summer of 1968, the UDI made a tremendous impact by hosting a delegation of three South Vietnamese resistance fighters, Ha Giang, Vo Thi The, and Mai Thi Tu. Accompanied by noted UDI leaders such as Marisa Rodano and Tommasina Materozzi, the three women toured the country visiting regional UDI chapters and meeting women workers. The UDI also arranged special sessions with the leaders of several political parties and trade unions, including the Christian Democratic Party; the Italian Socialist and Communist Parties; and the Catholic trade union, the ACLI. The firsthand accounts of the women's struggles against their American aggressors resonated with the Italian people and earned the UDI credibility for its autonomous actions.[26] Throughout 1968, the UDI continued to cover the war and to emphasize the roles of women in it. Nguyen Thi Binh, a member of the Central Committee for the National Front for the Liberation of the South, became the favorite heroine of many UDI members, who identified with her as a little woman in a small country fighting a well-oiled military machine.[27]

Violence and Revolution in Europe and the United States

In addition to the war in Vietnam, several major events in Europe and the United States, especially the Prague Spring and the assassinations of Martin Luther King, Jr., and Robert Kennedy galvanized the Italian women's associations. However, the UDI and the CIF reacted very differently to news coming from the communist bloc and the United States. The Catholic women remained sharp critics of the Soviets and continued to express their overall support of the Americans, especially during times of crisis. The women of the UDI, in contrast, expressed their solidarity with the women of eastern Europe and focused on the worst excesses of American life. Despite these general positions, however, UDI and CIF women's participation in Cold War dichotomies took more subtle forms in the mid- to late 1960s. Rather than uniformly applying ideology to every situation, the women became more astute political and cultural critics who approached matters on a case-by-case basis. They also delivered didactic messages to their members even when they did not call on them to take any direct social action. Their publications' cultural propaganda influenced current and potential members and presented carefully thought out political, economic, and social ideas that often upheld political divisions. As a result, the associations' silences and outcries reveal much about their own self-construction and the sort of ideal Italian woman they had helped to shape. For both the UDI and the CIF, political engagement meant at least being informed about global developments, if not involved in them. The associations thus continued to be active at the European and international levels but also placed great importance on the correct transmission of ideas to their members in Italy.

In 1964, the Soviet leadership ousted Nikita Khrushchev and replaced him with Leonid Brezhnev, who had gained popularity among the political elite, partly because of his dislike for the "brinkmanship and the crisis-mongering that had characterized Khrushchev's foreign policy since 1956."[28] When Brezhnev became Soviet premier, he directed the Soviet Union on a course toward détente but quickly deviated from it because of events unfolding in Czechoslovakia, where his own protégé, Alexander Dubček, was leading a series of reforms through the Action Program. At first endorsed by the Soviets, the Action Program called for some democratic political measures, such as the freedoms of assembly and expression, but retained the hegemony of the Communist Party. During the spring of 1969, reform spiraled into revolution, in part because of writer Ludvik Vaculík's manifesto "Two Thousand Words." Brezhnev was forced to act to preserve the Soviet Union's place in central Europe. Historian Vladislav Zubok has likened the Soviet leader's need to prevent "falling dominoes" in Central Europe to U.S. President Johnson's argument that the same strategy was required in Southeast Asia.[29] By August, the so-called Prague Spring came to end when Brezhnev called the Warsaw Treaty into action and ordered more than five thousand tanks to enter Czechoslovakia and crush the rebellion. Several hundred people were killed, and images and stories of the Soviet-led actions circulated the globe and generated a public outcry in the Western world, although no military action ensued. Moreover, the fact that Dubček remained in power until April 1969 signaled to some Westerners that the Soviet Union was not fully in control of the situation.

In Italy, events in Czechoslovakia provoked a number of reactions.[30] The Christian Democrats had welcomed Dubček's promises of reform with great hope and viewed the Action Program as an important step in loosening the hold of the Soviets in eastern Europe. In a report in *Cronache e Opinioni* on the events of August, *Osservatore romano* journalist Sergio Trasatti communicated his thoughts that "whomever freely looks at the facts of Prague concludes that communism is in crisis like never before. It is in political crisis because it is not able to maintain its form of neocolonialism of satellite countries without resorting to arms; it is in economic crisis more now than yesterday precisely because financial questions give birth to so-called counterrevolutionary unrest to then develop a polemic on more or less liberal grounds."[31] Trasatti's words reinforced the sentiments of the CIF and underscored the fact that not all Soviet bloc countries were content to live under the watchful eyes of the Kremlin. The Italian Communist Party responded to the crisis with some trepidation, however. In his study of communist daily *l'Unità* and weekly *Rinascita*, political scientist Alessandro Frigerio has argued that the party remained vague and submissive on Soviet actions in Czechoslovakia. The absence of serious coverage on the events in Prague in the communist publications, in Frigerio's estimation, is evidence that the party was more "capable of smoky verbal thinness and redundant theoretical analyses" than critical reflection on the Czechoslovak challenge to Soviet hegemony in eastern Europe.[32] Historian Maud Bracke has pointed out, moreover, that Italian Communist Party Secretary Luigi Longo was open to reform but ultimately resisted the idea of pluralism in Czechoslovakia, preferring to see the Czech Communists retain their privileged position.[33] In any case, it was relatively easy for the Italian left to make unfavorable comparisons between U.S. and Soviet military interventions. When examined in a global framework, "the massive bloodletting incurred by the war in Vietnam placed the Warsaw Pact's almost bloodless occupation of Czechoslovakia in a relatively benign light."[34] Many of the Italian Communist Party's leaders, in fact, preferred to remain focused on U.S. rather than Soviet actions, even men such as Longo and Giancarlo Pajetta who condemned the use of military force in Czechoslovakia. As these communists saw it, there was no immediate threat to socialism in the country. Moreover, Longo and Pajetta feared the West would take advantage of the inopportune moment to advance its anti-Soviet propaganda machine.[35]

The UDI reacted to the Prague Spring and the repression of reforms proposed by Ludvik Vaculík and Alexander Dubček by focusing primarily on the experiences of women in Czechoslovakia. An article in *Noi Donne* recounted the story of Bozena Machacova, the minister of light industry, who was the official head of the Czechoslovak government for seven days following the arrests of Dubček and other reformers. Many women also played important roles during the crisis simply by remaining focused and resolute. "To women, passive resistance meant to continue to go regularly to work, not allow themselves to be taken by panic because of rumors (there was no hoarding of food, for example), to be in the front lines of peaceful demonstrations and in the actions aimed at convincing the occupying forces of the rightness of the cause of the Czechoslovak people."[36] Although it stopped short of a full attack on the Soviets, the UDI sympathized with the people of Czechoslovakia. The UDI's Executive Committee also developed a working relationship with the Czechoslovak Women's Union, which in June had corresponded with the Rome office to let the UDI know that the Czech association was again active and to highlight specific features of its new Action Program for women. After the invasion of Warsaw Pact troops in August, the UDI expressed its grief for the loss of life the Czechoslovak people had endured and asked the Czechoslovak Women's Union to take advantage of an invitation it had previously extended and come to Italy in October to discuss recent events in a hospitable environment.[37] During the visit, Emilia Sedlakova, vice president of the Slovak committee of the Czechoslovak's Women's Union, emphasized less the events that had unfolded in Prague than the current situation of women in her country. Many Czech women, it seemed, had begun to question the socialist line: "We believed that the launching of the building of a socialist society meant automatically resolving the woman question; this was our error."[38] As Sedlakova and her companions explained, socialism had not ultimately liberated them; instead, most women found themselves working all day and then being responsible for household chores at home at night. It was now not uncommon, they said, to hear women articulating their desire just to be housewives. As a result, the Czechoslovak Women's Union was now actively seeking ways to address the problem of *doppio lavoro*, work inside and outside the home, and to advance women's emancipation. Since the women of the UDI had years of experience working on just these sorts of issues, the Czechoslovak women expressed their desire to exchange information and strategies with them.

Like the violence in Czechoslovakia, the violence that ended the lives of American reformers and peace activists Martin Luther King, Jr., and Robert Kennedy shocked and troubled the women of both the UDI and the CIF. King's assassination on April 4, 1968 provoked a massive outcry and led to rioting in dozens of American cities. His killing and Kennedy's shooting death two months later contributed to the highly tumultuous environment at the Democratic Party National Convention in Chicago that August. The UDI and the CIF's commentaries on the assassinations took sharply divergent directions and revealed how differently their relationships with the United States had evolved. The UDI had long been highly critical of "the American system," but during the mid- to late 1960s, *Noi Donne*'s writers found even more news coming from the United States that reinforced their notions that American life was full of contradictions and that American violence was endemic to the country's foundations on private property and individual interests. As characterized by *Noi Donne* during these years, the United States was a nation that celebrated democracy without granting it. Ghettoes, the Ku Klux Klan, and King's assassination served as evidence of deeply rooted racism. Standardization, conformism, and isolation ran rampant in America's suburbs, which served primarily to separate the classes.[39] Martin Luther King, Jr., and

Robert Kennedy, wrote one editorial contributor identified only as GC, were brought down by the very violence they had worked to end. Kennedy had not gone far enough in his critique of American society, she said: "Bob Kennedy had criticized certain moments in American politics and society, but he stayed far away from a rejection of the 'system,' and he never questioned the problem of the true roots of the evils that afflict Johnson's 'great society.' It's precisely from these roots that the shots that killed him also sprang."[40] American imperialism and the violence the government used to uphold it, some UDI women argued, ran deep within the nation and thus had also informed the U.S. approach to foreign affairs. The Soviet Union, for all its faults, valued the lives of its citizens and placed human dignity above individual gain.[41]

The CIF's America was a much different place—troubled but full of hope. Although the *Cronache*'s writers certainly did not ignore problems of racism and violence in the United States, they cast America as a leader of Christian nations whose values of democracy and justice benefited not only Americans but also women and men around the world. For instance, in an article about the life and death of Martin Luther King, Jr., Catholic journalist Mauro Bellabarba focused on King's use of nonviolent protest and his Christian messages, including his question "How many times must Christ die before all men are granted equal dignity?"[42] In her biographical article about Robert Kennedy, CIF member and international children's rights activist Emma Cavallaro emphasized Kennedy's efforts to bring help to poor nations and peace to the world and featured quotations by Vatican and Italian government officials on the tragedy of his loss.[43] Neither association took a categorical approach to the tragic events in Prague or the United States. They did not issue outright proclamations from the national headquarters or insist on following a particular political line. Instead, UDI and CIF members and supporters interpreted events through the historical lenses of their experiences and offered their thoughts for discussion and debate. The separation of ideology and world events indicates less commitment to a Cold War paradigm even though a general attachment to one of the two blocs nevertheless stood.

Youth, Gender, and Values in Modern Society

Back in Italy, generational conflicts became especially apparent when, in 1967, protests erupted first at the University of Trento and then at the

Catholic University in Milan. As university students in France would later do, Italian students questioned the carefully proscribed lives their parents, teachers, and politicians had laid out for them. Unlike in France, however, the first student protestors in Italy were enrolled in Catholic institutions where they were being groomed to become new Catholic leaders in industry and government. Christian Democracy, in particular, had accepted many graduates of the Catholic University of Milan into its highest ranks. By the early 1960s, however, Italian universities were overcrowded and understaffed, and matriculation rates were low. Between 1960 and 1968, the number of students enrolled in Italian universities grew from 268,000 to more than 450,000, of which about one-third were women. The system was unprepared to manage them with too few and often inaccessible professors, inadequate classroom space, and few opportunities for funding. Students who were able to overcome obstacles and complete their degrees often left the university with few prospects for employment in the fields they had prepared to enter. In response to such poor conditions in higher education, university students staged a series of sit-ins and nonviolent protests. In mid-November 1967 in Milan, students occupied the university until the police forcefully expelled them. Fury at the use of force and the perceived justness of the protestors' objections provoked the ire of students in Turin, who in late November occupied the Faculty of Letters campus building and questioned the quality of education they were receiving. By early 1968, the student movement had grown rapidly, touching nearly every university and even many secondary schools.[44] The student movement also began to encompass discussions of and protests against the Vietnam War, especially following the Tet offensive in January 1968.

Italian politicians reacted to the student protests with indignation. The students were breaking away from the established political parties and creating a new extraparliamentary political movement. Critical of both the Christian Democrats and the Italian Communists, the students set off a series of hostile responses from both parties. Giovanni Benzoni, of the Federation of Italian Catholic Universities, wrote a highly critical article in *Cronache e Opinioni* detailing the unfair, one-sided objections of the students. In his estimation, Italian universities had improved enormously since the 1950s, especially because of the "presence in all the schools considered, of a larger number of girls for whom a regularity of studies superior to that of boys can be noted."[45] Many students, however, he explained, had become spoiled and their expectations overblown. He noted that dreaming about becoming a doctor, for example, did not make you one, but too few students were realistic about their capabilities and wanted access to opportunities beyond their talents. Benzoni suggested that the students reevaluate themselves before attacking the university system. Many communists responded with equal irritation, accusing the students of being immature and misdirecting their energies, but some influential party members welcomed the social disruption the student movement had provoked.[46] Luigi Longo, secretary of the Communist Party, for example, published an article in the communist weekly *Rinascita* with the title "The Student Movement in the Anti-capitalist Struggle," in which he dissented from the general condemnation of the students espoused by other party members. The UDI covered the student protests with greater frequency once the movement spread to France in May and encompassed cities throughout Europe; the violence used by governments to break up marches and protests especially troubled writers for *Noi Donne*. As communist journalist Bruna Bellonzi editorialized, "From Rome to Torino to Marseilles to Paris to Bonn to Berlin to Madrid, the youths-with-books-under-their-arms have constructed a very long front line against which attacks and counterattacks are occurring in the context of a real war that sees lined up, on one side, the younger generations working to claim a diverse structure in schools and society and, on the other, the old conservative forces that don't know how to oppose the just requests of the young people but with batons, tear gas, and criminal trials."[47] The UDI's solidarity with the students, however, would face some challenges when the association entered into dialogue with young women activists.

Major world events and tragedies captured the public's attention during the mid- to late 1960s and put youth activism and culture into focus. It certainly appeared to many contemporary commentators of the day that the newest generation to come of age was overturning the values of their parents and grandparents. While this particular characterization of the '68 generation is not completely wrong, it does overlook some of the intricacies that developed along the lines of gender and generation. Historians Paolo Capuzzo, Federico Romero, and Elisabetta Vezzosi have pointed to the need for a deepening in the Italian historiography of the era that recognizes not only the young protagonists who led a break with the identities and structures of the past, but also reflects on agents of change, such as consumerism and women's culture, that contributed to a mutation in values and behaviors.[48] Seen in this way, 1968 is not just the culmination of a series of frustrations but part of a historical trajectory that reflects multiple mutations and convergences. In fact, an examination of the historic Italian and international women's organizations lends credibility to this interpretation since the women's groups contributed to a larger discourse about women's roles and values without necessarily transforming their key points of view on fundamental questions of gender difference. At the same time, however, the women's groups showed their engagement with changes under way. The older women of the organizations opened dialogues with the younger members and looked to integrate their needs and experiences into the associations' agendas.

A short article published in the November 1964 issue of *Cronache e Opinioni* appositely reveals some of the persistent ideological clashes over gender roles between women of the Marxist-inspired left and Catholic women that continued to characterize their interactions throughout the 1960s. Following a roundtable on the "Education for Family Life and Opportunities for Mothers for a Better Knowledge of Home Economics" held by the World Movement of Mothers in October, the UDI published a two-page article in *Noi Donne* criticizing the conclusions reached by the WMM, particularly those also espoused by the sociologist Archille Ardigò in his 1964 book *Emancipazione femminile e urbanesimo* [Women's Emancipation and Urbanization] that continued to champion the domestic sphere as women's ideal domain. In response to the UDI's critique, a CIF member identified only as Emma sarcastically editorialized that "the big mistake of the World Movement of Mothers was that of underscoring the fundamental role of mothers in the first years of a baby's life and to hope for measures from the State for mothers who work only for material necessity and who would not work if such measures were in place. But, oh dear, the terrible truth, the women of the WMM dared to hope that in a not too distant future a modern and efficient teaching of home economics could prepare young ladies to take on family problems with greater awareness and preparation."[49] According to Emma, the UDI continued to uphold its assertion that women's emancipation could only come through insertion in the productive system, that is, through employment outside the home, and thus failed to recognize that there were many "normal families in which mothers and housewives did not feel at all oppressed by their 'ancient subjection.'" The CIF and the World Movement of Mothers took offense at the UDI's claim that the average housewife would need five college degrees and a van to run a household according to their standards and suggested instead that common sense and a basic knowledge of the world around her would serve her just fine. The Catholic women also took issue with the UDI's labeling of all points of view that did not correspond to its own as "bourgeois" and stressed that the CIF's perspective "is not liberal bourgeois individualism; it is Christian communitarian personalism. This is rooted in us, not only in our way of thinking but in all our being and therefore in our mode of operating."[50] As had been the case many times before throughout the Cold War era, the philosophical differences between the women of the UDI and the CIF and the World Movement of Mothers provoked disagreements, and while this umpteenth call of the UDI to work with women above and beyond the limitations of the political parties may have resonated with women across the socialist/communist divide, it did not persuade the Catholic women's organizations to change course.

The latest confrontations between the women's associations did, however, reveal old and new elements in their attitudes about the futures of young women and their approaches to resolving the fundamental problems of daily life. Both the UDI and the CIF recognized the challenges of *doppio lavoro*, women's employment outside the home that did not free them from their domestic responsibilities or from antiquated attitudes that kept them in a position of legal and social inferiority in the domestic sphere. The Italian Civil Code of 1942 had, after all, granted married men legal dominance over their wives and children and had not yet been effectively challenged by women legislators. While the question of women's work inside and outside the home thus remained at the heart of the associations' activities, a newer set of questions entered their purview as well. In particular, and driven largely by the concerns of younger generations of women, the family code and its related issues, such as divorce, adultery, and birth control, began to garner greater attention. The Catholic women's organizations chose to face such matters through education and special programs that placed an emphasis on the family as a spiritual center whose proper balance would grant women the dignity and options they deserved. The UDI, in contrast, began a more systematic analysis of contemporary gender roles. Beginning with its *tesi* (theses) prepared for the 1964 national congress, the UDI labeled modern society "masculin-ist," which signified deemphasizing capitalism as the source of women's oppression and seeing gender as a distinct category to be addressed. In the work of Catholic women and women on the left, however, generational disparities proved hard to overcome.

The CIF and the World Movement of Mothers identified the thorough and proper education of young people, especially young women, as the main way to overcome women's inferior status in the household and thereby eliminate the need for divorce, birth control, or extramarital af-fairs. According to the Catholic women's associations, if women and men entered into marriage and parenthood with a full understanding of what they entailed and were equipped with a complete set of skills to confront the challenges of family life, the family would receive a much-needed revitalization. Family life, they argued, was to be entered into with con-sciousness and free will: "The family is a community based on love in which all members have equal dignity and whose basis for existence is stability and absolute loyalty among its members; each person must know how to fully assume his/her responsibilities, and the family must be built on free and responsible choice."[51] This is not to say that the women's or-ganizations did not want women to have full and equal status with men in family law in Europe and around the world; they did. However, they did not regard laws and customs as equivalent. In preparation for its 1966 in-ternational congress, "Family Life: Improvisation or Matter of Education?" the World Movement of Mothers initiated a series of studies to under-stand the relationship between laws and ideals. According to interviews of mothers and young people conducted by the organization's national members, at times legislation seemed to move more quickly than social values. Young people, said the international organization, "seemed to show a tendency to get rid of traditional laws while attempting as quickly as possible to adapt to new discoveries and innovations."[52] At times, the opposite was true: "Mothers feel unprepared, fearful and defenseless faced with the rapid evolution of customs and the decline of moral and tradi-tional values."[53] In other words, youths of the 1960s appeared eager to modernize and overturn the systems of their parents' generation but with-out having a full grasp of what the consequences might be. The results of nearly six hundred questionnaires the CIF helped to collect from mothers and daughters (and thirteen sons) about social customs and relationships found that young women and men took marriage very seriously but rarely talked to their mothers about it and that they considered flirting a sufficient test of possible marriage partners. Moreover, 56 percent of the 288 daughters who responded asserted that they would raise their children according to an upbringing different from their own.[54] Such results pointed to a need for greater coordination of education across private and public institutions. As the World Movement of Mothers' vice president, Paule Chapelle, put it: "To achieve the final goal of all our work and achieve a practical and effective work for the benefit of families, and particularly mothers, the WMM will not only collaborate with government and private authorities, but will determine a concrete course of action as well. It will do its utmost and deploy all its energies to ensure that, in all countries where it operates, the various powers translate these initiatives and suggestions into appropriate action within national or international law, in educational reform programs, in bodies of continuing education for adults before and after marriage, and in institutions for mothers."[55] The CIF and World Movement of Mothers believed the traditional family could not only be saved but strengthened.

The UDI was less concerned with saving the family than with protecting the advancement of women's emancipation. In Italy, the UDI was able to point to its many contributions to pro-woman legislation but also bemoaned the indissolubility of the family that men continued to legally head; here, too, it was clear that values and laws had not arrived at the same point. "At the root of this disharmony between law and custom," according to Alessandro Galante Garrone, a historian and former member of the Partito d'Azione writing for *Noi Donne*, "there's a social-political reason. It's useless to talk about the parties of the right, which, in our country, are of more openly conservative or reactionary tendencies. We know all too well why these parties are persistently hostile, still today, to recognize the full position of equality of women in the family."[56] The UDI did not, however, limit its criticisms to the parties of the right. Women of the UDI and the Italian Communist Party recalled in interviews with historian Lucia Chiavola Birnbaum that when they introduced certain women's concerns to the party's central committee in the 1960s, more than half the men walked out.[57] The UDI did not limit its considerations to the Italian context, either, but placed the situation of Italian women in an international framework. In preparation for its seventh national con-

gress, the UDI's leaders made known that "the woman question, therefore, is not only not absorbed by the development of modern society but
it presents itself, even with strong differentiations in diverse national contexts, as a global problem that is still not resolved in any part of the world,
not even in those societies where the gains are strongest."[58] The UDI's
work with the Women's International Democratic Federation had revealed that while women in the people's democracies enjoyed fuller equality in the workplace, their lives were met with many of the same challenges
as those of women elsewhere. An article by Bruna Bellonzi, for example, said that Soviet men, although much more likely to help around the
home than their Italian counterparts, did not carry an equal burden in
household chores, and she noted that women were obligated to work outside the home. Many Soviet women responded to this inequity by letting
the dust accumulate on their furniture.[59] American women, the UDI repeated on many occasions, were actually among the most repressed in the
world despite the deceptive appearance of their growing employment.
With few social services in place to help them, "in reality the roots of the
modern subordination of the American woman are rooted in the entire
organization of the society."[60] Only Swedish women, as the UDI saw it,
seemed to have achieved something coming close to full emancipation.

The changing values and priorities of the younger generations of European women sometimes perplexed the women of the Resistance generation who were celebrating twenty years of political and social activity.
Consumerism now appeared to take precedence over spirituality or community, and sexuality over other basic rights. To take on recent social and
cultural tendencies, the Catholic women's organizations wanted to give
young women a stronger set of tools to create priorities in their lives. In
particular, they worked on reshaping a model of femininity that had
emerged with the economic boom, namely, one that celebrated domesticity, consumption, and passivity and that denigrated education, public involvement, and service. The CIF's leaders asked, for example, if all the
members of the family really needed to work to be able to afford the items
associated with the latest interior decorating trends, especially if such
items meant the children would be denied an education or participation
in extracurricular activities that helped them develop as young people.[61]
Lidia Menapace, a teacher and CIF member from Novara whose biography
includes the Resistance and memberships in the Christian Democratic

and Communist Parties, questioned whether gender roles had been transformed just to the point that men earned money and women spent it—
and not on their families' futures but on makeup, clothing, and trashy
novels. The devaluation of religion, she noted, seemed to account for a
decline of morals in the United States where barriers to women's public
life were being removed without new systems being put in place to help
them. She cautioned, "When we ask that these protective structures be
removed we must prepare people to avoid falling with them."[62] It was not
that the CIF had given up on the housewife but that the sort it esteemed
was an educated, emancipated woman who provided much more to her
household than ornamentation or cleaning and cooking.

The women of the CIF wanted to see the religious core of the family
reinforced to avoid a downward spiral into the emptiness of consumption.
On a list of values in crisis, the CIF placed at no. 7 a "crisis of religious
values in contemporary society" and stated, "We think that the attention
should be placed on the increased pressure of secular thoughts and attitudes." Therefore, when the World Movement of Mothers began to revise
the *Mother's Charter*, the CIF's Maria Penco insisted on certain modifications and complained that the text did not place sufficient value on
spiritual formation as a mother's work. She refused to accept various proposals that would have added specifics about training and education that
she thought downplayed the spiritual aspect.[63] The organization's International Council agreed to make the requested changes. In Italy, the CIF
held educational sessions on holding onto spirituality in a secularizing
society. In one such session, young people were invited to engage in a dialogue with Mons. Filippo Franceschi, who had been named to advise the
youth section of Catholic Action. At the end of their meeting, he concluded: "All considered this is a great historic occasion for the Church:
more favorable than one might think. The Church today is, in fact, the
only one to offer man the meaning of life with a prophetic word and a
sense of his destiny and thus to give him new hope."[64] According to the
Catholic women's groups, in a time of uncertainty and chaos, religious
values could help young people make sense of their lives.

The UDI, meanwhile, worried that the generation of women coming
of age had lost sight of central objectives that promoted women's emancipation. Reporting from the association's eighth national convention, UDI
Executive Committee member Giulietta Ascoli asked, "What do today's

women want?" Did they really want sexual freedom and birth control pills or equality in the workplace, daycare centers, and fewer tasks in the home when they returned in the evening? The UDI's leaders were ultimately not really sure what young women wanted or how they planned to obtain it. As they saw it, women were right to shed old attitudes and seek newer and more immediate forms of protest that overcame the notion of a political elite. At the same time, they did not think that they and their ways of operating no longer had a place in contemporary society. Journalist and UDI Executive Committee member Miriam Mafai explained, "We don't want to lead 'for' women or 'with' women: we want women to lead themselves. This is what we call the 'self-management' of the struggle, a method that can only allow the growth of a consciousness of emancipation."[65] The UDI's leaders did not oppose divorce, access to birth control, or the expression of femininity through sexuality, but they did not want such concerns to overshadow longstanding and unresolved battles for women's economic and political rights. Some younger UDI women accused the association of hesitating on some of these issues anyway because of the association's relationships with the political parties.[66] While party loyalty may have been a factor for a few of the UDI's leaders, many UDI members held personal beliefs they were not yet ready to shed, and others fully embraced the new direction of young people.[67]

There was no uniform response to the emerging group of feminists. In fact, rank-and-file members of the UDI, such as Maria Belli, who joined the association in 1958, highlighted the historic association's role in developing a feminist agenda. "As I see it," she said, "the UDI shaped a collective of politically active women both at the national and local levels, but women got to know about the specificity of femininity inside the UDI. Then the feminism of '68 arrived, a feminism that was aggravating in certain ways, which I agree with in some respects. But, I believe that feminism would not have existed if the UDI had not been there first."[68] Giuseppina Carbonetti of Chieti was twenty years old when she joined the UDI in 1969, just as new feminist collectives were emerging from student and other extraparliamentary groups. Carbonetti preferred to work for women's rights within the UDI, however, because of its established political history. As she recalls, "The feminists were revisiting themes that we had already dealt with, such as self-determination. We had already begun to undertake these discussions before feminism."[69] The same reflection on feminism could not be said to be held by a majority of the CIF's leaders and members, who supported the Vatican's pronouncements on birth control and divorce and mostly avoided open discussions of sexuality outside marriage, contending that most Italians were good Catholics who held conservative points of view on these matters.[70] The CIF did not ignore the influence of the new social movements and the advent of feminism, however, and in 1970 changed its structure from that of a federation to that of an association to better respond to the new political and social challenges.[71]

Conclusion

By the end of the 1960s, the Cold War world was a much different place. The West had shown it was not willing to fight a war with the Soviets over the Eastern European satellites but was willing to engage them in proxy wars in the developing world. A new generation coming of age, however, questioned the choices made by their elders and openly challenged them through organized protest, especially on the war in Vietnam. Moreover, the generation born after World War II reflected the changing values of society. Young people wanted more options in their educational and personal lives and professional development. Politicians and religious leaders responded to the youths of the 1960s in a multitude of ways, many with surprise, others with disdain, and some with admiration. Whatever their reaction, older men and women recognized that the students of the 1960s were a force to be taken seriously. Contemporary society was moving in new directions that required dialogue across cultures and generations if accord was to be found. The challenges presented to the historic women's associations, especially by young women activists, led to a reassessment of their priorities and tactics. Ultimately, the UDI and the CIF remained true to their core values and veered very little from the paths they had constructed over the previous twenty-five years. In the 1968 generation, they saw hope for the future of Italy and the world at large. But they looked to carefully guide the young women newly entering the complicated world of political and associational activity. The CIF reasserted the primacy of the family, the benefits of healthy capitalist societies, and the need for spirituality in a secularizing world. In Italy, and through its work with the World Movement of Mothers, the CIF attempted to educate and prepare young women to become the kind of Catholic wives and mothers who would preserve traditional values while seeking fulfillment and balance in their lives inside and outside the home. The UDI used its exchanges with the younger generation to explore the deeper meanings of gender roles. Through interactions and studies with women inside and outside Italy, the women of the UDI reached the conclusion that a society founded on Marxist principles was not sufficient to guarantee women's emancipation; they began to look for new solutions to the problems women had long faced.

In addition to their direct interactions with the generation of *Sessantotto*, the women's associations also found themselves educating and directing women on a variety of European and international issues. *Noi Donne* and *Cronache e Opinioni* had always been important tools for the Italian women's associations, but during the 1960s they became even more important indicators of the UDI's and the CIF's main political and economic interests on the world stage. What the publications covered and what they ignored showed that the associations were now responding to individual events rather than making global pronouncements. The UDI, for example, focused especially on the war in Vietnam and the coup in Greece and downplayed the unrest in Czechoslovakia, whereas the CIF covered the European Economic Community and women in Africa and only rarely referred to these other important struggles. For both associations, the lives of women in the United States and the Soviet Union continued to serve as points of reference for social and cultural changes in Italy, particularly as new issues pertaining to the domestic sphere entered into public debate. The associations also highlighted the work of men such as Pope Paul VI and Martin Luther King, Jr., whose emphasis on international peace transcended the lines of political partisanship and created new models for dialogue. However, the UDI and the CIF did not completely let down their guard when it came to the bipolar split. The CIF remained suspicious of Soviet communism, and the UDI remained a fervent critic of the United States. Both called on their members to uphold their long-standing principles and vote accordingly. While the CIF's lengthy relationship with the World Movement of Mothers deepened and reinforced their shared Christian values, the UDI's rupture with the Women's International Democratic Federation left the Italian women forging ahead to construct new international relationships based on their peace initiatives. Transnational connections therefore led to exchanges with Vietnamese, Greek, and Czechoslovak women outside the structure of the organization that had for so long been the center of the UDI's international work. Crisis and transformation shaped the international women's movements as they looked back to their origins in the Resistance and ahead to a new generation of leaders. As the CIF had stated in advance of its Twelfth National Congress, "We talk about crisis because we are aware that the intense social transformations taking place require a modification in mentality, not because we think that everything today is wrong and that things were going well only long ago."[72] Political experience and maturity guided the women's associations through the crises of the late 1960s and enabled them to survive their transmutations.

Conclusion

The Results of Women's Cold War Political Activism

All four of the main women's organizations discussed in this book are still active today–the Unione Donne Italiane, the Centro Italiano Femminile, the World Movement of Mothers, and the Women's International Democratic Federation. Each continues to be active in the promotion of gender equality and reflects some of the current preoccupations of worldwide women's movements. In 2003, the UDI changed its name from Unione Donne Italiane [Union of Italian Women] to Unione Donne in Italia [Union of Women in Italy] to account for the important changes in Italy's demographics, which includes the influx of large numbers of migrant women.[1] The association has recently pursued several campaigns to include: the 50/50 initiative to require that political parties' electoral lists include at least 50 percent women; the Relay [*staffetta*] against Domestic Violence; and the Friendly Images project to promote a positive image of women in the media.[2] The Centro Italiano Femminile has been a principle organizer of several programs focusing on professional training for young women. Migrants, development, and globalization have also been of central interest to the CIF, which in 2008 and 2010 held its national conventions on related themes. In 2010, the UDI and the CIF cooperated together on an internship program, "Archiving Gender Difference," in which twenty female students interested in working in libraries and archives were selected to participate in a project to digitalize archival documents. The UDI and the CIF benefited from the assistance to help preserve their records, and the women interns gained valuable experience and built their résumés.[3] In 2004, the World Movement of Mothers was granted General Consultative Status at the United Nations, a higher level than its previous "Category B" Status, which means it can now send its own representatives to the UN, attend and speak at meetings of the Economic and Social Council, and distribute its own circulars. The organization is also involved in a European Commission project called the Family Platform to which it is contributing a report, "The Realities of Mothers in Europe."[4] And although the Women's International Democratic Federation suffered from the collapse of communism in Eastern Europe in 1989 and the breakup of the Soviet Union in 1991, it reconstituted itself in 1994 and is now based in São Paulo, Brazil. The association continues to tackle highly politicized problems. In 2007, its international congress, "For a World of Peace, Sovereignty, Work, and Equality," focused on its long-standing intertwined interests of peace and women's rights, this time centered on the wars in Iraq and Afghanistan, the ongoing struggle of the Palestinians, and women's needs for security and stability within each of these difficult contexts.[5]

It is highly significant that these four historic women's organizations have survived a myriad of challenges since the late 1960s and have outlasted a great number of the women's groups that emerged after 1968. In particular, many of the Italian feminist collectives that sprang from the student and workers' movements lasted just a few years. They, like their predecessors, certainly affected legislation, pushing through, for example, a divorce law in 1970, access to abortion in 1978, and anti–sexual violence legislation in 1985.[6] Despite all the negative attention on the women of the latest Berlusconi government, Italy's gender laws today are well in line with those of the other European Union countries and are perhaps even more advanced in the area of maternity benefits. Yet, female political participation in the Italian Parliament, which stands at 17 percent, lags behind that of the other original European Union members.[7] It should be pointed out, however, that this is the same percentage of women who currently serve in the U.S. Congress. Attempts are now being made to increase the female presence in business, a sector in which Italian women have typically fallen behind their counterparts in the rest of the European Union. According to a law passed in late June 2011, beginning in 2012, all private companies listed in the stock market as well as those with public holdings must include at least 20 percent women on their administrative councils; that number will increase to 33.3 percent in 2015. In its commentary on the law, the UDI noted a certain similarity to its own 50/50 campaign, but Pina Nuzzo, the UDI's archival director, critiqued the use of the term "quota rosa" [pink quota] to describe the new proposal, saying it was an example of the continued denigration of femininity.[8] In any case, it appears that although a great deal of work remains to be done to achieve gender equality in Italy, as most everywhere else, the UDI and the CIF are continuing to contribute their historical experiences and remain active public participants. The CIF, however, as a Catholic women's organization, has largely stayed on course on certain contentious issues, such as fertility rights and access to abortion, and thus engages very little with feminist organizations that promote women's full autonomy.

Clearly, the women's organizations analyzed in this book still matter, even though the historical context of the Cold War in which they were born has lost its immediacy. The fact that the Cold War ended but the UDI, CIF, World Movement of Mothers, and the Women's International Democratic Federation have kept their doors open underscores their relevance to the construction of a women's rights agenda, a focus that has consistently guided them through the ebb and flow of the contemporary era. The women of the Italian and international organizations inhabited a complex, male-led political world that was built in the aftermath of a devastating world war and they kept the spotlight on the needs of women, wherever they carried out their work. In doing so, they showed the value of female activism and autonomy. In Italy, the UDI and the CIF oversaw key legislative battles that opened careers, protected workers, and upheld the principles of gender equality established in the constitution of 1948. They influenced political outcomes by mobilizing millions of Italian women and reaching out to those who might be persuaded to come along. Their grassroots techniques, which included establishing strong local chapters, surveying members, distributing publications, and holding seminars, proved especially effective in consolidating the associations' bases and building on the strength of the leadership of the women who ran the Rome offices and established clear objectives. Outside Italy, the UDI and the CIF contributed to the extension of an international women's movement through their involvement in the highly influential Women's International Democratic Federation and World Movement of Mothers. Italian women held important positions in these organizations and used their global networks to build a dialogue about women's emancipation while tackling related issues, such as peace and social justice for women, mothers, workers, and children around the world. Using their access to the United Nations and the emerging components of the eventual European Union, the women's organizations were able to present clear and unified positions on all the matters that concerned them and thus establish points of view that did not always line up with those of the male (and female) politicians who were supposed to represent them.

In their activities between the conclusion of World War II and 1968, the UDI and the CIF were influenced by and responding to global Cold War political events taking place inside and outside Italy. While the United States and the Soviet Union competed to extend their global influence in the wake of their short-lived alliance, they drew the Italian political parties into the fray and faced the powerful influence of the Vatican. The UDI and the CIF lived through each of the Cold War conflicts that extended and modified global bipolarism in the Italian context. They reacted to the ways in which the United States and the USSR defended and conducted themselves during such key conflicts as the wars in Korea and Vietnam but also responded to the ways in which these other societies defined the status and roles of women. Cold War politics thus overlapped with the concerns of women, who saw themselves not as the passive recipients of decisions being made by politicians but as influential political actors in their own right who could draw on their experiences as women to guide and inform the political process. The discourse of motherhood and peace, for example, served as an important tool for the Italian and international women's organizations even if they approached it from opposite sides of the political spectrum. A widespread complicit acceptance of the idea of a maternal instinct that led women activists to want to make the world safe for its children worked in the women's favor as they introduced compelling arguments to protect women and children and direct the United States and USSR away from nuclear war.

Despite all their similarities, the women's organizations operated in separate though parallel worlds across which there was little possibility for meaningful, lasting cooperation. The UDI and the Women's International Democratic Federation were born from a strong tradition on the political left that made them vigilant against fascism, critical of the United States, and sympathetic to the world's people's democracies, especially the Soviet Union. The organizations' leaders believed in the promises of socialism and took a largely Marxist view of economic and social policies. But, unlike many of the male political leaders with whom they often worked, the women activists did not see the goal of women's emancipation as secondary to the cause of the working classes. They championed women's rights even in instances when it was not opportune to do so, and they challenged ideas about women's inferiority whenever and wherever necessary. As the decades progressed and the inequalities of socialist societies became better understood, the UDI and, to a lesser degree the WIDF, revised their thinking about how to guarantee women more rights even in the most "progressive" countries. The CIF and the World Movement of Mothers were created instead after declining to become members of associations like the UDI and the Women's International Democratic Federation. Although they were initially open to learning more about these first of the new postwar women's organizations, a strong Catholic identity, which included a rejection of "atheist" communist ideology, prevented the founders of these organizations from taking more than a cursory role as observers at the first meetings of the leftist women's organizations. No amount of enticing on the part of even the most committed Catholics of the UDI and the Women's International Democratic Federation, such as Ada Alessandrini, was enough to convince the women of the center-right that their interests would not be better served in organizations that were infused with a heavy dose of Christian values. In their own associations, the Catholic women struggled to uphold the strength of the traditional family through economic and social progress. They were fearful of communism but also suspicious of consumerism, and so they searched for ways to allow women to fulfill their mission as mothers but also find spiritual happiness within a Christian community. While at first hesitant to embrace the woman who works outside the home, and despite a tendency to see her as an unfortunate victim of tough economic times, women of both organizations later came to accept and assist her. They appreciated the democratic capitalist countries of western Europe and their historical basis in Christianity and they looked to uphold such values as community, family, and individual liberty. No other Italian women's associations reached the numbers of women the UDI and the CIF were able to reach.

The fundamental divisions between the UDI/Women's International Democratic Federation and the CIF/World Movement of Mothers proved formidable and insurmountable. Because of the absence in Italy of a strong secular liberal political approach after World War II, the Catholic/Popular Front divide was ultimately more determining than other factors in the creation and development of women's organizations, which continually delivered stinging criticisms of each other and found it extremely difficult to cooperate in all but the most selected cases. The Cold War heightened deep political divides that might otherwise have remained in the realm of less complicated disparities in their overall visions of gender roles. In Italy, the UDI and the CIF were subjected to but also advanced the constant animosity and squabbling that took place among Italy's main political parties. They were, after all, autonomous but certainly not separatist organizations. The fact that many of the UDI and the CIF's leaders represented the parties in Parliament and accepted money from them did raise questions from time to time about their positions on certain issues, especially those that involved taking sides in disputes involving the United States or the Soviet Union. Yet, overall the women more often than not reached their own conclusions after taking into consideration the different messages aimed at them by the political parties, the labor unions, and the Vatican as well as the news coming in from other parts of the world.

Between 1945 and 1968, the UDI and the CIF became much more expert in their own communications. They were able to anticipate criticisms and have responses ready for them. They were quick to point out hypocrisy and flaws in logic. They understood how to move their projects forward with or without the support of all Italian women. Over time, the women activists nonetheless became less reactionary and developed a more sophisticated conception of politics and more effective ways to disseminate their ideas and build women's movements. The UDI and the CIF's international networks further reinforced and replicated national Cold War divisions and proved to be conspicuous reminders of the challenges inherent in trying to balance the desire to advance women's rights and carry out social assistance work in the face of major political disaccord. The Women's International Democratic Federation and the World Movement of Mothers were perhaps even more opposite politically and rarely addressed each other directly. However, global Cold War entanglements did sometimes unravel on the national level. The Women's International Democratic Federation's highly politicized behavior, especially its unapologetically pro-Soviet tone, eventually led the UDI to question the validity of the organization's commitment to women's rights and to lessen its involvement in it. This, too, is an important reminder of the limitations of women's political cooperation, even when it involved women who were on the same side of the Cold War barrier. As studies of international women's activism continue, it is important not to lose sight of how both similar and divergent interests shape feminist strategies. By expanding and deepening a discussion of the global context of Italian Catholic and communist women's movements during the earlier decades of the Cold War, I hope I have demonstrated that the voices of liberal feminists have not been the only ones at the center of questions about women's rights in national and global politics, not even in western Europe.

Notes

Introduction

1. I prefer not to translate the names of the Unione Donne Italiane and the Centro Italiano Femminile, but they are sometimes translated as Union of Italian Women and the Italian Women's Center, respectively.

2. See my own *Immigrant Women and Feminism in Italy* (Aldershot, England: Ashgate, 2006) and "'Join Us in Rebuilding Italy': Women's Associations 1946–1963," *Journal of Women's History* 20, no. 4 (Winter 2008): 82–104.

3. For a good start to correcting this oversight, see the essays in Claire Duchen and Irene Bandhauer-Schoffman, eds., *When the War Was Over: Women, War, and Peace in Europe, 1940–1956* (New York: Leicester University Press, 2000). Recent monographs on women and the Cold War include Mire Koikari's *Pedagogy of Democracy: Feminism and the Cold War in the U.S. Occupation of Japan* (Philadelphia: Temple University Press, 2008) and Helen Laville's *Cold War Women: The International Activities of American Women's Organisations* (New York: Manchester University Press, 2002).

4. Paul Ginsborg, *A History of Contemporary Italy: Society and Politics, 1943–1988* (New York: Penguin, 1990).

5. Leila Rupp, *Worlds of Women: The Making of an International Women's Movement* (Princeton, N.J.: Princeton University Press, 1997).

6. Laville, *Cold War Women*.

7. Luisa Tasca, "The Average Housewife in Post–World War II Italy," *Journal of Women's History* 16, no. 2 (Summer 2004): 92–115.

8. Mario Del Pero, "Containing Containment: Rethinking Italy's Experience during the Cold War," *Journal of Modern Italian Studies* 8, no. 4 (2003): 532.

9. My own "Join Us in Rebuilding Italy" and "Emancipation or Liberation? Women's Associations and the Italian Movement," *Historian* 67, no. 1 (March 2005): 73–96, are examples. See also Lucia Chiavola Birnbaum, *Liberazione della donna: Feminism in Italy* (Middletown, Conn.: Wesleyan University Press, 1986); Perry Willson, *Women in Twentieth Century Italy* (Hampshire, England: Palgrave Macmillan, 2010), 136–44.

10. Patrizia Gabrielli, *La pace e la mimosa: l'Unione donne italiane e la costruzione politica della memoria (1944–1955)* (Rome: Donzelli Edirore, 2005); *Il club*

delle virtuose: UDI e CIF nelle Marche dall'antifascismo alla guerra fredda (Ancona, Italy: Il lavoro editoriale, 2000).

11. Fiorenza Taricone, *Il Centro Italiano Femminile dalle origini agli anni settanta* (Milan: FrancoAngeli, 2001).

12. See, for example, Fiorenza Taricone, "Il Centro Italiano Femminile e l'idea d'Europa," and Mimma De Leo, "L'Unione donne italiane fra rimozione e riforme," in *Cittadine d'Europa: Integrazione europea e associazioni femminili italiane*, ed. Beatrice Pisa (Milan: FrancoAngeli 2003), 21–92.

13. For a comprehensive overview of the historiography of Cold War Italy, see Antonio Varsori, "Cold War History in Italy," *Cold War History* 8, no. 2 (May 2008): 157–87.

14. Molly Tambor, "Red Saints: Gendering the Cold War, Italy 1943–1953," *Cold War History* 10, no. 3 (2010): 429–56.

15. Christopher Duggan, "Italy in the Cold War Years and the Legacy of Fascism," in *Italy in the Cold War: Politics, Culture, and Society, 1948–58*, ed. Christopher Duggan and Christopher Wagstaff (Washington, D.C.: Berg, 1995), 1–24.

16. Karen Garner, *Shaping a Global Women's Agenda: Women's NGOs and Global Governance, 1925–1985* (New York: Manchester University Press, 2010).

17. Ibid., 2.

18. Francisca De Haan, "Continuing Cold War Paradigms in Western Historiography of Transnational Women's Organisations: The Case of the Women's International Democratic Federation," *Women's History Review* 19, no. 4 (2010): 547–73; Karen Offen, *European Feminisms, 1700–1950: A Political History* (Stanford, Calif.: Stanford University Press, 2000), 11 and 386–88.

19. Gabrielli, *La pace e la mimosa*; Pojmann "'Join Us in Rebuilding'"; Willson, *Women in Twentieth Century Italy*, 136–44. Interpretations of the UDI as a tool of the Italian Communist Party, established in Birnbaum's *Liberazione della donna* and Donald B. Meyer's, *Sex and Power: The Rise of Women in America, Russia, Sweden, and Italy* (Middletown, Conn.: Wesleyan University Press, 1987), have been difficult to overturn. As recently as 2008, Chiara Ferrari uncritically perpetuated the view of the UDI as a flanking organization of the Communist Party in its first decades of operation. See Ferrari's "Contested Foundations: Postmodern Feminism and the Case of the Union of Italian Women," *Signs: Journal of Women in Culture and Society* 33, no. 3 (Spring 2008): 569–94.

20. Susan B. Whitney, *Mobilizing Youth: Communists and Catholics in Interwar France* (Durham, N.C.: Duke University Press, 2009).

21. Gabrielli, *Il club delle virtuose*; Taricone, *Il Centro Italiano Femminile*. Anna Scaratino, *Donne per la pace. Maria Bajocco Remiddi e l'Associazione internazionale madri per la pace nell'Italia della guerra fredda* (Milan: FrancoAngeli, 2006). I have not been able to identify any scholarly studies specifically about the World

Movement of Mothers but suggest Naomi Black, *Social Feminism* (Ithaca, N.Y.: Cornell University Press, 1989), 161–239, for a history of the Unione Féminine Civique et Sociale.

22. Myra Marx Ferree and Aili Mari Tripp, eds., *Global Feminism: Transnational Women's Activism, Organizing, and Human Rights* (New York: New York University Press, 2006); Mary E. Hawkesworth, *Globalization and Feminist Activism* (New York: Rowman & Littlefield, 2006); Cynthia Enloe, *The Morning After: Sexual Politics at the End of the Cold War* (Berkeley: University of California Press, 1993).

23. Rupp, *Worlds of Women*, 5.

24. Hawkesworth, *Globalization*.

25. De Haan, "Continuing Cold War Paradigms." Her forthcoming book *Cold War in the International Women's Movement: A Transnational History of the ICW, IAW, and WIDF, 1945–1990* is sure to shed even more light on these issues.

26. See for instance, Nitza Berkovitch, *From Motherhood to Citizenship: Women's Rights and International Organizations* (Baltimore, Md.: Johns Hopkins University Press, 1999); Julie Peters and Andrea Wolper, *Women's Rights, Human Rights: International Feminist Perspectives* (New York: Routledge, 1995).

27. See, for example, "I cattolici e la vita internazionale," *Cronache e Opinioni*, May 1952, 6, and "Istantanee alla scuola dell'Udi," *Noi Donne*, March 18, 1951, 7.

28. Ginsborg, *A History of Contemporary Italy*.

1. Daughters of the Resistance, 1943–1946

1. Unione donne italiane, "Costituzione dell'Unione Donne Italiane (September 15, 1944)," in *L'Unione donne italiane, 1944–1948*, ed. Silvana Casmirri (Rome: Quaderni della FIAP, 1978), 97–100.

2. Odd Arne Osted, *The Global Cold War: Third World Interventions and the Making of Our Times* (Cambridge: Cambridge University Press, 2007).

3. Anna Rossi-Doria, "Italian Women Enter Politics," in *When the War Was Over: Women, War and Peace in Europe, 1940–1956*, ed. Claire Duchen and Irene Bandhauer-Schoffman (New York: Leicester University Press, 2000), 89–102; and Anna Bravo and Anna Maria Bruzzone, *In guerra senza armi. Storie di donne* (Bari: Laterza, 1995).

4. Leila Rupp, *Worlds of Women: The Making of an International Women's Movement* (Princeton, N.J.: Princeton University Press, 1997).

5. Ibid.

6. Ibid., 16–17.

7. Anna Maria Mozzoni, "La questione dell'emancipazione della donna in Italia," in *La liberazione della donna*, ed. Franca Pieroni Bortolotti (Milan: G. Mazzotta, 1975), 112–23.

8. Anna Maria Mozzoni, "Discorso al congresso internazionale per il diritto delle donne a Parigi," in Bortolotti, *La liberazione della donna*, 136.

9. Karen Offen, *European Feminisms 1700–1950: A Political History* (Stanford, Calif.: Stanford University Press, 2000).

10. Daniela Rossini, "The Italian Translation of American Feminism: The CNDI and the International Women's Movement from *Belle Époque* to Fascism." Conference paper from the proceedings of the 20th AISNA Conference, Turin, Italy, September 24–26, 2009.

11. For a brief history of the National Council of Italian Women, see the organization's official website at www.cndi.it/index.php?lang=it&content=la_storia.

12. Pope Leo XIII, *Rerum Novarum*, Papal Encyclical of 1891 (available at www .vatican.va/holy_father/leo_xiii/encyclicals/documents/hf_l-xiii_enc_15051891 _rerum-novarum_en.html).

13. Claudia Frattini, *Il primo congresso delle donne italiane, Roma 1908: Opinione pubblica e femminismo* (Rome: Biblink, 2009).

14. Fiorenza Taricone, "Il Consiglio nazionale delle donne italiane," Donne e conoscenza storica website at www.url.it/donnestoria/testi/accardidonne/actut consiglio.htm.

15. Victoria De Grazia, *How Fascism Ruled Women: Italy 1922–1945* (Berkeley: University of California Press, 1992); Perry Willson, "The Fairytale Witch: Laura Marani Argnani and the Fasci Femminili of Reggio Emilia, 1929–1940," *Contemporary European History* 15, no. 1 (2006): 23–42.

16. Giovanni De Luna, *Donne in oggetto: L'antifascismo nella società italiana, 1922–1939* (Torino: Bollati Boringhieri, 1995).

17. Ibid., 96–97.

18. Gianni Corbi, *Nilde* (Milan: Rizzoli, 1993); Jo Marie Alano, *A Life of Resistance: Ada Prospero Marchesini Gobetti (1902–1968)*, doctoral dissertation, University of Rochester, 2002; Ada Gobetti, *Diario partigiano* (Turin: G. Einaudi, 1973); Marisa Rodano, *Del mutare dei tempi* (Rome: Edizioni Memori, 2008).

19. Richard Lamb, *War in Italy, 1943–1945. A Brutal Story* (London: Penguin, 1995); Massimo Legnani and Ferruccio Vendramini, eds. *Guerra, guerra di liberazione, guerra civile* (Milan: FrancoAngeli, 1990); Claudio Pavone, *Una guerra civile. Saggio storico sulla moralità della Resistenza* (Turin: Bollati Boringhieri, 1994).

20. Giuseppe Mammarella, *Italy after Fascism: A Political History, 1943–1965* (Notre Dame, Ind.: University of Notre Dame Press, 1966), 63–69.

21. Ibid., 67.

22. The books cited in note 19 have overturned the prevalence of one-sided heroic accounts of the Resistance. See Jane Slaughter, *Women and the Italian Resistance, 1943–1945* (Denver, Colo.: Arden, 1997); and Jomarie Alano, "Armed

with a Yellow Mimosa: Women's Defence and Assistance Groups in Italy, 1943–1945," *Journal of Contemporary History* 38, no. 4 (2003): 615–31.

23. Bravo and Bruzzone, *In guerra senza armi.*

24. For an overview of the historiography of women in the Resistance and its relationship to trends in the Italian women's movement, see Perry Willson, "Saints and Heroines: Re-Writing the History of Italian Women in the Resistance," in *Opposing Fascism: Community, Authority and Resistance in Europe*, ed. Tim Kirk and Anthony McElligott (Cambridge: Cambridge University Press, 1999), 180–98.

25. "Relazioni del Comitato provinciale femminile di Milano al Comitato nazionale dei Gruppi di difesa della donna (inverno 1944–45)," in *UDI: Laboratorio di politica delle donne; idee e materiali per una storia*, ed. Maria Michetti, Margherita Repetto, and Luciana Viviani (Rome: Cooperativa Libera Stampa, 1984), 20.

26. *Bollettino di Attività del Centro Italiano Femminile*, April 1945, 2.

27. *Noi Donne*, May 21, 1945, 3.

28. Alano, "Armed with a Yellow Mimosa," 628.

29. Iside Bertaccini, interviewed by Barbara Farinelli in *Volevamo cambiare il mondo: Memorie e storie delle donne dell'UDI in Emilia Romagna*, ed. Caterina Liotti, Rosangela Pesenti, Angela Remaggi, and Delfina Tromboni (Rome: Carocci editore, 2002), 105.

30. Eda Bussolari, interviewed by Mariangela Tedde and Ermanna Zappaterra in ibid., 113.

31. "Pane, lavoro e pace: Uguaglianza di diritto tra donne e uomini, ecco ciò che le donne chiedono al nuovo Governo," *Noi Donne*, June 25, 1945, 3.

32. "Progetto di volantino presentato al Comitato direttivo del 9.4.1946," in Michetti et al., *UDI: Laboratorio*, 45–46.

33. In fact, I have chosen not to include the National Council of Italian Women as a central organization in my study because of its diminished importance in the post–WWII era and minimal contributions even to the prewar international women's movement and the International Council of Women, as discussed by Rossini, in "The Italian Translation of American Feminism."

34. "L'Unità femminile non è più necessaria," *Noi Donne*, August, 31, 1945, 1.

35. *Bollettino di Attività del Centro Italiano Femminile*, June 1945, 1.

36. Anna Minguzzi, interviewed by Luana Vacchi in *Volevamo cambiare il mondo*, 186.

37. Grazia Gallone, "Promozione sociale, culturale, cristiana," interview in *Cronache e Opinioni*, special issue, December 2005, 91.

38. Paul Ginsborg, *A History of Contemporary Italy: Society and Politics, 1943–1988* (New York: Penguin, 1990), 70–71; Spencer M. Di Scala, *Italy from Revolution to Republic, 1700 to the Present*, 3rd ed. (Boulder, Colo.: Westview, 2004), 301–2.

39. Mirco Dondi, "The Fascist Mentality after Fascism," in *Italian Fascism: History, Memory, and Representation*, ed. R.J.B. Bosworth and Patrizia Dogliani (New York: Palgrave, 1999), 141.

40. There are surprisingly few studies on women's suffrage in Italy. See Anna Rossi-Doria, *Diventare cittadine: Il voto alle donne in Italia* (Firenze: Giunti Gruppo Editoriale, 1996). In English and for a condensed version of the same arguments, see Rossi-Doria, "Italian Women Enter Politics."

41. Maria Eletta Martini, "La Storia, le storie: Il ricordo di come nacque l'associazione," interview in *Cronache e Opinioni*, special issue, December 2005, 99.

42. Rossi-Doria, *Diventare cittadine*, 39.

43. See, for example, *Bollettino di Attività del Centro Italiano Femminile*, April and May 1945.

44. See, for example, the December 1946 issues of the CIF's *Bollettino di Attività del Centro Italiano Femminile* and the UDI's *Noi Donne* for discussions of Christmas preparations.

45. Maria Federici, "Circolare n. 40 alle presidenti dei comitati proviniciali," [1946?], Archives of Istituto Paolo VI, Unione Donne—Centro Italiano Femminile, Folder 68 (1945–53).

46. Maria Federici, "Per la Crisi degli Alloggi," *Bollettino di Attività del Centro Italiano Femminile*, February 1945, 4; "Progetto di volantino presentato al Comitato direttivo del 9.4.1946," in Michetti et al., *UDI: Laboratorio*, 45.

47. Clorinda Morante, "Fiducia nella Provvidenza e grande tenacia," interview in *Cronache e Opinioni*, special issue, December 2005, 87–88.

48. Montagnana, "Attività dell'Unione Donne Italiane," 37.

49. Letter dated December 20, 1946, UDI National Archives, DnM 45.1.

50. Adda Corti, "Tra l'UDI e il CIF per un'azione femminile unitaria," in Casmirri, *L'Unione donne italiane*, 120.

51. "Perché queste menzogne?" in Casmirri, *L'Unione donne italiane*, 122–24.

52. Mirco Dondi, *La lunga liberazione: Giustizia e violenza nel dopoguerra italiano*, 2nd ed. (Rome: Editori Riuniti, 2004).

53. Dondi, "The Fascist Mentality," 147.

54. Christopher Duggan, *The Force of Destiny: A History of Italy since 1796* (New York: Houghton Mifflin, 2008).

55. Ibid., 538–40.

56. Dondi, "The Fascist Mentality," 153.

57. Ginsborg, *A History of Contemporary Italy*, 49.

58. Mario Del Pero, "Containing Containment: Rethinking Italy's Experience during the Cold War," *Journal of Modern Italian Studies* 8, no. 4 (2003): 533–34.

59. Unsigned and untitled in *Sempre più alto*, January 1946.

60. Maria Federci, "Daremo sei milioni di voti," *Bollettino di Attività del Centro Italiano Femminile*, April 1946, 1.

61. Rita Montagnana, "Attività dell'Unione Donne Italiane nell'Italia centro-meridionale," in Michetti et al., *UDI: Laboratorio*, 32–39.

62. Duggan, *The Force of Destiny*, 542.

63. "Progetto di volantino presentato al Comitato direttivo del 9.4.1946," in Michetti et al., *UDI: Laboratorio*, 45.

64. "Cartolina di propaganda," in Michetti et al., *UDI: Laboratorio*, 53.

65. Patrizia Gabrielli, *Il 1946, le donne, la repubblica* (Rome: Donzelli, 2010).

66. "Le donne nell'Assemblea Costituente," *Voci di donne* 9 (March 8, 2007) Provincia di Potenza, L'Ufficio della Consigliera di Parità, 3–5.

67. Biographies, UDI National Archives, DnM 48.1/3.

68. Gabriella Fanello Marcucci, "Il contributo delle donne all'Assemblea Costituente," *Le donne e la Costituzione: Atti del Convegno promosso dall'Associazione degli ex-parlamentari, 22–23 March 1988* (Rome: Camera dei deputati, 1989), 119–32.

69. "L'Unione donne italiane a tutte le donne elette all'Assemblea Nazionale Costituente," in Casmirri, *L'Unione donne italiane*, 125–26.

70. Palmiro Togliatti, "L'Unione delle donne deve essere unicamente lo strumento di lotta di tutte le donne per la conquista dei loro diritti e della libertà," in Casmirri, *L'Unione donne italiane*, 127–43.

71. Maria Federici, "Combattiamo l'astensionismo femminile," in Biase, *I cattolici*, 158–60.

72. For a good overview of International Women's Day, see Temma Kaplan, "On the Socialist Origins of International Women's Day," *Feminist Studies* 11, no. 1 (Spring 1985): 163–71.

73. Alano, "Armed with a Yellow Mimosa," 624.

74. *Noi Donne*, April 1, 1945, 8.

75. Ibid.

76. Laura Rossi, "La giornata della donna in Italia e nel mondo," in *Noi Donne*, April 1, 1945.

77. Letter dated October 27, 1944, UDI National Archives, DnM 45.1.

78. English language brochure, UDI National Archives, DnM 45.1.

79. Women's International Democratic Federation, *Eugénie Cotton* (Berlin: Women's International Democratic Federation [1970?]).

80. Minutes of November 8, 1945, UDI National Archives, DnM 45.1.

81. "La nostra volontà di pace espressa dalla delegazione italiana," *Noi Donne*, November 30, 1945, 1–2.

82. "Messaggere di pace venute d'ogni paese," *Noi Donne*, December 15, 1945, 5.

83. Ibid.

84. Francisca De Haan, "Progressive Women's Aspirations for a Better World: The Early Years of the Women's International Democratic Federation," published in German as "Hoffnungen auf eine bessere Welt: Die frühen Jahre der Internationalen Demokratischen Frauenföderation (1945–1950)," *Feministische Studen* 27, no. 2 (November 2009): 241–57.

85. *Noi Donne*, December 15, 1945, 1.

86. Karen Garner, *Shaping a Global Women's Agenda: Women's NGOs and Global Governance, 1925–1985* (New York: Manchester University Press, 2010), 143–45, 182.

87. "Le donne di tutto il mondo s'uniscono per la democrazia e per la pace," *Noi Donne*, October 31–November 15, 1945, 2.

88. Maria Calogero, "Relazione sul Congresso Internazionale Femminile di Parigi," UDI, National Archives, DnM 45.1.

89. Federici, "Circolare."

90. See chapter 2.

91. Interview with Lina Merlin, *Noi Donne*, September 15, 1945, 2.

92. Perry Willson, *Women in Twentieth Century Italy* (New York: Palgrave Macmillan, 2010), 144. For her discussion of the UDI and the CIF, see pages 139–48.

93. Laura Levine Frader, *Breadwinners and Citizens: Gender in the Making of the French Social Model* (Durham, N.C.: Duke University Press, 2008), 22.

94. La Presidente Provinciale di Milano, ing. Rosita, "Il Cif presente nei congressi internazionali," *Bollettino di Attività del Centro Italiano Femminile*, November–December 1946, 5.

2. Cold War Housewives? 1947–1949

1. Relazione di lavoro della commissione Femminile dal 17 Maggio al 30 Giugno, dated July 10, 1949, Gramsci Institute, Moscow Collection, Box 233, Folder 73, Commissione Centrale Femminile, 1949–53.

2. "Preferenza assoluta per il lavoro casalingo," *Bollettino di attività del Centro italiano femminile*, October–November 1949, 1.

3. Luisa Tasca, "The 'Average Housewife' in Post-War Italy," *Journal of Women's History* 16, no. 2 (2004): 92–115.

4. Renata Talassi, interviewed by Liviana Zagagnoni in *Volevamo cambiare il mondo: Memorie e storie delle donne dell'UDI in Emilia Romagna*, ed. Caterina Liotti, Rosangela Pesenti, Angela Remaggi, and Delfina Tromboni (Rome: Carocci editore, 2002), 241–43.

5. See, for example, Andrea Mariuzzo's article about the Partisans of Peace, "Stalin and the Dove: Left Pacifist Language and Choices of Expression between the Popular Front and the Korean War, 1948–1953," *Modern Italy* 15, no. 1 (February 2010): 21–35; and Ruggero Giacomini, *I partigiani della pace. Il movimento*

pacifista in Italia e nel mondo negli anni della prima guerra fredda (Milan: Vangelista, 1984). The UDI participated in several of the organization's activities and featured its 1949 congress in many issues of *Noi Donne*.

6. Spencer M. Di Scala, *Italy from Revolution to Republic, 1700 to the Present*, 3rd ed. (Boulder, Colo.: Westview, 2004), 301–2; Giuseppe Mammarella, *Italy after Fascism: A Political History, 1943–1965* (Notre Dame, Ind.: University of Notre Dame Press, 1966), 120–21.

7. Mammarella, *Italy after Fascism*, 120–21.

8. Vera Zamagni, *The Economic History of Italy, 1860–1990* (Oxford: Clarendon Press, 1993), 324.

9. Di Scala, *Italy from Revolution*, 302.

10. Ibid., 306.

11. Zamagni, *The Economic History*, 331.

12. Mario Del Pero, "Containing Containment: Rethinking Italy's Experience during the Cold War," *Journal of Modern Italian Studies* 8, no. 4 (2003): 532–55.

13. Paul Ginsborg, *A History of Contemporary Italy: Society and Politics, 1943–1988* (New York: Penguin, 1990), 83.

14. David Ellwood, "The Propaganda of the Marshall Plan in Italy in a Cold War Context," *Intelligence and National Security* 18, no. 2 (2003): 225–36.

15. Alexander De Grand, *The Italian Left in the Twentieth Century: A History of the Socialist and Communist Parties* (Bloomington: Indiana University Press, 1989), 115.

16. Wendy Pojmann, "'Join Us in Rebuilding Italy': Women's Associations 1946–1963," *Journal of Women's History* 20, no. 4 (Winter 2008): 82–104.

17. Patrizia Gabrielli, *Il club delle virtuose: UDI e CIF nelle Marche dall'antifascismo alla guerra fredda* (Ancona: Il lavoro editoriale, 2000), 19.

18. Budapest 1948 WIDF Congress Documents titled, "Il movimento democratico internazionale femminile," UDI National Archives, DnM 48.1.

19. Intervention de Mme Fazio Longo—Italie," in *IIe Congrès International des Femmes: Compte rendu des travaux du congrès qui s'est tenu à Budapest (Hongrie) du Ier au 6 Décembre 1948*, ed. Fédération Démocratique Internationale des Femmes (Paris: WIDF, 1948[1949]), 221.

20. Minni Tatò, "La verità sul Patto Atlantico," *Noi Donne*, April 3, 1949, 3.

21. Alcide De Gasperi, "Discorso al I convegno nazionale del Movimento femminile della Dc," in *I cattolici e il voto alle donne*, ed. Paola Gaiotti de Biase (Turin: Società Editrice Internazionale, 1996), 162.

22. Cecilia Dau Novelli, "Il CIF e la società italiana (1944–1981)," in *Donne del Nostro Tempo: Il Centro Italiano Femminile (1945–1995)*, ed. Cecilia Dau Novelli (Rome: Edizioni Studium, 1995), 10.

23. Anna Maria Pazzaglia, "Donne pronte ad affrontare le sfide della società," interview in *Cronache e Opinioni*, special issue, December 2005, 90.

24. Ellwood, "The Propaganda of the Marshall Plan," 230.

25. Clementina Bertini, "Così ho incontrato l'associazione," and Cesarina Mittini, "Una vita spesa per le donne," interviews in *Cronache e Opinioni*, special issue, December 2005, 95 and 103.

26. Ginsborg, *A History of Contemporary Italy*, 105–10.

27. Ibid., 110.

28. "La donna alla Costituente della Terra," in *UDI: Laboratorio di politica delle donne, idee e materiali per una storia*, ed. Maria Michetti, Margherita Repetto, Luciana Viviani (Rome: Cooperativa Libera Stampa, 1984), 93–94.

29. Photo advertisement, *Noi Donne*, February 27, 1949, 11.

30. "Appello rivolto alle donne a conclusione della Costituente della Terra," in Michetti et al., *UDI: Laboratorio*, 95.

31. Ansalda Siroli, interviewed by Rosangela Pesenti in *Volevamo cambiare il mondo*, 234.

32. Maria Casalini, *Le donne di sinistra (1944–1948)* (Rome: Carocci editore, 2005), 143.

33. The July and August 1948 issues of the *Bollettino di attività del Cif* feature the *giornata* and *case del sole*.

34. Maria Cristina Giuntella, "Il rapporto con gli altri movimenti cattolici. L'esperienza della federazione," in *Donne del Nostro Tempo*, 51–76.

35. For population data, see ISTAT, *Sommario di statistiche storiche dell'Italia, 1861–1975* (Roma: Istituto centrale di statistiche, 1976). On the effects of population losses on the German women's movement, see Marilyn Rueschemeyer and Hanna Schissler, "Women in the Two Germanys," *German Studies Review* 13, special issue (1990): 71–85.

36. "La donna e la casa," in Michetti et al., *UDI: Laboratorio*, 96.

37. Ibid.

38. "Per le donne casalinghe," in Michetti et al., *UDI: Laboratorio*.

39. Ibid., 97.

40. "Discutendo del lavoro casalingo," *Bollettino di attività del Cif*, May 1949.

41. Centerfold questionnaire in *Bollettino di attività del Cif*, March 1949.

42. "I risultati dell'inchiesta Cif sul lavoro casalingo," *Bollettino di attività del Cif*, December 1949, 1–2.

43. "Giornate internazionali sulla famiglia," *Bollettino di attività del Cif*, no. 32, October–November 1949, 6.

44. Letter from Maria Federici to Maria Rimoldi dated March 11, 1947, Paolo VI Institute, Unione Donne—Centro Italiano Femminile, Box 68 (1945–53).

45. Susan Pedersen, *Family, Dependence, and the Origins of the Welfare State: Britain and France, 1914–1945* (Cambridge: Cambridge University Press, 1993), 395.

46. World Movement of Mothers, "The Mother's Charter," Paris, 1947 (available at www.mouvement-mondial-des-meres.org/eng/identity/charter.html).

47. Ibid.

48. "I compiti del movimento internazionale femminile nella lotta per la pace e la democrazia," 10. UDI National Archives, DnM 48.1/3.

49. Anna Scarantino, *Donne per la pace: Maria Bajocco Remiddi e l'Associazione internazionale madri unite per la pace nell'Italia della guerra fredda* (Milan: FrancoAngeli, 2006), 77.

50. Christopher Duggan, *The Force of Destiny: A History of Italy since 1796* (Boston: Houghton Mifflin Company, 2008), 544–46.

51. Giovanni De Luna, *Donne in oggetto: L'antifascismo nella società italiana, 1922–1939* (Torino: Bollati Boringhieri, 1995), 86.

52. T. Chiaretti, "Partenza per Mosca," interview with Maria Maddalena Rossi, *Noi Donne*, November 20, 1949, 2.

53. Pius XII, "La missione della donna," speech to the CIF on October 21, 1945, in *I cattolici*, 153.

54. "Tutela delle lavoratrici madri," *Bollettino di attività del Cif*, no. 18, June 1948, special insert.

55. "Relazione d'apertura," 80.

56. "Intervention de Mme Noce—Italie," in *IIe Congrès International des Femmes*, 351.

57. Del Pero, "Containing Containment."

58. It should be mentioned that not all of the CIF's members supported eradicating the monarchy.

59. "Si discute la nuova costituzione: Che cosa è?" *Bollettino di attività del Cif*, January 1947.

60. Ibid.

61. Ginsborg, *A History of Contemporary Italy*, 101.

62. See Casalini, *Le donne di sinistra*, 192–204, for a good discussion of the use of *Noi Donne* in promoting a maternalist message among ordinary women.

63. Ginsborg, *A History of Contemporary Italy*, 115.

64. Ibid., 115–17.

65. Dau Novelli, "Il CIF e la società italiana," 9.

66. Maria Federici, "Daremo sei milioni di voti," *Bollettino di attività del Cif*, April 1947, 1.

67. Robert A Ventresca, "The Virgin and the Bear: Religion, Society, and the Cold War in Italy," *Journal of Social History* 37, no. 2 (Winter 2003): 439.

68. Biographical information about Ada Alessandrini; Basso Foundation; Ada Alessandrini Collection.

69. Mariachiara Fugazza and Maria Cassamagnaghi, eds. "Italia 1946: le donne al voto," Istituto Lombardo di Storia Contemporanea, 2006, 58 (available at www.insmli.it/pubblicazioni/35/Voto%20donne%20versione%20def.pdf).

70. "Relazione d'apertura di Rosetta Longo al II Convegno nazionale dell'U.d.i.," in Michetti et al., *UDI: Laboratorio*, 78.

71. Ibid., 79.

72. Gabriella Vergoni, interviewed by Giovanna Azzini in *Volevamo cambiare il mondo*, 255–57.

73. "Elezioni del 18 aprile 1948," *Bollettino di attività del Cif*, May 1948, 8.

74. "Consiglio Nazionale," *Bollettino di attività del Cif*, April–May 1950, 2 and 6.

75. Mariuccia Salvati, "Behind the Cold War: Rethinking the Left, the State, and Civil Society (1940s–1970s)," *Journal of Modern Italian Studies* 8, no. 4 (2001): 563.

76. "Relazione d'apertura," in Michetti et al., *UDI: Laboratorio*, 81.

77. There are too many examples to cite them all here. Nearly every issue of *Noi Donne* in 1949, for instance, includes at least one such story.

78. "Nella Giornata Internazionale della Pace, appello della Federazione Democratica Internazionale Femminile alle donne di tutto il mondo 1948," in Michetti et al., *UDI: Laboratorio*, 89.

79. Maria Federici, "A proposito della Giornata della Pace," *Bollettino di attività del Cif*, April 1948, 5.

80. Francisca De Haan, "Progressive Women's Aspirations for a Better World: The Early Years of the Women's International Democratic Federation," published in German as "Hoffnungen auf eine bessere Welt: Die frühen Jahre der Internationalen Demokratischen Frauenföderation (1945–1950)" *Feministische Studen* 27, no. 2 (November 2009): 241–57; 20 in English version.

81. Chronicle of conference, UDI National Archives, DnM 48.1.

82. "I compiti del movimento internazionale femminile nella lotta per la pace e la democrazia," UDI National Archives, DnM 48.1/3.

83. Speech of Magda Jóboru chief secretary of the Democratic Union of Hungarian women, Fondazione Basso, Collection: Ada Alessandrini, Series 8: Federation democratique des femmes, Box UA 1: Congresso internazionale FDIF 1948 Budapest.

84. Rosetta Longo, "Le italiane si sono impegnate a difendere la pace minacciata," *Noi Donne*, January 2, 1949, 7.

85. Christopher Duggan, "Italy in the Cold War Years and the Legacy of Fascism," in *Italy in the Cold War: Politics, Culture, and Society, 1948–58*, ed. Christopher Duggan and Christopher Wagstaff (Washington D.C.: Berg, 1995), 10.

86. Ada Alessandrini, "La pace può divenire una realtà," *Noi Donne*, January 9, 1949, 7. I did not find any such letters in subsequent issues.

87. Longo, "Le italiane si sono impegnate," 7.

88. "Intervention de Mme Noce—Italie," in *IIe Congrès International des Femmes*, 350–57.

89. Del Pero, "Containing Containment," 536.

90. Ibid.

91. "La Lutte de la FDIF et ses sections nationales pour la paix," Fondazione Basso, Fondo: Ada Alessandrini, Serie 8: Federation democratique des femmes, UA 2: Consiglio della Fdif, Mosca, November 1949.

92. Dina Rinaldi, "Stalin per un'intesa di pace," *Noi Donne*, February 13, 1949, 3.

93. Pietro Nenni, "Il compito delle donne: imporre la pace," *Noi Donne*, March 6, 1949, 3.

94. "Le donne italiane a Truman," *Noi Donne*, April 17, 1949, 5.

3. Mothers for Peace, 1950–1955

In this chapter, I make arguments similar to those I made in "For Mothers, Peace and Family: International (Non)-Cooperation among Italian Catholic and Communist Women's Organisations during the Early Cold War," *Gender and History* 23, no. 2 (August 2011): 415–29.

1. Clotilde Cassigoli, "Intervento al Congresso Mondiale delle Madri—Losanna 7–10 Luglio 1955," UDI National Archives, DnM 55.1/17.

2. Ibid.

3. Giuseppe Mammarella, *Italy after Fascism: A Political History, 1943–1965* (Notre Dame, Ind.: University of Notre Dame Press, 1966), 201–4.

4. Ibid., 202–3.

5. Alexander De Grand, *The Italian Left in the Twentieth Century: A History of the Socialist and Communist Parties* (Bloomington: Indiana University Press, 1989), 119–20, 122.

6. Mario Del Pero, "Containing Containment: Rethinking Italy's Experience during the Cold War," *Journal of Modern Italian Studies* 8, no. 4 (2003): 532–55.

7. Paul Nitze, "A Report to the National Security Council—NSC 68," April 12, 1950. President's Secretary's File, Truman Papers. Harry S. Truman Library, Independence, Missouri, 13 (available at www.trumanlibrary.org/whistlestop /study_collections/coldwar/documents/sectioned.php?pagenumber=17&documentid=10-1&documentdate=1950-04-12).

8. Ibid., 17.

9. Del Pero, "Containing Containment," 537–38.

10. Melvyn P. Leffler, *The Specter of Communism: The United States and the Origins of the Cold War, 1917–1953* (New York: Hill and Wang, 1994), 94–95.

11. Vladislav M. Zubok, *A Failed Empire: The Soviet Union in the Cold War from Stalin to Gorbachev* (Chapel Hill: University of North Carolina Press, 2007), 78–79.

12. Leffler, *The Specter of Communism*, 98.

13. Del Pero, "Containing Containment," 545.

14. Ruggero Giacomini, *I partigiani della pace* (Milan: Vangelista, 1984).

15. "We Accuse: Report of the Committee of the Women's International Democratic Federation in Korea," May 16–27, 1951, Berlin, 1.

16. Ibid., 24.

17. Ibid., 18.

18. Ibid., 19.

19. Francisca De Haan, "Progressive Women's Aspirations for a Better World: The Early Years of the Women's International Democratic Federation," published in German as "Hoffnungen auf eine bessere Welt: Die frühen Jahre der Internationalen Demokratischen Frauenföderation (1945–1950)," *Feministische Studen* 27, no. 2 (November 2009): 241–57; 20 in English version.

20. Ibid., 21. The Women's International Democratic Federation was not readmitted until 1967.

21. Karen Garner, *Shaping a Global Women's Agenda: Women's NGOs and Global Governance, 1925–1985* (New York: Manchester University Press, 2010), 181.

22. UDI National Archives, Box Pace, Folder 2, File 17.

23. Ibid., File 19.

24. Marisa Ombra, ed., *Donne manifeste: L'UDI attraverso i suoi manifesti, 1944–2004* (Rome: Il Saggiatore, 2005), 49.

25. Fiorenza Taricone, *Il Centro Italiano Femminile dalle origini agli anni settanta* (Milan: FrancoAngeli, 2001). See especially chapter 2 on the 1950s.

26. On the Christian Democratic Party during the war in Korea, see Sergio Chillè, "I riflessi della guerra di Corea sulla situazione politica italiana negli anni 1950–1953: Le origini dell'ipotesi degasperiana di 'democrazia protetta'," *Storia contemporanea* 18, no. 5 (October 1987): 895–926.

27. Renato Moro, "The Catholic Church, Italian Catholics, and Peace Movements: The Cold War Years, 1947–1962," *Contemporary European History* 17, no. 3 (2008): 376.

28. Peter C. Kent, *The Lonely Cold War of Pope Pius XII: The Roman Catholic Church and the Division of Europe, 1943–1950* (Ithaca, N.Y.: McGill-Queen's University Press, 2002), 256.

29. Pope Pius XII, "Summi Maeroris (On Public Prayers for Peace)," July 19, 1950 (available at www.ewtn.com/library/ENCYC/P12MAERO.HTM).

30. Moro, "The Catholic Church, Italian Catholics, and Peace Movements," 366.

31. Christopher Duggan, "Italy in the Cold War Years and the Legacy of Fascism," in *Italy in the Cold War: Politics, Culture, and Society, 1948–58*, ed. Christopher Duggan and Christopher Wagstaff (Washington, D.C.: Berg, 1995), 13.

32. Emanuela Scarpellini, *L'Italia dei consumi. Dalla belle epoque al nuovo millennio* (Rome: Laterza, 2008).

33. Stephen Gundle, *Between Hollywood and Moscow: The Italian Communists and the Challenge of Mass Culture, 1943 to 1991* (Durham, N.C.: Duke University Press, 2000), 9.

34. This is the case in Victoria De Grazia's *Irresistible Empire: America's Advance through Twentieth-Century Europe* (Cambridge, Mass.: Belknap, 2005). Italian scholars such as Emanuela Scarpellini have used a model of "hybridization" to explain how American culture and society were adapted by the Italians. See her "Shopping American Style: The Arrival of the Supermarket in Postwar Italy," *Enterprise and Society* 5, no. 4 (December 2004): 625–68. See also Elisabetta Bini, Enrica Capussotti, Giulietta Stefani, Elisabetta Vezzosi, "Genere, consumi, comportamenti negli anni cinquanta: Italia e Stati Uniti a confronto," *Italia contemporanea* no. 224 (September 2011): 1–17 (available at www.insmli.it/pubblicazioni/1/ic_224_bini.pdf).

35. Maria Rosa Cutrufelli, Elena Doni, Paola Gaglianone et al., eds., *Il Novecento delle italiane. Una storia ancora da raccontare* (Rome: Editori Riuniti, 2002), 195.

36. Enrica Capussotti, *Gioventù perduta. Gli anni Cinquanta dei giovani e del cinema in Italia* (Florence: Giunti, 2004), 45–100.

37. Luciana Viviani, "Salviamo l'infanzia," *Noi Donne*, May 13, 1951, 2.

38. Gian Luigi Rondi, "Relazione," in *Atti del IV Congresso Nazionale del Centro Italiano Femminile*, Rome, March 8–11, 1951, reprinted in *Inchiesta sulla cinematografia per ragazzi*, ed. Centro Italiano Femmminile (Rome: Crea Poligrafiche Riunite, 1952), 11–12.

39. Duggan, "Italy in the Cold War Years," 14; and Paul Ginsborg, *A History of Contemporary Italy: Society and Politics, 1943–1988* (New York: Penguin, 1990), 187–88.

40. Nicola Perrotti, "Rapporto sulla salute," document prepared for the International Defense of Children Conference, UDI National Archives, DnM 52.1.

41. Preparatory Committee of the International Conference, International Conference in Defense of Children, Program brochure, UDI National Archives, DnM 52.1.

42. Nicola Perrotti, "Children's Health," in *The Children of the World Call to Us*, ed. International Conference in Defense of Children (Berlin: Secretariat of the Conference, 1952), 43.

43. Dr. Groscurth, "The Influence of Literature, the Press, the Radio, Cinema and Art on the Moral and Cultural Development of Children," in ibid., 63.

44. "Le proposte di legge," in *Inchiesta sulla cinematografia per ragazzi*, ed. Centro Italiano Femmminile (Rome: Crea Poligrafiche Riunite, 1952), 152–58.

45. "Risposta CIF al questionario del M.M.M.," 1–2, CIF National Archives, B1429 F01 EB746 NS 38 MMM.

46. Amalia di Valmarana, "Speech at the IV Congresso Nazionale del Cif, March 8–11, 1951," in *Problemi relativi alla vita del fanciullo* (Rome: Centro Italiano Femminile, 1951), 54.

47. Flavia Crespi, "Il congresso di Colonia," CIF National Archives, B1432 O4 354 25.

48. "Inauguriamo l'anno sociale del nostro Circolo," in *UDI: Laboratorio di politica delle donne, idee e materiali per una storia*, ed. Maria Michetti, Margherita Repetto, Luciana Viviani (Rome: Cooperativa Libera Stampa, 1984), 145–53.

49. Ibid., 152.

50. Maria Casalini, *Famiglie comuniste* (Bologna: Il Mulino, 2010).

51. Mariuccia Salvati, "Behind the Cold War: Rethinking the Left, the State, and Civil Society in Italy (1940s–1970s)," *Journal of Modern Italian Studies* 8, no. 4 (2001): 561.

52. Marilyn Rueschemeyer and Hanna Schissler, "Women in the Two Germanys," *German Studies Review* 13, special issue (1990): 73.

53. Maria Cacioppo, "Condizione di vita familiare negli anni cinquanta," *Memoria: Rivista di storia delle donne* no. 6 (1982): 83–90, here 84.

54. "Risposta CIF," 2.

55. "I cattolici e la vita internazionale," *Cronache e Opinioni*, May 1952, 6.

56. Clara Valente, "Comunismo e donna," *Cronache e Opinioni*, July–August 1954, 7.

57. Cecilia Dau Novelli, "Le Presidenti del CIF," in *Donne del Nostro Tempo: Il Centro Italiano Femminile (1945–1995)*, ed. Cecilia Dau Novelli (Rome: Edizioni Studium, 1995), 149–51.

58. Amalia di Valmarana, "Family, Social and Civic Education: Social Conditions Which Facilitate or Hinder Education of Youth," report presented by the central president of the Centro Italiano Femminile, World Movement of Mothers, International Congress, Brussels, June 1953, CIF National Archives, B1429 F01 EB746 NS 38 MMM.

59. Ibid.

60. Bini et al., "Genere, consumi, comportamenti," 8–9.

61. Executive Committee, "Resolution sur les droits des femmes," Basso Foundation, Ada Alessandrini Collection, Series 8: Fédération démocratique des femmes, UA 3: Comitato esecutivo Fdif, Bucharest July 18–22, 1952.

62. Rina Piccolato, "Intervention sur le duexieme point: les droits des femmes," 2; speech at the Executive Committee meeting of the WIDF, Bucharest, July 18–22, 1952. Ibid.

63. Ibid., 9.

64. Maria Antonietta Macciocchi, "Che cos'e' *Noi Donne*?" *Noi Donne*, March 8, 1951, 2.

65. Ibid.

66. See for example, *Noi Donne*, March 18, 1951, 12–13.

67. Lorenza Bartolotti, interviewed by Luana Vacchi in *Volevamo cambiare il mondo: Memorie e storie delle donne dell'UDI in Emilia Romagna*, ed. Caterina Liotti, Rosangela Pesenti, Angela Remaggi, and Delfina Tromboni (Rome: Carocci editore, 2002), 96.

68. Taricone, *Il Centro Italiano Femminile*, 138.

69. Amalia di Valmarana quoted in ibid., 135.

70. Correspondence and notes, Paolo VI Institute, Unione Donne—Centro Italiano Femminile, Box 68 (1945–53).

71. Letter dated March 22, 1954 to Carmen Rossi for UDACI from Tittoni, in ibid.

72. Letter from the Vatican to the Centro Italiano Femminile, dated June 21, 1956, Paolo VI Institute, Unione Donne—Centro Italiano Femminile, Box 68 (1945–53).

73. "Giornata della Donna Cristiana," May 1955[est.], in ibid.

74. Maria Antonietta Macciocchi, "Perché è impossibile l'intesa?" *Noi Donne*, May 29, 1955, 1.

75. Giuliana Dal Pozzo, "Troppe rinunce al VI Congresso del CIF," *Noi Donne*, May 8, 1955, 17.

76. Mammarella, *Italy after Fascism*, 251–55; and Ginsborg, *A History of Contemporary Italy*, 141–44.

77. Michetti et al., *UDI: Laboratorio*, 114.

78. Letters dated January 11 and February 16, 1952 from M. M. Rossi to Segreteria del PCI Roma, Gramsci Institute, Moscow Collection, UDI 1952, Folder 193.

79. Correspondence, UDI National Archives, DnM 53.1/13.

80. Amalia di Valmarana, "La donna valido baluardo del regime democratico," *Cronache e Opinioni*, April 1953, 2.

81. Documents and Notes from Congrès Mondial des Femmes, UDI National Archives, DnM 53.1/13.

82. Translation into Italian of Brochure from Congrès Mondial des Femmes, DnM 53.1/13, UDI National Archives.

83. Taricone, *Il Centro Italiano Femminile*, 131.

84. Paola Gaiotti, "La situazione politica," *Cronache e Opinioni*, June 1953.

85. Mario Del Pero, "The United States and 'Psychological Warfare' in Italy, 1948–1955," *Journal of American History* 87, no. 4 (March 2001): 1328. For more on the ambassadorship of Clare Boothe Luce, see Del Pero's "American Pressures and Their Containment in Italy during the Ambassadorship of Clare Boothe Luce, 1953–1956," *Diplomatic History* 28, no. 3 (June 2004): 407–39.

86. Piero Ottone, "Lo 'spirito di Ginevra' base della propaganda russa," *Corriere della Sera*, October 28, 1955, 8.

87. Pietro Pastorelli, "Italy's Accession to the United Nations Organization," conference paper (available at www.diplomatie.gouv.fr/fr/IMG/pdf/ONU_pietro _pastorelli.pdf).

88. Giuliana Nenni, "Les femmes s'unissent pour leur émancipation et pour la paix," *Femmes du Monde Entier*, April 1955, 20–21.

89. WIDF, "Message to the United Nations Organization," World Congress of Mothers, Documents, Lausanne, July 7–10, 1955, Smith College Archives, Sophia Smith Collection 594, Box 2.

4. The Push for Autonomy and Women's Rights, 1956–1959

1. Letter dated March 20, 1956 from Maria Maddalena Rossi to Amalia di Valmarana, UDI National Archives, Folder 517.

2. Letter dated April 11, 1956 from Amalia di Valmarana to Maria Maddalena Rossi, UDI National Archives, Folder 517.

3. "Qualcosa di nuovo e di grande è avvenuto nel nostro paese," *Noi Donne*, April 22, 1956, 5. According to Michetti et al., the UDI reached about 3 million women in 1956, though not all were official members. See Maria Michetti, Margherita Repetto, Luciana Viviani, eds., *UDI: Laboratorio di politica delle donne, idee e materiali per una storia* (Rome: Cooperativa Libera Stampa, 1984), 173.

4. Vladislav M. Zubok, *A Failed Empire: The Soviet Union in the Cold War from Stalin to Gorbachev* (Chapel Hill: University of North Carolina Press, 2007), 101–2.

5. William Taubman, *Khrushchev: The Man and His Era* (New York: W.W. Norton, 2003), 270–99.

6. Zubok, *A Failed Empire*, 113.

7. Mark Kramer, "Power, Politics, and the Long Duration of the Cold War," in *Reinterpreting the End of the Cold War: Issues, Interpretations, Periodizations*, ed. Silvio Pons and Federico Romero (London: Frank Cass, 2005), 24–25.

8. Alexander De Grand, *The Italian Left in the Twentieth Century: A History of the Socialist and Communist Parties* (Bloomington: Indiana University Press, 1989), 124–25.

9. Ibid.

10. Zubok, *A Failed Empire*, 118.

11. Kramer, "Power, Politics," 25.

12. De Grand, *The Italian Left*, 125.

13. Paul Ginsborg, *A History of Contemporary Italy: Society and Politics, 1943–1988* (New York: Penguin, 1990), 207.

14. Giovanni Scirocco, "La lezione dei fatti. Il 1956, Nenni, il PSI e la sinistra italiana," *Storia contemporanea* 27, no. 2 (1996): 203–68.

15. "Rassegna del Mese," *Cronache e Opinioni*, July–August 1956, 11.

16. Letter dated September 19, 1956, UDI National Archives, DnM 56.1/21.

17. Clara Valente, "Lettere a Ida. Qualche novità per l'Europa," *Cronache e Opinioni*, December 1956, 3. (The all-caps HUNGARY is in the original.)

18. "Rassegna del Mese," *Cronache e Opinioni*, February 1956, 5.

19. Paola Gaiotti, "La distruzione del mito di Stalin," *Cronache e Opinioni*, March 1956, 4.

20. Valente, "Lettere a Ida."

21. "Dopo un mese di martiro, l'accorta richiesta di aiuto delle eroiche donne ungheresi," *Cronache e Opinioni*, December 1956, 10.

22. Ibid.

23. "Risoluzione della Segreteria Nazionale sulla Questione Egiziana," November 2, 1956, UDI National Archives, DnM 56.1/21.

24. "Le donne per la pace," *Noi Donne*, December 23, 1956, 10.

25. Baldina di Vittorio Berti, Intervento, La responsibilità della donna nell'era atomica, Brunate, July 10–12, 1959, UDI National Archives, DnM 59.1/24.

26. I will address the effects on the UDI's relationship with the Women's International Democratic Federation more thoroughly in chapter 5.

27. Michetti et al., "Facendoci carico dell'universo," in *UDI: Laboratorio*, 221–35.

28. "Campagne de Union des Femmes Italiennes contre les armements atomiques," *Bulletin d'Information edite par la FDIF*, no. 4, March 1, 1958, 4. Basso Foundation, Ada Alessandrini Collection, Series 8: Fédération démocratique des femmes, UA 5B Bollettini e pubblicazioni.

29. "Telegrammi ai Presidenti Eisenhower e Kruscev del Consiglio Nazionale dell'Unione Donne Italiane. Un telegramma anche al Presidente De Gaulle sulla questione dell'esplosione nel Sahara," UDI National Archives, DnM 59.1/24.

30. Lina Merlin quoted in Luisa Melograni, "Le donne dell'era atomica," *Noi Donne*, July 26, 1959, 19.

31. "Il vicepresidente americano a Mosca," *Noi Donne*, August 9, 1959, 9.

32. "Speranza in tutto il mondo," *Noi Donne*, August 16, 1959, 8–9.

33. "Telegrammi."

34. Liliana Piccinini, "La visita di Nikita Kruscev negli Stati Uniti," *Cronache e Opinioni*, September 1959, 5.

35. Linda Risso, "Cracks in a Facade of Unity: The French and Italian Christian Democrats and the Launch of the European Integration Process, 1945–1957," *Religion, State, and Society* 37, no. 1 (March 2009): 110.

36. Maurizio Carbone, "Between Ambition and Ambivalence: Italy and the European Union's Mediterranean Policy," *Modern Italy* 13, no. 2 (May 2008): 155–68.

37. Giuseppe Mammarella, *Italy after Fascism: A Political History, 1943–1965* (Notre Dame, Ind.: University of Notre Dame Press, 1966), 304.

38. Spencer M. Di Scala, *Italy from Revolution to Republic, 1700 to the Present,* 3rd ed. (Boulder, Colo.: Westview, 2004), 335.

39. Anonymous, "Il mercato comune europeo," *Cronache e Opinioni,* March 1957, 1.

40. Ivo Murgia, "Discorso alle donne sull'Europa," *Cronache e Opinioni,* April 1955, 23.

41. "Scopi del mercato comune," *Cronache e Opinioni,* February 1959, 4.

42. Ada Alessandrini, *Tutte le mamme contro la CED* (Rome: Unione Donne Italiane, 1954), 4.

43. On the Italian economic miracle, see Duggan 554–59; Di Scala, *Italy from Revolution to Republic,* 333–49; Ginsborg, *A History of Contemporary Italy,* 210–53; and Vera Zamagni, *The Economic History of Italy, 1860–1990* (Oxford: Clarendon Press, 1993), 337–78.

44. Women's International Democratic Federation, "Memorandum sent to the United Nations," Supplement to *Women of the Whole World,* no. 11, November 1957, 1.

45. "You will not prevent Algeria from becoming independent," *Women of the Whole World,* no. 2, February 1958, 11. Djamila Bouhired was one of the three women who famously planted bombs in public places during the Battle of Algiers.

46. Vo-Thi-The, "My Part in the Struggle for National Liberation," interview with Nguyen Khoa Dieu Hong, *Women of the Whole World,* no. 9, September 1959, 18–20, 34.

47. Eslanda Goode Robeson, "Africa for the Africans," *Women of the Whole World,* no. 3, March 1959, 11–14. Robeson and her husband, Paul, were investigated by the Un-American Activities Committee, and their passports revoked until just before the conference in Ghana.

48. "Possibilità di nuovi orientamenti e nuove attività dell'U.d.i." Documento del Comitato direttivo per la discussione nei Comitati provinciali," July 1956, in Michetti et al., *UDI: Laboratorio,* 214.

49. Ibid., 217.

50. Ibid.

51. Ermanna Zappaterra, interviewed by Mariangela Tedde in *Volevamo cambiare il mondo: Memorie e storie delle donne dell'UDI in Emilia Romagna,* ed. Caterina Liotti, Rosangela Pesenti, Angela Remaggi, and Delfina Tromboni (Rome: Carocci editore, 2002), 264.

52. Amalia di Valmarana, "L'organizzazione del C.I.F. come strumento di educazione democratica," speech at the Eighth National Congress, Vallombrosa, July 19–22 (Rome: Centro Italiano Femminile, 1957), 195–96.

53. Ibid., 199–200.

54. Elisabetta Bini, Enrica Capussotti, Giulietta Stefani, Elisabetta Vezzosi, "Genere, consumi, comportamenti negli anni cinquanta: Italia e Stati Uniti a confronto," *Italia contemporanea* no. 224, September 2011, 1–17 (available at www .insmli.it/pubblicazioni/1/ic_224_bini.pdf); Maria Casalini, *Famiglie comuniste* (Bologna: Il Mulino), 2010.

55. On prostitution, see Molly Tambor, "Prostitutes and Politicians: The Women's Rights Movement in the Legge Merlin Debates," in *Women in Italy, 1945–1960*, ed. Penelope Morris (New York: Palgrave Macmillan, 2006), 131–46.

56. *Noi Donne,* March 10, 1957, 9–10.

57. Letter dated July 13, 1956 from Marisa Rodano to the CIF, UDI National Archives, Folder 517.

58. Amalia di Valmarana, "L'azione del C.I.F. per un'attiva partecipazione della donna alla vita democratica," in her speech at the Eighth National Congress, CIF, 150.

59. Ibid.

60. Irene Rosa Colizzi, "Dentro la storia, al passo con i tempi," interview in *Cronache e Opinioni*, special issue, December 2005, 89.

61. Rosanna Galli, quoted by Delfina Tromboni, in *Volevamo cambiare il mondo*, 53.

62. Anna Maria Pazzaglia, "Donne pronte ad affrontare le sfide della società," interview in *Cronache e Opinioni*, special issue, December 2005, 90.

63. Fiorenza Taricone, *Il Centro Italiano Femminile dalle origini agli anni settanta* (Milan: FrancoAngeli, 2001), 146–47.

64. Giuliana Dal Pozzo, "La Magistratura ha detto: L'articolo 37 è legge," *Noi Donne*, October 9, 1955, 5–6.

65. "Les salaries feminins en Italie et la mise en application de la Convention no. 100 du BIT Position et action de l'UDI pour egalité de salaries," *Bulletin d'Information edite par la FDIF*, no. 15, November 20, 1957, 2–9.

66. Ines Pidorni Cerlesi, "Continuing Our Discussion on Women's Right to Work: The Movement for Equal Pay in Italy," *Women of the Whole World*, no. 12, December 1959, 27.

67. "Les salaries feminins en Italie."

68. Alda Miceli, "Una nostra inchiesta: La valutazione del lavoro femminile in casa e fuori," *Cronache e Opinioni*, May 1957, 4. The exact number of responses was not specified.

69. Ibid.

70. Valmarana, "L'azione del C.I.F.," 160.

71. Ibid., 155.

72. Wendy Pojmann, "'Join Us in Rebuilding Italy': Women's Associations 1946–1963," *Journal of Women's History* 20, no. 4 (Winter 2008): 82–104.

73. Nilde Jotti, "La pensione alle casalinghe come riconoscimento del valore sociale del loro lavoro," in Michetti et al., *UDI: Laboratorio*, 187.

74. Anna Matera, "Introduzione," Assemblea nazionale per la pensione alle casalinghe, in Michetti et al., *UDI: Laboratorio*, 281.

75. Ibid.

76. Valmarana, "L'azione del C.I.F.," 150–51.

77. "Conclusioni delle giornate del MMM," Paris June 9–16, 1958; CIF National Archives, Series 39–Rapporti con enti e organizzazioni nazionale e internazionali, Folder 1432, File 10.

78. "Sulla pensione alla casalinga," *Cronache e Opinioni*, July–August 1957, 3 and 12.

79. For a recent comprehensive study of divorce in Italy, see Mark Seymour, *Debating Divorce in Italy: Marriage and the Making of Modern Italians, 1860–1974* (New York: Palgrave Macmillan, 2006).

80. Ibid.

81. "Un centro di studi per le delusioni matrimoniali," *Noi Donne*, February 24, 1957, 30–31.

82. "Il dito sulla piaga," *Noi Donne*, February 10, 1957, 23.

83. "Il matrimonio è la tomba dell'amore? Con cinque coppie di sposi la cui esperienza va da mezzo secolo a due anni di vita coniugale," interview by Giovanni Cesareo, reprinted in Michetti et al., *UDI: Laboratorio*, 273.

84. Valmarana, "L'azione del C.I.F.," 164.

85. In the 1958 elections, the Christian Democratic Party won 42.3 percent of the vote (compared with 40.1 percent in 1953), the Italian Communist Party 22.7 percent (.1 percent higher than in 1953 despite the Hungarian crisis), and the Italian Socialist Party 14.2 percent (up from 12.7 percent in 1953). See Mammarella, *Italy after Fascism*, 310–11.

5. Opening to the Center, 1960–1963

1. Amalia di Valmarana, "Un aiuto al Movimento Mondiale Madri," *Cronache e Opinioni*, April 1963, 9.

2. Letter dated May 21, 1963 from Maria Penco to Amalia di Valmarana, CIF National Archives, Series 39, Binder 1432, Folder 4.

3. Paul Ginsborg, *A History of Contemporary Italy: Society and Politics, 1943–1988* (New York: Penguin, 1990), 258.

4. Leopoldo Nuti, "A Delicate Balancing Act: The Place of Western Europe in JFK's Foreign Policy," *Journal of Transatlantic Studies* 8, no. 3 (2010): 244.

5. Maria Rosa Cutrufelli, Elena Doni, Paola Gaglianone et al., eds., *Il Novecento delle italiane. Una storia ancora da raccontare* (Rome: Editori Riuniti, 2002), 220.

6. Leopoldo Nuti, "The United States, Italy, and the Opening to the Left, 1953–1963, *Journal of Cold War Studies* 4, no. 3 (Summer 2002): 36–55.

7. Ibid. Nuti's article offers a more nuanced assessment of the "opening to left" than is available in most of the related literature.

8. Liliana Piccinini, "Il Congresso Socialista," *Cronache e Opinioni*, April 1961, 9.

9. Elisa Bianchi, "La dottrina sociale cristiana chiede un impegno unitario per essere realizzata," *Cronache e Opinioni*, March 1963, 3.

10. Alda Miceli, "L'unità dei cattolici nell'attuale situazione politica," *Cronache e Opinioni*, February 1963, 3. See pp. 2–4 of the April 1963 issue of *Cronache* for a list of women's issues and women candidates to support.

11. Letter dated May 23, 1963 to CIF federation and provincial offices, signed Leone Bentivoglio; Istituto Paolo VI, UD 70—CIF 1963–66.

12. Anna Matera quoted in Enrica Lucarelli, "Un impegno per l'emancipazione," *Noi Donne*, April 2, 1961, 29.

13. Maria Michetti, Margherita Repetto, Luciana Viviani, eds., *UDI: Laboratorio di politica delle donne, idee e materiali per una storia* (Rome: Cooperativa Libera Stampa, 1984), 305–6.

14. Arthur M. Schlesinger, Jr., *A Thousand Days: John F. Kennedy in the White House* (New York: Mariner, 2002).

15. Liliana Piccinini, "Il Messaggio di Kennedy," *Cronache e Opinioni*, January 1961, 5.

16. Liliana Piccinini, "Dopo John Kennedy, Oggi si tratta di continuare," *Cronache e Opinioni*, December 1963, 4.

17. "The Struggle between Two Lines at the Moscow World Congress of Women," Smith College Archives, Sophia Smith Collection, MS 594, Box 2, Folder 3.

18. As it reported on the assassination of Robert Kennedy, *Noi Donne* sustained that JFK's death was just one more example of the consequences of the violence and hatred ripe in American society. See, for example, GC, "Robert Kennedy l'ultimo caduto sulla strada della violenza," *Noi Donne*, June 15, 1968, 5–7.

19. Cecilia Dau Novelli, "Il CIF e la società italiana (1944–1981)," in *Donne del Nostro Tempo: Il Centro Italiano Femminile (1945–1995)*, ed. Cecilia Dau Novelli (Rome: Edizioni Studium, 1995), 16. She makes this claim but does not elaborate on it.

20. Elisa Bianchi, "Riflessioni dopo le elezioni," *Cronache e Opinioni*, May 1963, 3. See also Alberto Melloni, *Pacem in Terris. Storia dell'ultima enciclica di Papa Giovanni* (Rome: Laterza, 2010), esp. 75–91.

21. See, for instance, Don Angelo Rebora, "La preparazione dei cattolici al Concilio Ecumenico," *Cronache e Opinioni*, September 1962, 3. On the broader

effects of Vatican II, see Guido Formigoni, *Alla prova della democrazia. Chiesa, cattolici e modernità nell'Italia del '900* (Trento: Il Margine, 2008), esp. chapter 7.

22. Alda Miceli, *Tra storia e memoria* (Rome: Centro Italiano Femminile, 1994).

23. Amalia di Valmarana, "Il ruolo del CIF in ordine al problema della donna nella famiglia e nel lavoro," speech delivered at the X Congresso nazionale, La donna nella famiglia e nel lavoro, December 6–10, 1960, 102.

24. John XXIII, "L'apostolato della donna nella famiglia e nel lavoro," excerpts from speech at the CIF's 1960 National Congress, *Cronache e Opinioni*, June 1963, 7.

25. John XXIII, *Pacem in terris: On Establishing Universal Peace in Truth, Justice, Charity, and Liberty*, April 11, 1963 (available at www.vatican.va/holy_father/john_xxiii/encyclicals/documents/hf_j-xxiii_enc_11041963_pacem_en.html).

26. Miceli, *Tra storia e memoria*.

27. Mons. Leone Bentivoglio, "Io vo' gridando pace, pace, pace," *Cronache e Opinioni*, May 1963, 2.

28. Bruna Bellonzi, "La Pace in Marcia," *Noi Donne*, June 29, 1963, 27.

29. Ada Alessandrini, "L'importanza della Enciclica Pacem in Terris di papa Giovanni XXIII per l'affermazione dei diritti della donna e per la pacifica convivenza," Basso Foundation, UA 8 Congresso mondiale delle donne (Mosca 24–29 Giugno 1963).

30. Ibid.

31. Eugénie Cotton, "The WIDF in the Struggle for Peace, National Independence, Women's Rights and the Happiness of Children," *World Congress of Women, Moscow 1963* (Berlin: Women's International Democratic Federation, 1963), 11.

32. Mark Kramer, "Power, Politics, and the Long Duration of the Cold War," in *Reinterpreting the End of the Cold War: Issues, Interpretations, Periodization*, ed. Silvio Pons and Federico Romero (London: Frank Cass, 2005), 28.

33. Ibid., 28–30.

34. Liliana Piccinini, "Rassegna del Mese," *Cronache e Opinioni*, January 1960, 5.

35. CIF, "Mozione," *Cronache e Opinioni*, November 1961, 3.

36. CIF, "Nuove potentissime armi contro ogni aggressione," *Cronache e Opinioni*, November 1961, 5.

37. Ivo Murgia, "Le estreme nel ritorno della democrazia," *Cronache e Opinioni*, January 1963, 2.

38. Baldina di Vittorio Berti, "Intervento," presentation at conference La responsabilità della donna nell'era atomica, July 10–12, 1959, Como, Italy. UDI National Archives, DnM 59.1/24.

39. Ibid.

40. See the 1962 issues of *Femmes du Monde Entier*, Baldina di Vittorio Berti, "Les femmes italiennes pour un monde sans guerre et sans armes," no. 4, 16–17, and "La lutte des femmes italiannes pour la paix," no. 9, 10.

41. La Presidenza Nazionale dell'Unione Donne Italiane, untitled statement of October 24, 1962, *Noi Donne*, November 4, 1962, 6.

42. "Documenti presentati dalla Unione Donne Italiane alla F.D.I.F., Bureau di Praga, Maggio 1962," *Posta della settimana. Numero straordinario: Contributo dell'Unione Donne Italiane alla preparazione ed impostazione del 'Congresso Mondiale delle Donne',*" nos. 7–9 (May–June 1963): 5. UDI National Archives, DnM 63.1/33.

43. Serena Madonna, "Rapporto fra l'Unione Donne Italiane e la F.D.I.F," in ibid., 11.

44. Amalia di Valmarana, "Libertà e socialità nel programma del CIF," speech delivered at the Eleventh National Congress, Il CIF per la libertà e la socialità nella vita italiana contemporanea, December 15–19, 1962, 54.

45. "La donna e la politica," *Cronache e Opinioni*, September 1962, 6–7.

46. "Circolare," no. 487, January 24, 1961, Archives of Catholic Action, Series UD, Folder 69 CIF 1957–58, 1959, 1960, 1962.

47. CIF National Archives, Series 39, Binder 1433, File 2.

48. Letter dated May 12, 1961 from Amalia di Valmarana to Lea Ermini, president of the Italian section of the MMM, CIF National Archives, Series 39, Binder 1433, File 3.

49. Letter dated May 21, 1963 from Maria Penco to Amalia di Valmarana, CIF National Archives, Series 39, Binder 1432, File 4.

50. Report of meeting of the Bureau International du MMM in Paris, January 15–16, 1965, CIF National Archives, Series 39, Binder 1432, File 8.

51. Report of the Riunione del comitato italiano del MMM, Rome, June 19, 1964, CIF National Archives, Series 39, 1433, File 3.

52. Letter from Maria Penco to Amalia di Valmarana dated November 12, 1966, CIF National Archives, Series 39, 1432, File 9.

53. Undated note from Maria Penco to Alda Miceli, CIF National Archives, Series 39, 1432, File 9.

54. Letter from Penco to Valmarana, November 12, 1966.

55. Ibid.

56. Madonna, "Rapporto fra l'Unione Donne Italiane e la F.D.I.F.," 15.

57. "Mozione presentata dell'UDI per essere iscritta all'ordine del giorno del V Congresso della FDIF," in ibid., 8.

58. Ibid., 9.

59. Francisca De Haan has also noted a shift in the federation's balance between women's rights and world politics, which she argues had occurred by the 1948 Budapest convention. See her "Progressive Women's Aspirations for a Better

World: The Early Years of the Women's International Democratic Federation," published in German as "Hoffnungen auf eine bessere Welt: Die frühen Jahre der Internationalen Demokratischen Frauenföderation (1945–1950)," *Feminist-ische Studen* 27, no. 2 (November 2009): 241–57.

60. "Documenti presentati dalla Unione Donne Italiane alla F.D.I.F.," in ibid., 6.

61. "The Struggle between Two Lines at the Moscow World Congress of Women."

62. The Italian press widely reported on the UDI's dramatic actions. See, for example, "La delegazione italiana abbandona la seduta al Congresso mondiale delle donne a Mosca," *Il Messaggero*, June 25, 1963 and "Vivaci critiche all'internazionale della donna," *L'Avanti*, July 12, 1963; UDI National Archives, DnM 63.1/33.

63. "Vivaci critiche."

64. "No, anche a Mosca," in Michetti et al., *UDI: Laboratorio*, 317–27.

65. Luisa Melograni, "Il vocabulario delle idee nuove per la donna d'oggi," *Noi Donne*, June 20, 1964, 8–11.

66. The official title of the CIF's congress was "La donna nella famiglia e nel lavoro" [Woman in the Family and Work], and the UDI's was "Il lavoro della donna e la famiglia" [The Work of Woman and the Family].

67. Clelia d'Inzillo, "La famiglia americana," *Cronache e Opinioni*, July–August 1961, 10.

68. Mara Selvini Palazzolo, "Lavoro della donna e suoi riflessi sulla vita psich-ica," speech delivered at the Tenth National Congress, La donna nella famiglia e nel lavoro, December 6–10, 1960, 158.

69. The "crisis of the American family" remained a popular theme in *Noi Donne* throughout the 1960s.

70. Silvia Fatuzzo, "Le consumatrici di fronte al Mercato Comune," *Cronache e Opinioni*, July–August 1960, 2.

71. "L'azione della donna nella Comunità Europea," *Cronache e Opinioni*, April 1961, 5.

72. Amalia di Valmarana, "Il ruolo del CIF in ordine al problema della donna nella famiglia e nel lavoro," speech delivered at the Tenth National Congress, La donna nella famiglia e nel lavoro, December 6–10, 1960, 118.

73. Comitato di associazioni femminili per la parità di retribuzione, "La parità di retribuzione nella Comunità economica europea," Milano, September 30–October 2, 1963, program brochure, UDI National Archives, DnM 63.1/32.

74. Comitato di associazioni femminili per la parità di retribuzione, "Conclu-sioni del convegno di studio sulla parità di retribuzione nella Comunità eco-nomica europea," UDI National Archives, DnM 63.1/32.

75. "Partecipazione del CIF al convegno dell'UFCS," *Cronache e Opinioni*, July 1966, 21.

76. Ibid. Also a founding member of the World Movement of Mothers, the Union Féminine Civique et Sociale had remained active in France throughout the Cold War era and operated similarly to the CIF. See chapter 2.

77. Liliana Piccinini, "L'Europa è sulla strada dell'autonomia," *Cronache e Opinioni*, March–April 1967, 11.

78. Liliana Piccinini, "L'atomo al servizio dell'Europa," *Cronache e Opinioni*, June 1967, 11.

79. Documents, Congresso Mondiale per la Pace, Helsinki, July 10–15; and "Cinquième question à l'ordre du jour: L'emploi des femmes ayant des responsabilité familiales," conference international du travail, UDI National Archives, DnM 65.1/36.

80. In *Cronache e Opinioni* issues from 1962, see, "La Purezza Oggi," April, 6–7; "L'influenza dei mezzi di comunicazione di massa," June, 6–7, "La femminilità . . . che ci sia ognun lo dice, cosa sia nessun sa," May, 4–5.

81. Simonetta Piccone Stella, "Crescere negli anni '50," *Memoria: rivista di storia delle donne*, no. 2 (1981): 22.

82. Liliana Piccinini, "La crisi del Vietnam," *Cronache e Opinioni*, September 1963, 5.

6. Confronting the Youth Generation, 1964–1968

1. "1968: Il lungo cammino della pace," *Cronache e Opinioni*, December 1968, special insert.

2. "Donne dell'anno," *Noi Donne*, December 21, 1968, 5.

3. Peter Hebblethwaite, *Paul VI: The First Modern Pope* (New York: Paulist Press, 1993).

4. Ibid., 438–39.

5. Pope Paul VI, *Populorum Progressio, Encyclical of Pope Paul VI on the Development of Peoples, March 26, 1967* (available at www.vatican.va/holy_father/paul_vi /encyclicals/documents/hf_p-vi_enc_26031967_populorum_en.html).

6. Elisa Bianchi, "È ancora utile l'attività missionaria?" *Cronache e Opinioni*, July 1966, 16–17.

7. Irène Mancaux, "Abidjan 1961—Paris 1966," *Vie familiale: improvisation ou formation? VIIIe Congres International du Mouvement Mondial des Meres, Paris, Novembre 1966* (Paris: World Movement of Mothers, 1966), 147–50.

8. Ibid., 145–46.

9. Pope Paul VI, *Christi Matri, Encyclical of Pope Paul VI on Prayers for Peace during October, September 15, 1966* (available at www.vatican.va/holy_father/paul _vi/encyclicals/documents/hf_p-vi_enc_15091966_christi-matri_en.html).

10. Centro Italiano Femminile, "Lavorare per la pace," *Cronache e Opinioni*, October 1966, 3–4.

11. Ibid., 4.

12. Paul Ginsborg, *A History of Contemporary Italy: Society and Politics, 1943–1988* (New York: Penguin, 1990), 301–2.

13. Christopher Gosha and Maurice Viasse, eds., *La guerre du Vietnam et l'Europe, 1963–1973* (Brussels: Bruylant, 2003).

14. Leopoldo Nuti, "L'Italie et l'escalade de la guerre du Vietnam," in ibid., 131–50.

15. Richard Drake, "Catholics and the Italian Revolutionary Left of the 1960s," *Catholic Historical Review* 94, no. 3 (July 2008): 453.

16. Quoted in Luisa Melograni, "Il vocabolario delle idee nuove per la donna d'oggi," *Noi Donne*, June 20, 1964, 11.

17. Carmen Zanti, "Una pioniera della lotta per l'emancipazione femminile," *Noi Donne*, July 1, 1967, 41.

18. Bruna Bellonzi, "Da vent'anni sangue e lacrime nel Vietnam," *Noi Donne*, February 27, 1965, 6–9.

19. See, for example, the *Noi Donne* articles, "Parole di Donne," April 10, 1965, 6–9, and "L'America contro Johnson," April 13, 1968, 8–9.

20. Ugo D'Ascia, "Un appuntamento difficile," *Noi Donne*, October 2, 1965, 28–29.

21. "Alle donne del Vietnam, siamo con voi per la pace e la libertà," *Noi Donne*, March 6, 1965, 9.

22. Postcard insert, *Noi Donne*, December 11, 1965.

23. "Delegazione dell'UDI a Ginevra," *Noi Donne*, July 16, 1966, 10.

24. "La marcia per la pace e per la libertà," *Noi Donne*, December 9, 1967, 11.

25. Ibid.

26. Coverage of the visit appears in Giulietta Ascoli, "Viaggio attraverso l'Italia con le eroiche donne del Vietnam. È stato un lungo abbraccio al Vietnam," *Noi Donne*, July 20, 1968, 5–10, and "Le tre responsabilità delle donne vietnamite," *Noi Donne*, August 3, 1968, 5–7. See also related correspondence and press coverage in UDI National Archives, DnM 68.3/47.

27. Several *Noi Donne* stories feature her. See three stories by Giulietta Ascoli, "Nguyen Thi Binh con questa donna l'America deve trattare la pace," November 16, 1968, 4–6; "Binh vuol dire pace ma c'è chi ha paura della pace," November 23, 1968, 6–8; and "Undici guerrigliere contro i marines," December 14, 1968, 24–25.

28. Vladislav M. Zubok, *A Failed Empire: The Soviet Union in the Cold War from Stalin to Gorbachev* (Chapel Hill: University of North Carolina Press, 2007), 203.

29. Ibid., 207.

30. Alessandro Brogi, "France, Italy, the Western Communists, and the Prague Spring," in *The Prague Spring and the Warsaw Pact Invasion of Czechoslo-*

vakia in 1968, ed. Gunter Bischof, Stefan Karner, and Peter Ruggenthaler (New York: Lexington Books, 2010), 283–315.

31. Sergio Trasatti, "Il silenzio di Praga," *Cronache e Opinioni*, September 1968, 4–5.

32. Alessandro Frigerio, "1968, Praga e il silenzio del PCI" (available at www .storiain.net/arret/num143/artic1.asp).

33. Maud Bracke, *Which Socialism? Whose Detente? Western European Communism and the Czechoslovak Crisis of 1968* (Budapest: Central European University Press, 2007), 167–75.

34. Joan Barth Urban, *Moscow and the Italian Communist Party: From Togliatti to Berlinguer* (Ithaca, N.Y.: Cornell University Press, 1986), 255.

35. Ibid., 254–56.

36. F.D.S., "Una donna a capo del governo," *Noi Donne*, September 7, 1968, 4.

37. "Czechoslovakia," UDI National Archives, DnM 68.3/46.

38. Bruna Bellonzi, "Il nuovo corso dell'emancipazione," *Noi Donne*, November 2, 1968, 10.

39. See for example, "La setta dell'odio bianco, KKK," *Noi Donne*, January 15, 1966, 5–9; Giovanna Marini, "Canto l'America," *Noi Donne*, October 22, 1966, 10–14; "L'America malata di violenza," *Noi Donne*, April 20, 1968, 12–13.

40. GC, "Robert Kennedy l'ultimo caduto sulla strada della violenza," *Noi Donne*, June 15, 1968, 6–7.

41. Bruna Belonzi, "Tre ragazze alla scoperta dell'URSS," *Noi Donne*, March 19, 1966, 6–10; "Come si vive in Unione Sovietica? La donna in serie A," *Noi Donne*, April 6, 1968, 22–23;

42. Mauro Bellabarba, "L'America ferita," *Cronache e Opinioni*, May 1968, 4–5.

43. Emma Cavallaro, "In memoria di Robert Kennedy, un lutto per la pace," *Cronache e Opinioni*, June 1968, 6–8.

44. Jan Kurz and Marica Tolomelli, "Italy," in *1968 in Europe: A History of Protest and Activism*, ed. Martin Klimke and Joachim Scarloth (New York: Palgrave Macmillan, 2008), 83–96; Ginsborg, *A History of Contemporary Italy*, 298–309.

45. Giovanni Benzoni, "Flash sull'università," *Cronache e Opinioni*, September 1968, 17–19.

46. Ginsborg, *A History of Contemporary Italy*, 307.

47. Bruna Bellonzi, "Da Roma a Parigi studenti in prima linea," *Noi Donne*, May 18, 1968, 21.

48. Paolo Capuzzo, Federico Romero, and Elisabetta Vazzosi, the introduction to Paolo Capuzzo, ed., *Genere, generazione e consumi: L'Italia degli anni sessanta* (Rome: Carocci editore, 2003), 11–16.

49. Emma, "Perché no?" *Cronache e Opinioni*, November 1964, 8.

50. "Non si può prescindere dalle ideologie quando si parla di problemi di fondo: si può andare d'accordo?" *Cronache e Opinioni*, May 1964, 6.

51. "Nuovi documenti del CIF," *Cronache e Opinioni*, April 1968, 19.

52. World Movement of Mothers, "Family Life: Improvisation or Matter of Education?" conference invitation, CIF National Archives, Series 39, Binder 1432, Folder 9.

53. Questionnaire summary, CIF National Archives, Series 39, Binder 1432, Folder 9.

54. Ibid.

55. Paule Chapelle, "Role specifique de la mere dans la formation des jeunes a leur vie conjugale et familiale," *Vie familiale: improvisation ou formation? VIIIe Congres International du Mouvement Mondial des Meres, Paris, Novembre 1966* (Paris: World Movement of Mothers, 1966), 37.

56. Alessandro Galante Garrone, "La donna nuova e il codice vecchio," *Noi Donne*, March 8, 1964, 62.

57. Lucia Chiavola Birnbaum, *Liberazione della donna: Feminism in Italy* (Middletown, Conn.: Wesleyan University Press, 1986), 62-63.

58. "I termini attuali della questione femminile, dalle tesi per la preparazione del VII Congresso nazionale," in *UDI: Laboratorio di politica delle donne, idee e materiali per una storia*, ed. Maria Michetti, Margherita Repetto, Luciana Viviani (Rome: Cooperativa Libera Stampa, 1984), 357.

59. Bruna Bellonzi, "Meglio la polvere sui mobili che la muffa sul cervello," *Noi Donne*, May 7, 1966, 6-9.

60. Giovanni Cesareo, "Una bomba fra i miti," *Noi Donne*, March 8, 1964, 81. His article details the results of a report commissioned under John F. Kennedy and led by Eleanor Roosevelt that concluded that American women were not so advanced in terms of daily lives or legislation. In particular, as workers, American women were not protected and were often the last hired and first fired, underemployed, and employed mostly in sectors that paid less than others. Girls were excluded from studying math and science. There were no rights for employed women with children, and only a few states even allowed maternity leave. American women had few social services to help them, and once their kids were grown, they had little to look forward to. In "Giornalisti e scrittori commentano il progresso della donna nel mondo," published in the same issue, Sergio Perucchi reports that Swedish women have full equality with men.

61. "Verso il XII Congresso Nazionale, Crisi di valori nella società in trasformazione," *Cronache e Opinioni*, July-August 1964, 6-7.

62. Lidia Menapace, "Come si comporta la donna oggi di fronte all'evoluzione sociale," *Cronache e Opinioni*, November 1965, 9.

63. Conseil International Mouvement Mondial des Meres, "Relazione delle riunioni del 3 e 4 maggio 1964 Amsterdam," CIF National Archives, Series 39, Binder 1433, Folder 5.

64. Filippo Franceschi, "La logica del dissenso giovanile, un no alle tre M," *Cronache e Opinioni*, October 1968, 20.

65. Miriam Mafai, "Il silenzio della stampa femminile sul congresso dell'UDI," *Noi Donne*, November 30, 1968, 8.

66. See Chiara Ferrari, "Contested Foundations: Postmodern Feminism and the Case of the Union of Italian Women," *Signs: Journal of Women in Culture and Society* 33, no. 3 (2008): 569–94, on *doppia militanza* and direct challenges to the subordination of gender to class within the Italian Community Party in the 1970s and 1980s. I disagree, however, with Ferrari's characterization of the UDI as a "flanking organization" of the party.

67. The range of opinions expressed by UDI members in articles in *Noi Donne* between 1964 and 1968 makes this evident. See for example, Ea Mori, "La crisi è donna?" May 23, 1964, 6–9; "La parità è tutto?" June 6, 1964, 6–10; Sandro De Cesare, "La pillola sotto bianco," February 12, 1966, 6–9; and Pina Canale, "Il pudore non è più di moda?" January 6, 1968, 8–11.

68. Maria Belli, interviewed by Delfina Tromboni in *Volevamo cambiare il mondo: Memorie e storie delle donne dell'UDI in Emilia Romagna*, ed. Caterina Liotti, Rosangela Pesenti, Angela Remaggi, and Delfina Tromboni (Rome: Carocci editore, 2002), 101.

69. Giuseppina Carbonetti, interviewed by Angela Remaggi, in ibid., 117.

70. In *Cronache e Opinioni*, see, for example, Clelia D'Inzillo, "Il divorzio e la Costituzione," March 1966, 12, and "Le donne italiane e l'unità della famiglia," July–August 1966, 12–14.

71. Cecilia Dau Novelli, "Il CIF e la società italiana (1944–1981)," in *Donne del Nostro Tempo: Il Centro Italiano Femminile (1945–1995)*, ed. Cecilia Dau Novelli (Rome: Edizioni Studium, 1995), 28–30.

72. "Verso il XII Congresso Nazionale," 6.

Conclusion: The Results of Women's Cold War Political Activism

1. Wendy Pojmann, *Immigrant Women and Feminism in Italy* (Aldershot, England: Ashgate, 2006).

2. See the UDI's website at http://unionedonne.altervista.org/.

3. See the CIF's website at www.cifnazionale.it/.

4. The WMM's website is at www.mouvement-mondial-des-meres.org/.

5. The WIDF's website is at www.fdim-widf.com.br/indexingles.htm. It appears to be updated less frequently than do the other organizations' websites.

6. Paola Bono and Sandra Kemp, eds., *Italian Feminist Thought: A Reader* (Oxford: Blackwell, 1991); Perry Willson, *Women in Twentieth Century Italy* (Hampshire, England: Palgrave Macmillan, 2010), 149–67.

7. Data on women in politics and government in the European Union countries can be found on the European Commission's website at http://ec.europa.eu /social/main.jsp?catId=764&langId=en and on the European Women's Lobby's website at www.womenlobby.org.

8. Pina Nuzzo, "Quote rosa nei consigli di amministrazione" (available at http://unionedonne.altervista.org/).

Selected Bibliography of Secondary Sources

Alano, Jo Marie. "Armed with a Yellow Mimosa: Women's Defence and Assistance Groups in Italy, 1943–1945," *Journal of Contemporary History* 38, no. 4 (2003): 615–31.

———. "A Life of Resistance: Ada Prospero Marchesini Gobetti (1902–1968)." Doctoral dissertation, University of Rochester, 2002.

Berkovitch, Nitza. *From Motherhood to Citizenship: Women's Rights and International Organizations.* Baltimore, Md.: Johns Hopkins University Press, 1999.

Bini, Elisabetta, Enrica Capussotti, Giulietta Stefani, and Elisabetta Vezzosi. "Genere, consumi, comportamenti negli anni cinquanta: Italia e Stati Uniti a confronto." *Italia contemporanea* no. 224 (September 2011): 1–17. Available online at www.insmli.it/pubblicazioni/1/ic_224_bini.pdf.

Birnbaum, Lucia Chiavola. *Liberazione della donna: Feminism in Italy.* Middletown, Conn.: Wesleyan University Press, 1986.

Black, Naomi. *Social Feminism.* Ithaca, N.Y.: Cornell University Press, 1989.

Bono, Paola, and Sandra Kemp, eds. *Italian Feminist Thought: A Reader.* Oxford: Blackwell, 1991.

Bosworth, R.J.B. *Italy and the Wider World, 1860–1960.* London: Routledge, 1996.

Bracke, Maud. *Which Socialism? Whose Detente? Western European Communism and the Czechoslovak Crisis of 1968.* Budapest: Central European University Press, 2007.

Bravo, Anna, and Anna Maria Bruzzone. *In guerra senza armi. Storie di donne.* Bari: Laterza, 1995.

Brogi, Alessandro. "France, Italy, the Western Communists, and the Prague Spring." In *The Prague Spring and the Warsaw Pact Invasion of Czechoslovakia in 1968,* edited by Gunter Bischof, Stefan Karner, and Peter Ruggenthaler, 283–315. New York: Lexington Books, 2010.

Cacioppo, Maria. "Condizione di vita familiare negli anni cinquanta." *Memoria: Rivista di storia delle donne* no. 6 (1982): 83–90.

Capussotti, Enrica. *Gioventù perduta. Gli anni Cinquanta dei giovani e del cinema in Italia.* Florence: Giunti, 2004.

Capuzzo, Paolo, Federico Romero, and Elisabetta Vazzosi. Introduction to *Genere, generazione e consumi: L'Italia degli anni sessanta,* edited by Paolo Capuzzo, 11–16. Rome: Carocci editore, 2003.

Carbone, Maurizio. "Between Ambition and Ambivalence: Italy and the European Union's Mediterranean Policy." *Modern Italy* 13, no. 2 (May 2008): 155–68.

Casalini, Maria. *Le donne di sinistra (1944–1948).* Rome: Carocci editore, 2005.

———. *Famiglie comuniste.* Bologna: Il Mulino, 2010.

Chillè, Sergio, "I riflessi della guerra di Corea sulla situazione politica italiana negli anni 1950–1953: Le origini dell'ipotesi degasperiana di 'democrazia protetta.'" *Storia contemporanea* 18, no. 5 (October 1987): 895–926.

Corbi, Giann. *Nilde.* Milan: Rizzoli, 1993.

Cutrufelli, Maria Rosa, Elena Doni, Paola Gaglianone et al., eds. *Il Novecento delle italiane. Una storia ancora da raccontare.* Rome: Editori Riuniti, 2002.

Dau Novelli, Cecilia. "Il CIF e la società italiana (1944–1981)." In *Donne del Nostro Tempo: Il Centro Italiano Femminile (1945–1995),* edited by Cecilia Dau Novelli, 3–35. Rome: Edizioni Studium, 1995.

De Grand, Alexander. *The Italian Left in the Twentieth Century: A History of the Socialist and Communist Parties.* Bloomington: Indiana University Press, 1989.

De Grazia, Victoria. *How Fascism Ruled Women: Italy 1922–1945.* Berkeley: University of California Press, 1992.

———. *Irresistible Empire: America's Advance through Twentieth-Century Europe.* Cambridge, Mass.: Belknap, 2005.

De Haan, Francisca. "Continuing Cold War Paradigms in Western Historiography of Transnational Women's Organisations: The Case of the Women's International Democratic Federation." *Women's History Review* 19, no. 4 (2010): 547–73.

———. "Progressive Women's Aspirations for a Better World: The Early Years of the Women's International Democratic Federation." Published in German as "Hoffnungen auf eine bessere Welt: Die frühen Jahre der Internationalen Demokratischen Frauenföderation (1945–1950)." *Feministische Studen* 27, no. 2 (November 2009): 241–57.

De Leo, Mimma. "L'Unione donne italiane fra rimozione e riforme." In *Cittadine d'Europa: Integrazione europea e associazioni femminili italiane,* edited by Beatrice Pisa, 65–92. Milan: FrancoAngeli 2003.

De Luna, Giovanni. *Donne in oggetto: L'antifascismo nella società italiana, 1922–1939.* Turin: Bollati Boringhieri, 1995.

Del Pero, Mario. "American Pressures and Their Containment in Italy during the Ambassadorship of Clare Boothe Luce, 1953–1956. *Diplomatic History* 28, no. 3 (June 2004): 407–39.

———. "Containing Containment: Rethinking Italy's Experience during the Cold War." *Journal of Modern Italian Studies* 8, no. 4 (2003): 532–55.

———. "The United States and 'Psychological Warfare' in Italy, 1948–1955." *Journal of American History* 87, no. 4 (March 2001): 1304–34.

Di Scala, Spencer M., ed. *Italian Socialism: Between Politics and History*. Amherst: University of Massachusetts Press, 1996.

———. *Italy from Revolution to Republic, 1700 to the Present*. 3rd ed. Boulder, Colo.: Westview, 2004.

Dondi, Mirco. "The Fascist Mentality after Fascism." In *Italian Fascism: History, Memory, and Representation*, edited by R.J.B. Bosworth and Patrizia Dogliani, 141–60. New York: Palgrave, 1999.

———. *La lunga liberazione: giustizia e violenza nel dopoguerra italiano*. 2nd ed. Rome: Editori Riuniti, 2004.

Drake, Richard. "Catholics and the Italian Revolutionary Left of the 1960s." *Catholic Historical Review* 94, no. 3 (July 2008): 450–75.

Duchen, Claire, and Irene Bandhauer-Schoffman, eds. *When the War Was Over: Women, War, and Peace in Europe, 1940–1956*. New York: Leicester University Press, 2000.

Duggan, Christopher. *The Force of Destiny: A History of Italy since 1796*. New York: Houghton Mifflin, 2008.

———. "Italy in the Cold War Years and the Legacy of Fascism." In *Italy in the Cold War: Politics, Culture and Society, 1948–58*, edited by Christopher Duggan and Christopher Wagstaff, 1–24. Washington, D.C.: Berg, 1995.

Ellwood, David. "The Propaganda of the Marshall Plan in Italy in a Cold War Context." *Intelligence and National Security* 18, no. 2 (2003): 225–36.

Enloe, Cynthia. *The Morning After: Sexual Politics at the End of the Cold War*. Berkeley: University of California Press, 1993.

Ferrari, Chiara. "Contested Foundations: Postmodern Feminism and the Case of the Union of Italian Women." *Signs: Journal of Women in Culture and Society* 33, no. 3 (Spring 2008): 569–94.

Ferree, Myra Marx, and Aili Mari Tripp, eds. *Global Feminism: Transnational Women's Activism, Organizing, and Human Rights*. New York: New York University Press, 2006.

Filippini, Nadia Maria, and Anna Scattigno, eds. *Una democrazia incompiuta: Donne e politica in Italia dall'Ottocento ai nostri giorni*. Milan: FrancoAngeli, 2007.

Formigoni, Guido. *Alla prova della democrazia. Chiesa, cattolici e modernità nell'Italia del '900*. Trento: Il Margine, 2008.

Frader, Laura Levine. *Breadwinners and Citizens: Gender in the Making of the French Social Model*. Durham, N.C.: Duke University Press, 2008.

Frattini, Claudia. *Il primo congresso delle donne italiane, Roma 1908*. Rome: Biblink editori, 2008.

Fugazza, Mariachiara, and Maria Cassamagnaghi, eds. "Italia 1946: Le donne al voto." Istituto Lombardo di Storia Contemporanea, 2006. Available online at www.insmli.it/pubblicazioni/35/Voto%20donne%20versione%20def.pdf.

Gabrielli, Patrizia. *Il club delle virtuose: UDI e CIF nelle Marche dall'antifascismo alla guerra fredda*. Ancona: Il lavoro editoriale, 2000.

———. *Il 1946, le donne, la Repubblica*. Rome: Donzelli Editore, 2010.

———. *La pace e la mimosa: L'Unione donne italiane e la costruzione politica della memoria (1944–1955)*. Rome: Donzelli Editore, 2005.

Garner, Karen. *Shaping a Global Women's Agenda: Women's NGOs and Global Governance, 1925–1985*. New York: Manchester University Press, 2010.

Giacomini, Ruggero. *I partigiani della pace*. Milan: Vangelista, 1984.

Ginsborg, Paul. *A History of Contemporary Italy: Society and Politics, 1943–1988*. New York: Penguin, 1990.

Giuntella, Maria Cristina. "Il rapporto con gli altri movimenti cattolici. L'esperienza della federazione." In *Donne del Nostro Tempo: Il Centro Italiano Femminile (1945–1995)*, edited by Cecilia Dau Novelli, 51–76. Rome: Edizioni Studium, 1995.

Gosha, Christopher, and Maurice Viasse, eds. *La guerre du Vietnam et l'Europe, 1963–1973*. Brussels: Bruylant, 2003.

Gundle, Stephen. *Between Hollywood and Moscow: The Italian Communists and the Challenge of Mass Culture, 1943 to 1991*. Durham, N.C.: Duke University Press, 2000.

Hawkesworth, Mary E. *Globalization and Feminist Activism*. New York: Rowman & Littlefield, 2006.

Hebblethwaite, Peter. *Paul VI: The First Modern Pope*. New York: Paulist Press, 1993.

Kaplan, Temma. "On the Socialist Origins of International Women's Day." *Feminist Studies* 11, no. 1 (Spring 1985): 163–71.

Kent, Peter C. *The Lonely Cold War of Pope Pius XII: The Roman Catholic Church and the Division of Europe, 1943–1950*. Ithaca, N.Y.: McGill-Queen's University Press, 2002.

Koikari, Mire. *Pedagogy of Democracy: Feminism and the Cold War in the U.S. Occupation of Japan*. Philadelphia: Temple University Press, 2008.

Kramer, Mark. "Power, Politics, and the Long Duration of the Cold War." In *Reinterpreting the End of the Cold War: Issues, Interpretations, Periodizations*, 21–38, edited by Silvio Pons and Federico Romero. London: Frank Cass, 2005.

Kurz, Jan, and Marica Tolomelli. "Italy." In *1968 in Europe: A History of Protest and Activism*, edited by Martin Klimke and Joachim Scarloth, 83–96. New York: Palgrave Macmillan, 2008.

Lamb, Richard. *War in Italy, 1943–1945. A Brutal Story*. London: Penguin, 1995.

Laville, Helen. *Cold War Women: The International Activities of American Women's Organisations*. New York: Manchester University Press, 2002.

Leffler, Melvyn P. *The Specter of Communism: The United States and the Origins of the Cold War, 1917–1953*. New York: Hill & Wang, 1994.

Legnani, Massimo, and Ferruccio Vendramini, eds. *Guerra, guerra di liberazione, guerra civile*. Milan: FrancoAngeli, 1990.

Mammarella, Giuseppe. *Italy after Fascism: A Political History, 1943–1965*. Notre Dame, Ind.: University of Notre Dame Press, 1966.

McNamara, Patrick. *A Catholic Cold War: Edmund A. Walsh, S. J., and the Politics of American Anticommunism*. New York: Fordham University Press, 2005.

Melloni, Alberto. *Pacem in Terris: Storia dell'ultima enciclica di Papa Giovanni*. Rome: Laterza, 2010.

Meyer, Donald B. *Sex and Power: The Rise of Women in America, Russia, Sweden, and Italy*. Middletown, Conn.: Wesleyan University Press, 1987.

Miceli, Alda. *Tra storia e memoria*. Rome: Centro Italiano Femminile, 1994.

Michetti, Maria, Margherita Repetto, and Luciana Viviani, eds. *UDI: Laboratorio di politica delle donne, idee e materiali per una storia*. Rome: Cooperativa Libera Stampa, 1984.

Moro, Renato. "The Catholic Church, Italian Catholics, and Peace Movements: The Cold War Years, 1947–1962." *Contemporary European History* 17, no. 3 (2008): 365–90.

Newell, James L. *The Politics of Italy: Governance in a Normal Country*. Cambridge: Cambridge University Press, 2010.

Nuti, Leopoldo. "A Delicate Balancing Act: The Place of Western Europe in JFK's Foreign Policy." *Journal of Transatlantic Studies* 8, no. 3 (2010): 236–46.

———. "L'Italie et l'escalade de la guerre du Vietnam." In *La guerre du Vietnam et L'Europe*, edited by Christopher Goscha and Maurice Vaïsse, 131–50. Brussels: Bruylant, 2003.

———. "The United States, Italy, and the Opening to the Left, 1953–1963." *Journal of Cold War Studies* 4, no. 3 (Summer 2002): 36–55.

Offen, Karen. *European Feminisms, 1700–1950: A Political History*. Stanford, Calif.: Stanford University Press, 2000.

Oliva, Gianni. *Le tre Italie del 1943: Chi ha veramente combattuto la guerra civile*. Milan: Mondadori, 2004.

Ombra, Marisa, ed. *Donne manifeste: L'UDI attraverso i suoi manifesti, 1944–2004*. Rome: Il Saggiatore, 2005.

Osted, Odd Arne. *The Global Cold War: Third World Interventions and the Making of Our Times*. Cambridge: Cambridge University Press, 2007.

Pastorelli, Pietro. "Italy's Accession to the United Nations Organization." Conference paper. Available online at www.diplomatie.gouv.fr/fr/IMG/pdf/ONU_pietro_pastorelli.pdf.

Pavone, Claudio. *Una guerra civile. Saggio storico sulla moralità della Resistenza*. Turin: Bollati Boringhieri, 1994.

Pedersen, Susan. *Family, Dependence, and the Origins of the Welfare State: Britain and France, 1914–1945*. Cambridge: Cambridge University Press, 1993.

Peters, Julie, and Andrea Wolper. *Women's Rights, Human Rights: International Feminist Perspectives*. New York: Routledge, 1995.

Piccone Stella, Simonetta. "Crescere negli anni '50." *Memoria: Rivista di storia delle donne*, no. 2 (1981): 9–35.

Pojmann, Wendy. "Emancipation or Liberation? Women's Associations and the Italian Movement." *Historian* 67, no. 1 (March 2005): 73–96.

———. *Immigrant Women and Feminism in Italy*. Aldershot, England: Ashgate, 2006.

———. "'Join Us in Rebuilding Italy': Women's Associations 1946–1963." *Journal of Women's History* 20, no. 4 (Winter 2008): 82–104.

Risso, Linda. "Cracks in a Facade of Unity: The French and Italian Christian Democrats and the Launch of the European Integration Process, 1945–1957." *Religion, State, and Society* 37, no. 1 (March 2009): 99–114.

Rodano, Marisa. *Del mutare dei tempi*. Rome: Edizioni Memori, 2008.

Romero, Federico. *Storia della guerra fredda: L'ultimo conflitto per l'Europa*. Turin: Giulio Einaudi, 2009.

Rossi-Doria, Anna. *Diventare cittadine: Il voto alle donne in Italia*. Florence: Giunti Gruppo Editoriale, 1996.

———. "Italian Women Enter Politics." In *When the War Was Over: Women, War, and Peace in Europe, 1940–1956*, edited by Claire Duchen and Irene Bandhauer-Schoffman, 89–102. New York: Leicester University Press, 2000.

Rossini, Daniela. "The Italian Translation of American Feminism: The CNDI and the International Women's Movement from *Belle Époque* to Fascism." Conference paper from the Proceedings of the 20th AISNA Conference, Turin, Italy, September 24–26, 2009.

Rueschemeyer, Marilyn, and Hanna Schissler. "Women in the Two Germanys." *German Studies Review* 13 (special issue, 1990): 71–85.

Rupp, Leila. *Worlds of Women: The Making of an International Women's Movement*. Princeton, N.J.: Princeton University Press, 1997.

Salvati, Mariuccia. "Behind the Cold War: Rethinking the Left, the State, and Civil Society (1940s–1970s)." *Journal of Modern Italian Studies* 8, no. 4 (2001): 556–77.

Scaratino, Anna. *Donne per la pace. Maria Bajocco Remiddi e l'Associazione internazionale madri per la pace nell'Italia della guerra fredda*. Milan: FrancoAngeli, 2006.

Scarpellini, Emanuela. *L'Italia dei consumi. Dalla belle epoque al nuovo millennio*. Rome: Laterza, 2008.

———. "Shopping American Style: The Arrival of the Supermarket in Postwar Italy." *Enterprise and Society* 5, no. 4 (December 2004): 625–68.

Schlesinger, Jr., Arthur M. *A Thousand Days: John F. Kennedy in the White House*. New York: Mariner, 2002.

Scirocco, Giovanni. "La lezione dei fatti. Il 1956, Nenni, il PSI e la sinistra italiana." *Storia contemporanea* 27, no. 2 (1996): 203–68.

Seymour, Mark. *Debating Divorce in Italy: Marriage and the Making of Modern Italians, 1860–1974.* New York: Palgrave Macmillan, 2006.

Slaughter, Jane. *Women and the Italian Resistance, 1943–1945.* Denver: Arden, 1997.

Smith, E. Timothy. *The United States, Italy, and NATO, 1947–52.* New York: St. Martin's Press, 1991.

Soddu, Paolo. *L'Italia del dopoguerra, 1947–1953. Una democrazia precaria.* Rome: Editori Riuniti, 1998.

Sperling, Valerie. *Organizing Women in Contemporary Russia: Engendering Transition.* Cambridge: Cambridge University Press, 1999.

Tambor, Molly. "Prostitutes and Politicians: The Women's Rights Movement in the Legge Merlin Debates." In *Women in Italy, 1945–1960,* edited by Penelope Morris, 131–46. New York: Palgrave Macmillan, 2006.

———. "Red Saints: Gendering the Cold War, Italy 1943–1953." *Cold War History* 10, no. 3 (2010): 429–56.

Taricone, Fiorenza. *Il Centro Italiano Femminile dalle origini agli anni settanta.* Milan: FrancoAngeli, 2001.

———. "Il Centro Italiano Femminile e l'idea d'Europa." In *Cittadine d'Europa: Integrazione europea e associazioni femminili italiane,* edited by Beatrice Pisa, 21–64. Milan: FrancoAngeli 2003.

———. "Il Consiglio nazionale delle donne italiane." Donne e conoscenza storica website. Available online at www.url.it/donnestoria/testi/accardidonne/actut consiglio.htm.

Tasca, Luisa. "The Average Housewife in Post–World War II Italy." *Journal of Women's History* 16, no. 2 (Summer 2004): 92–115.

Taubman, William. *Khrushchev: The Man and His Era.* New York: W.W. Norton, 2003.

Urban, Joan Barth. *Moscow and the Italian Communist Party: From Togliatti to Berlinguer.* Ithaca, N.Y.: Cornell University Press, 1986.

Varsori, Antonio. "Cold War History in Italy." *Cold War History* 8, no. 2 (May 2008): 157–87.

Ventresca, Robert A. "The Virgin and the Bear: Religion, Society, and the Cold War in Italy." *Journal of Social History* 37, no. 2 (Winter 2003): 439–56.

Whitney, Susan B. *Mobilizing Youth: Communists and Catholics in Interwar France.* Durham, N.C.: Duke University Press, 2009.

Willson, Perry. "The Fairytale Witch: Laura Marani Argnani and the Fasci Femminili of Reggio Emilia, 1929–1940." *Contemporary European History* 15, no. 1 (2006): 23–42.

————. "Saints and Heroines: Re-Writing the History of Italian Women in the Resistance." In *Opposing Fascism: Community, Authority, and Resistance in Europe*, edited by Tim Kirk and Anthony McElligott, 180–98. Cambridge: Cambridge University Press, 1999.

————. *Women in Twentieth Century Italy*. Hampshire, England: Palgrave Macmillan, 2010.

Zamagni, Vera. *The Economic History of Italy, 1860–1990*. Oxford: Clarendon, 1993.

Zubok, Vladislav M. *A Failed Empire: The Soviet Union in the Cold War from Stalin to Gorbachev*. Chapel Hill: University of North Carolina Press, 2007.

Index